in **DETAIL** Solar Architecture

in **DETAIL**

Solar Architecture
Strategies · Visions · Concepts

Christian Schittich (Ed.)

Edition Detail – Institut für internationale
Architektur-Dokumentation GmbH & Co. KG
München

Birkhäuser – Publishers for Architecture
Basel · Boston · Berlin

Editor: Christian Schittich
Project manager: Andrea Wiegelmann
Editorial Services: Henning Bouterwek, Alexander Felix, Christina Kimmerle,
Julia Liese, Thomas Madlener, Christina Reinhard

Translation German/English: Peter Green (pp. 72–159),
Elizabeth Schwaiger (pp. 8–71, 160–175)
Drawings: Kathrin Draeger, Bettina Brecht, Daniel Gärtner, Norbert Graeser, Christiane
Haslberger, Olli Klein, Andrea Saiko, Andrea Sommer, Claudia Toepsch
DTP: Peter Gensmantel, Andrea Linke, Cornelia Kohn, Roswitha Siegler

This book is a cooperation between
DETAIL – Review of Architecture and
Birkhäuser – Publishers for Architecture

A CIP catalogue record for this book is available
from the Library of Congress, Washington D.C., USA

Bibliographic information published by Die Deutsche Bibliothek
The Deutsche Bibliothek lists this publication in the Deutsche Nationalbibliografie;
detailed bibliographic data is available on the Internet at <http://dnb.ddb.de>.

© 2003 Institut für internationale Architektur-Dokumentation GmbH & Co. KG,
P.O. Box 33 06 60, D-80066 München, Germany and Birkhäuser –
Publishers for Architecture, P.O. Box 133, CH-4010 Basel, Switzerland

Printed on acid-free paper produced from chlorine-free pulp (TCF ∞).

Printed in Germany
Reproduction: Karl Dörfel Reproduktions-GmbH, München
Printing and binding: Kösel GmbH & Co. KG, Kempten

ISBN 3-7643-0747-1

9 8 7 6 5 4 3 2 1

Contents

Toward Solar Architecture

Christian Schittich

The energy potential, which the sun places at our disposal on a daily basis, seems inexhaustible. The incident radiation on the landmasses of the earth alone is 3000 times greater than the worldwide demands. Yet we continue to meet these demands almost exclusively with non-renewable energies generated primarily from fossil fuels. The resultant environmental problems – air pollution, acid rain, greenhouse effect and climate change – are only too well known. As if this weren't bad enough, annual consumption is climbing dramatically. For affluence is on the rise and some of the most populous countries of the world, such as China and India, are about to adopt the extravagant lifestyle of the West. This will lead to nearly immeasurable ecological and political consequences in the near future since the conventional energy resources are finite and will soon be exhausted. The fight for access to and control over these energy resources, first and foremost oil, will intensify even more. Seen from this perspective, a solar agenda is not only a sensible environmental policy it is also a contribution to peace. It is high time, therefore, to finally adopt a new philosophy and to embark on the road towards sustainable development based on renewable energy resources. Energy resources, in other words, that are directly or indirectly linked to the sun such as solar radiation, wind- and hydro power generation or biomass.

Architecture and building play a key role in this context. For nearly half of all the energy consumed in Central Europe is expended in the operation of buildings, that is, for heating, cooling and lighting. The last two factors, especially, were neglected for a long time. When solar architecture gained in importance in the early 1970s as a result of the two oil crises, attention was initially focused entirely on avoiding heat loss, on utilizing solar energy to heat buildings in winter and to heat domestic water. However, in office buildings especially, cooling is generally a far greater problem and a major factor in energy consumption. Office buildings are subject to heat gains caused not only by climate, but also by the heat radiating from occupants, equipment such as computers and monitors, and above all by the use of artificial lighting. One need only consider that roughly three times the amount of energy is required to cool a room by one degree in comparison to heating the same space by one degree, to grasp the significance of cooling with renewable energy resources and the importance of natural lighting. Moreover, the comparison illustrates the degree to which the various factors are interdependent: solar architecture cannot be reduced to isolated measures such as collectors or photovoltaic installations on the roof. Rather, a building must be understood as a complex configuration – a total energy concept – that makes the best possible use of locally available natural resources such as solar energy, wind and geothermal energy for a variety of requirements. Passive and active measures complement one another in this approach, from the orientation and division of the building to the integration of systems for the generation of warm water or power. Flexible envelopes, regulated by intelligent control systems and capable of reacting to varying influences and weather conditions are making increasingly important contributions. It goes without saying that such a complex configuration calls for comprehensive interdisciplinary concepts, integrated planning, in other words, where all participating experts are involved at an early stage.

But energy-conserving architecture cannot be limited to the operation of the buildings. It begins with urban planning and includes consideration of the energy content of the employed materials as well as the material cycles. Production techniques, transportation routes, assembly and the recyclability of building components are all included in the approach. Renewable and local building materials such as timber or clay are preferable over those, which can only be manufactured by consuming large amounts of energy (generated from fossil fuels). The latter also cause high levels of pollutant emissions in production and must be transported across great distances. Yet what are the concrete criteria, which an architect can apply to evaluate materials? There is still a scarcity of available information and the primary energy demand of building materials is still insufficiently evaluated even in the case of solar architecture, although great strides have recently been made in this area.

The environmental declaration of building products in Vorarlberg (Austria), where the allocation of government subsidies for residential construction is based on ecological criteria, is a model worth emulating. A point catalogue is used to take not only the heating requirements into consideration, but also the environmental compatibility of each individual building material as well as the employment of renewable energy sources. In Germany, by comparison, subsidies for residential housing are currently dispersed on the basis of the principle of 'equal shares for all' and, as if that weren't enough, new building projects are given preference over rehabilitation projects. Ecologically speaking, the opposite approach would be required. For the primary principle of resource conservation is to utilize the most important available resource, that is, buildings that already exist.

Support should also favour dense housing development over the construction of single-family houses. Since neither detached single-family houses, nor high-rises for that matter, are capable of being truly ecological, these two building tasks are not included in the examples featured in this volume. In the case of single-family houses, land consumption and the traffic-related energy required to provide access tip the balance towards the negative. The high percentage of heat-emitting and material-consuming exterior surfaces is another unfavourable factor. High-rises, on the other hand, are associated with comparatively large access areas, but above all with a considerable increase in material consumption for the load-bearing structure and the facade in order to satisfy the structural requirements resulting from the high own weight and the extreme wind forces. High-rise facades are moreover almost exclusively realized with materials characterized by a very high primary energy demand, such as glass, steel and aluminium.

When DETAIL first published an issue on the topic of solar architecture precisely one decade ago (in 1993), it was still difficult to document convincing examples. It was all too rare that technologically functioning measures were satisfactorily integrated from a design perspective into mature architectural concepts. And the few successful examples placed excessive emphasis on the solar installations (as was the case in the shading system on Norman Foster's vocational school in Fréjus in southern France) – in keeping with the then dominant High-Tech architecture. (Fig. 1.2).

It was a time when every building that had anything at all to do with energy conservation was profitably advertised as a solar building. Much has changed in the meantime. There are many more functioning and usefully integrated solar concepts and individual measures, and they are rarely trumpeted as unique achievements today. Many outstandingly designed low-energy buildings are barely recognizable as such from the outside. In office buildings, aspects such as building component heating and cooling seem to have almost become routine for many architects. But we are still a long way from achieving our goals. The percentage of renewable energy resources employed to operate buildings is still far too low. There are still too few truly comprehensive concepts, and the conflict between aesthetics and function remains. It is still far too rare, for example, that collectors of photovoltaic modules are usefully integrated into a comprehensive concept. They are all too frequently simply placed any which way on top of conventional covered roofs. This is not only unsatisfying from an aesthetic perspective, but also with regard to costs and material consumption – if they were designed as roof or facade panels, they could be part of the building skin. Every now and then one cannot escape the impression that some measures are merely employed to salve someone's conscience or to pocket subsidies. Especially when monstrous, energy- and resource-guzzling suburban villas are topped by a collector. In the overall picture, the use of renewable energy resources thus far fulfils little more than the function of an alibi. Even if the Federal government of Germany should achieve its ambitious goal of increasing the percentage from 2.2 per cent to 4.2 per cent in 10 years, this cannot negate the fact that the total energy demand continues to increase unabated and that solar energy resources are essentially doing little more than covering surplus demands. Bluntly put, this means that the total volume of conventional energy consumption remains unchanged with all the aforementioned consequences this entails.

If we do not succeed in bringing about a lasting change to our wasteful lifestyle and drastically diminish energy consumption, the only possible solution will be to rely overwhelmingly on renewable energy resources in the near future. True solar architecture, therefore, becomes a necessity. It will be far more than simply a new style. Its principles will become the basis for all building. It will change the face of architecture. Integrating the technical and functional requirements of solar architecture into an aesthetically satisfying comprehensive concept presents both a challenge and an opportunity for architecture. This book aims to make a contribution towards achieving this goal.

1.1   Service centre tax offices Munich (2003), Bernhard Peck
       Photovoltaic modules mounted on shading louvres
1.2   Vocational school, Fréjus, France (1993), Norman Foster
       dramatic shading system
1.3   Administration building, Kronberg (2000), Schneider + Schumacher
       Climate facade with double windows   1.3

From Passive Utilization to Smart Solar Architecture

Manfred Hegger

Sustainability has become a dominant theme in the debate on architecture and building in recent years, although the meaning of the term has been stretched to the extreme. Some interpretations embrace Berlin's "stone architecture" as readily as experimental solar buildings. An EU commission is currently at work to clarify this confusion.[1] However, there is no disputing that the consideration of solar radiation and the passive use of solar energy in buildings is a central characteristic of sustainable architecture. In other spheres of life, the term sustainability always possessed a clear, unambiguous meaning.

Sustainable meant nourishing meals such as Grandma's pea soup, responsible forest management or solid buildings with a long lifespan. But a recent poll[2] revealed much confusion: only 10 per cent of citizens knew the meaning of the word – at least, somewhat. But nearly 90 per cent were in favour of a concept, the meaning of which they cannot fully comprehend. There seems to be a need for clarification. As a collective term, the word sustainability, originally employed to describe long-term forest management, is used to describe the correct treatment of the environment. The UN commission, chaired by former Norwegian Prime Minister Brundtland, formulated a succinct definition: "Sustainability is development, which satisfies the needs of the current generations, without influencing the opportunities of future generations."[3] This is relevant to building on many levels. On the one hand, in terms of its economic importance – more than half of the entire investment capital in Germany is tied to the building sector –, and, on the other hand, because it is the greatest factor in resource consumption. Even though the built environment is a long-term asset in its own right, it produces more than half of all "waste," recycling is still an underdeveloped aspect in construction.

Buildings account for roughly 40 per cent of the total energy consumption in Germany, higher than transportation or industry.[4]
Clearly, energy conservation and the intelligent utilization of incident solar radiation should play a role in a sustainable building. Fossil fuels, which are the foundation of our energy supplies, particularly for heating our homes, are limited. The annual discoveries of new deposits have been less than consumption for years, costs are rising, and the conflicts surrounding access to the sources are unbearable. The deleterious impact of fossil fuels on the environment is equally grave, since they are changing our global climate. Many alternatives have proven deceptive because they are ulti-

mately also based on finite resources, are difficult to manage from a technological viewpoint and are linked to harmful side effects. Perhaps the era of intensive fossil fuel use for our buildings will soon be seen as a phase. After all, why should we utilize solar energy stored in fossils to such an extent if we can put it to use directly? It doesn't interfere with the natural global balance; on the contrary, it is the very foundation of that balance. We are familiar with it as a source of light and energy. It would be short-sighted, however, to do no more than revive old principles. "Back to nature" is a popular slogan, but it isn't very logical. We cannot build houses in the same manner as before the start of the fossil age. The comfortable and almost universally available supply of energy has raised our expectations and demands considerably, and it is unlikely that we will give up this comfort in the future. No doubt, architecture that makes use of the sun will be able to adopt some ancient principles of clever solar use in buildings. Conversely, in its role as intelligent architecture, it will have to go beyond such principles in order to be accepted and satisfy today's demands. While passive use of solar energy was the only option available prior to the beginning of the fossil age (if necessary, complemented by fire pits for the combustion of renewable raw materials), fossil heating sources and the technologies derived from them allow for active temperature control today, completely independent of conditions in the environment, and the form and materials of our homes. The stages of first passive and then active energy supply in buildings are being overtaken by interactive or smart building concepts, which adopt certain passive systems and complement them with intelligent components.

Passive Use
Passive use of solar radiation functions without the need for technical systems. The building itself makes direct use of solar energy by virtue of its placement, geometry, building components and materials. This is the simplest and, at the same time, the most effective form of solar architecture. The building and its components are interpreted as a solar system. A carefully thought-out design can adapt a building to the natural energy potential in order to utilize it efficiently. The clever selection of the site, placement, shape and orientation, deliberate window arrangement, considered selection

2.1   Church Community Centre, Schwindkirchen (2001); arc Architects.
      An old stable is used as a climate buffer for the timber construction of
      the vicarage.

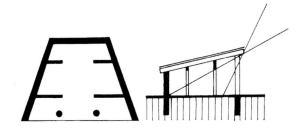

2.2

of materials and wall structures – these are the factors that make it possible to absorb and store solar heat, to maintain comfortable temperatures in a climate-conscious envelope and to utilize light to the best effect. In paying attention to a few simple rules, solar architecture is thus the most effective and progressive form of gaining and conserving energy in buildings. Heating demand is reduced, while the heating season and the periods for supplementary heating are considerably shorter. Building thus makes a considerable contribution to environmental protection by reducing CO_2 emissions; CO_2-neutral building materials also contribute to the reduction. Building and living with the sun also means more comfort. Bright interiors flooded with light have measurable positive physiological and psychological effects on human beings. Solar architecture, therefore, achieves more than environmental protection and energy conservation. It also increases comfort; sunshine penetrating deep into the house enhances one's sense of well-being just as much as the higher surface temperatures of well-insulated exterior walls. This is accompanied by an increased use of daylight, which, in turn, reduces the energy demand for artificial light while also having a positive effect on the users of such a building.

A Brief History
Insolation has fundamentally influenced the location, orientation, shape, construction and material selection of buildings since the beginning of architectural history. Together with other climate characteristics, it determined the evolution of house types and regional building styles. Socrates' Megaron House[5] (470–399 BC) has archetypical characteristics of solar architecture. The compact structure opens to the south. The trapezoidal plan makes the most of this orientation and simultaneously minimizes the northern surface turned away from the sun. This is where the cool storage room is located, functioning at the same time as a buffer zone to the living area. Walls and ceilings/floors are massive and thus have a high storage capacity. The roof overhang on the south side provides shade when the sun is high in the sky in summer, and allows the lower sun to penetrate into the building in winter (Fig. 2.2). The house concept exemplifies essential, timeless principles of solar architecture:
• minimizing of the surface (advantageous A/V-ratio),
• open towards to the sun,
• solar zoning – cool rooms on the north side, warm rooms on the south side,
• selective shading, protection against high solar altitude in summer,
• utilization of storage masses for temperature compensation

In the 19th century, new opportunities for solar architecture arose with the evolution of cost-efficient production processes for large-area glazing. The early glass houses created artificial exotic worlds, made possible through the greenhouse effect of glass, which was used to transform ultraviolet radiation into infrared thermal radiation and capture it behind glass (Fig. 2.3).

In the early 20th century, transparency, light, air and sun became the credo of the Modern. The artists and architects of the Gläserne Kette propagated crystalline structures as ideal models and designed environments that were an alternative to the dark and unhygienic cities that were caused by

the industrial revolution. However, these ideas were only realized in the Modern, although the glazed facades of that era
were often subject to considerable structural problems. At
the beginning of the 1930s – right in the middle of the misery
of the world economic crisis – an architecture evolved, which
anticipated the ideas of ecological building from the 1970s.
The Berlin competition for "Das wachsende Haus" inspired
house concepts that were large and autonomous in terms of
supply and passive-solar in design.[6]

The Third Reich brought an abrupt end to these first steps. It
would take forty years before the same ideas were taken further, albeit under changed conditions: space travel (the cir-
cumnavigation of the earth by Gagarin in 1961, the first
manned flight to the moon in 1969) offered the first view of
the earth from beyond and emphasized both the uniqueness
and the vulnerability of our planet. The energy crisis (1973)
demonstrated our dependence on fossil fuels and the finite-
ness of these resources. The warnings about the limitations
of growth, issued by the Club of Rome and published for the
first time in 1972[7], were assuming the stark mantle of reality.
These were the conditions under which so-called ecological
building developed. Its topics were the return to traditional
building forms, the use of natural materials, renewable
energy resources and, in particular, solar energy. Ignored at
first by the architectural establishment, the movement
evolved into that of solar and, finally, sustainable building.
The intelligent use of solar radiation remained a constant in
this approach, regardless of the changes to other goals. The
following pages describe the characteristics that constitute
solar architecture. They all influence sustainability and
energy efficiency. However, paying attention to these constit-
uents to the exclusion of everything else, won't take us any
further because overarching aspects of sustainability from
the areas of urban planning, transportation or other parameters are ignored. The decision to not fulfil a particular criterion
may, therefore, be completely reasonable and can generally
be compensated with the help of other measures (e.g., com-
pensating a microclimatically unfavourable location with
better insulation, or the absence of wind protection with
better sealing).

Location and Microclimate
The energy requirement of a building is not only dependent
on its structural characteristics, but also, and to the same
extent, on its location and the local climate conditions. Naturally, the global climate zones have the greatest impact:
typical temperatures per season and time of day, humidity,
insolation, wind velocities and directions. In addition, each
microclimate has its own typical characteristics determined
by topography, plants and groundcover, trees, location near
open bodies of water, etc. When selecting a building site,
one should therefore seek to locate the best possible microclimate. The position of the building on the site alone has an
influence on its energy balance.

2.3

2.2   Megaron House (circa 400 BC), Socrates. Opening towards the sun in
      a cone shape and equipped with buffer rooms to the north, this is the
      first design of a solar house.
2.3   Conservatory in Sefton Park, Liverpool (1896); Design and execution
      by Mackenzie & Moncur.

Topography

The topography has a decisive influence on the temperature conditions of the site. Elevated locations generally mean lower average temperatures. Conversely, low-lying locations may be subject to cold fronts or cold-air corridors as well as to ground fog, which result in temperatures that are considerably lower than those in adjacent sites.

Cold-air pressure regions are characterized by low temperature means as a result of the prevailing temperature lows at night; accordingly, energy requirements for heating are higher in these locations. Cold-air pressure regions, where no other means of influencing the microclimate is possible, should therefore be avoided. They are recognizable, among others, by adjacent fog fields, dew and hair-frost precipitation, and frost damage on plants.

Favourable building positions and vegetation screens prevent cold-air pressure near built structures and, thus, unnecessary heat losses. Cold-air influences can be deflected with the help of measures such as embedding the building in the earth, earth walls, hedges or neighbouring buildings. Slope sites are characterized by pronounced differences in insolation, depending on orientation, and, therefore, differences in ground and surface air temperatures. The insolation conditions for buildings on such sites are similarly different. It goes without saying that south-facing slopes are warmest – southwest slopes in winter, and south to south-east slopes in summer.

Wind Protection

High average wind velocities lead to correspondingly high transmission losses in the building. Sites that are sheltered from the wind are preferable, therefore, or, if that isn't possible, one should initiate wind protection measures. These may take the form of plantings such as hedges and dense rows of trees, planted facades or embankments. Hedges and tree groupings block cold air streams and simultaneously redirect them into desired channels. Sites that are naturally sheltered from wind and active wind protection measures greatly improve the site conditions for a building. Moreover, plants near the building contribute to cooling the immediate surroundings as a result of evaporation and transform carbon dioxide into oxygen. When properly selected and located, they also provide shade in summer. Evergreens shade the building in winter because they reduce insolation in that season. Deciduous trees, on the other hand, shed their leaves in fall and allow the warming rays of the sun to penetrate into the building interior. Studies of identical buildings at different sites demonstrate the impact of location on the energy consumption of buildings. Based on a detached single-family house in a standard location with 100 per cent energy consumption, an identical building at different locations may have considerably higher or lower heating requirements.[8]

Form

Optimized, energy-conscious building forms take climate concerns into consideration and respond to the microclimatic particularities. Urban planning and other overarching factors often make it impossible to achieve this ideal. However, in the interest of getting as close to the ideal as possible, it is worthwhile to return to traditional local building forms and models

2.4

2.5

2.6

in nature in addition to scientific parameters.

Indigenous Building Forms as Models
Traditional building types, which have been developed and improved over many centuries, are excellent indicators of suitable building forms. Structurally, they are adapted to the local economy and user requirements, and take the availability of building materials and the regional climate conditions into consideration. Indigenous building forms have always responded to the last factor, and, upon closer examination, usually in a very clever manner. Windy locations led to buildings lowered into the ground or with roofs that were pulled far down toward the ground. In extremely cold regions, the heat-radiating surfaces are kept to a minimum and the buildings are correspondingly compact. Homes in moderate climate zones are oriented toward the sun and have, since early times, utilized the greenhouse effect of glazed areas via large openings; trees and hedges are used to diminish heat loss through wind and provide shade in summer (Figs. 2.4– 2.6).

Bionics – Nature as a Model
Animals and plants in their many life forms adapt to the conditions in the natural environment, in particular, to climate conditions. What is a matter of survival for them can be an important source of inspiration for architecture. Yet for a long time we simply did not have the structural and technological expertise to apply such exemplary solutions to the discipline of building. Today, we have gained the expertise: the formal repertory of architecture has expanded tremendously and the resulting freedom can be usefully employed. Let's look at an example from an extreme climate zone: beneath their white, translucent fur, polar bears have black skin. The hair of the fur guides the solar rays to the black skin, which is warmed by them. But the fur does not only transport sun to the body, it also acts as an insulating layer.

A/V-ratio
In buildings, too, the correct design of the surfaces can be used to gain energy and to preserve heat. This is particularly important in regions, where internal temperatures are higher than external temperatures for most of the year, for example, in Central Europe. The logical solution is to minimize surfaces in order to keep undesired transmission heat losses as low as possible.

However, minimizing losses is not the only issue: surfaces

that offer good wind protection and insulation as well as effective utilization of natural light and solar heat, are elaborate and expensive. In other words, economy and ecology are closely linked. One useful value in determining an optimized building form is the so-called A/V-ratio, which expresses the relationship between the heat-radiating surfaces of a building (A) and its volume (V). A low A/V-ratio saves costs and energy. Following are some examples for clarification. A sphere has the best A/V-ratio. Since a sphere is not practical as a building form and poses problems for use (plan), the half-sphere comes closest to the ideal as a building shape. An igloo, for example, utilizes an optimum A/V-ratio and is particularly suitable for the climate conditions in cold regions. As the volume of the compact forms increases, the area decreases and the transmission heat loss is diminished. Smaller volumes always have a less favourable A/V-ratio than larger volumes. Compact structures and density, therefore, considerably reduce the cooling surfaces in comparison to a detached, free-standing building. Large and compact buildings are therefore preferable to small buildings divided into compartments (Fig. 2.8). However, if the latter are necessary, the disadvantages of their geometry can be compensated with the help of improved insulation and augmented use of solar radiation. Once again, the aforementioned principle applies: there is little sense in adhering exclusively, and at all costs, to a climate-conscious building form as a criterion. A/V-optimized cubes alone do not create truly habitable solar architecture.

Embedding
Embedding a building in the ground also diminishes heat losses, since the ground is far less susceptible to temperature fluctuation and dampens the impact of the changing external climate. Buildings that are earth-sheltered on the north side and oriented toward the sun can offer a comfortable indoor climate.

2.4 Traditional Faroe Island house. A tarred wood construction on a base of local basaltic rock and covered in a lush grass roof. In addition to wind and storm protection, the south or south-west orientation, chosen to utilize the insolation, is a key characteristic.
2.5 Earth-sheltered housing in Shaanxi/China. The effect of balancing temperatures in a region with extreme climate fluctuations is remarkable: in winter, the indoor climate is 10 °C warmer, and in summer 10 °C cooler, than on the outside.
2.6 Mountain village in Ticino, Switzerland. The stone houses are covered with stone shingles and built into the slope without mortar.

17

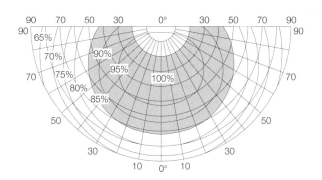

Recommended area orientation
Maximum annual insolation 1055 kWh/m²

2.7

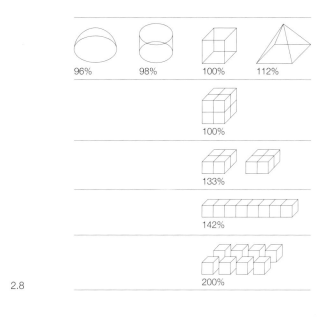

2.8

2.9

a		1:1		
b		1:16		
c		1:2		
d		1:3		
	1	2		3

1 Climate zone
2 Height/ width ratio
3 Orientation

Orientation and Insolation
In the early stages of solar architecture, orientation to the sun was seen as an unalterable law. In moderate climate zones, such as Central Europe, this naturally meant complete or partial southern orientation. In hot regions, on the other hand, protection from the sun is an important factor. However, this rule is too one-dimensional and limits the possibilities of urban planning and spatial articulation. Technical advances in building today permit considerable solar gains for other orientations as well. High insulation standards in combination with constantly high internal loads (artificial lighting, equipment, number of occupants) may suggest the opposite choice; that is, turning away from the sun in order to avoid additional solar gains. The decision must be made for each individual case, in particular for building types with high internal loads (e.g., offices with high occupancy rates, laboratories). Orientation to the sun, daylight penetration and shading should also always be evaluated in advance for urban projects. Simple solar altitude diagrams are classic assessment tools, although CAD programmes and specialized CAD tools are more commonly used to today to gather reliable data as well as static and moving images.

Shading from neighbouring buildings, vegetation and topography must all be taken into consideration. Once again: in moderate or northern latitudes, (e.g. Europe), southern orientation – especially of the principal rooms in apartments and homes – can be advantageous. It allows sunshine to penetrate into the interior, even in denser developments and in winter, and contributes high solar gains. Moreover, it is easier to provide sun protection for southern exposure than for east or west orientation; the steeper angle of incidence of solar radiation results in a higher degree of reflection on the external surface of the glazing. Shading systems and daylighting are more readily harmonized, again due to the steeper angle of incidence. In the warm season, east- and west-facing openings lead to high solar gains because the shallow angles allow sun to penetrate the glazing. In this case, effective shading will come at the price of diminished daylight incidence – unless complex shading systems are used. In winter, on the other hand, solar gains are lower in comparison to south orientation. Nevertheless, greater compactness and improved insulation qualities, for example, are increasingly contributing to good results even for west orientation, in some cases achieving a passive building quality. North orientation is ideal for uses with low heating requirements or high internal loads. It is worth remembering, that high-grade glazing can produce an energy surplus even in the case of complete north orientation.

Zoning
The zoning of a building is based on the premise that rooms have different quality requirements with regard to their use and indoor climate. This is especially relevant to housing. Temperature requirements for living rooms and work areas are fundamentally different than those for bedrooms and auxiliary rooms. For other building types, thermal differentiation according to use is equally helpful: for example, between work and recreation rooms, office and production/manufacturing spaces, or exhibition and storage/warehouse spaces. In cases where various requirements are given, it is useful to divide the building into zones according to their

uses. The classic zoning approach divides the spatial structure into concentric layers, like an onion.

Rooms that are constantly occupied and, therefore, warm are located at the core, while cooler and less frequently used rooms lie along the periphery. However, this concept does not make allowances for the effect of solar radiation. Solar zoning, by contrast, begins by orienting the building to the south. Core rooms with the greatest heat requirements face in that direction and utilize the solar radiation. They are surrounded on the three remaining sides by rooms with lower thermal requirements. This ideal spatial arrangement is generally not feasible, however. The solution lies in linear zoning, where rooms are generally arranged in rows: the prime rooms with higher heat requirements face south, the less important rooms are located on the north side. A circulation and distribution zone is frequently placed between these rows. Additions for temporary uses or buffer zones can complement this structure to the south and to the north. Structured zoning makes sense not only from the perspective of energy efficiency: it introduces order into the various functions, clarifies the building structure, and facilitates efficient building use and operation. Zoning creates orders – an essential condition for the evolution of architecture.

Building Skin
The building skin provides weather protection, creates comfort in the interior, allows daylight to fall into the building and allows for visual contact with the outside. The utilization of solar energy further expands the already complex functional spectrum of the envelope. The interface between interior and exterior must be understood as a dynamic system, which responds to the permanent variability in external radiation, climate conditions and internal requirements. Simple rules such as ensuring excellent quality in insulation are by no means nullified as a result, they are, however, placed into a larger context.

Insulation and Wind Protection
The good insulation quality of a building skin is essential for the passive use of solar energy. There is little sense in capturing solar radiation if it cannot be effectively stored in the interior. Efficient insulation of the building skin is usually created with the help of building components with a high insulating capacity: in the opaque facade areas, these are insulating materials or insulating components, in the transparent areas, these are high-grade glazing, transparent insulating materials or multi-layered facades. Thermal bridges must be reliably avoided through careful planning. Modern energy simulation systems or programmes for the calculation of the EnEV (German Energy Savings Regulation)[9] assist the architect in identifying and removing any thermal bridges. High insulating values can be achieved in opaque building components with corresponding superstructures. The costs lie less in the materials than in the installation effort. In choosing the insulation thickness, it is essential to take the installation requirements

2.7   Solar altitude diagram and recommended orientation
2.8   Changes in heating demands of a building for different surface areas but identical volume
2.9   Influence of climate on building form and orientation, and efficient placement of thermal storage masses

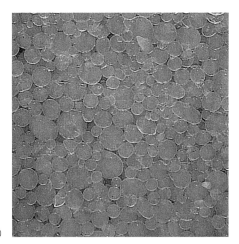

2.10

2.11

and the architectural appearance into account. The extreme thickness of insulating layers for passive houses, for example, is a particular challenge for architects. Vacuum insulation, originally developed for refrigerators and subsequently employed for space travel, are an innovation in the field of building. They can achieve an extraordinarily high quality of insulation with only a few centimetres of insulating layer. However, the installation problems, especially the treatment of butt joints, are largely unresolved, particularly for vertical installation. Insulation is ineffective without proper wind protection. To control unwanted ventilation heat losses, in addition to the transmission heat losses, the building skin must be designed to be airtight according to code; the effectiveness can only be tested empirically by means of blower-door-tests. Recent studies and design, however, have demonstrated that other means may be equally effective in creating facades with high energy-efficient qualities. The prerequisite is that the building skin is no longer interpreted as a static system, but as a dynamic envelope that reads and computes the conditions in the environment. This so-called cybernetic interpretation leads to completely new solutions, which make such efficient use of insolation either directly or through intermediate storage in building components, that this kind of truly interactive system is capable of largely replacing (traditional) insulation. The first buildings are already in operation and the dynamic simulations are promising.[10] To what extent these solutions will succeed in the everyday environment is still unanswered, however.

Openings
The openings of a house offer the greatest opportunities and, at the same time, pose the greatest risks for passive solar use. Given appropriate dimensions, arrangement, orientation and execution, they can make a considerable contribution today to the energy supply of a building and the comfort of its users. Conversely, they are a source of considerable heat loss, cooling or overheating – all factors in diminished indoor comfort. The calculations of the EnEV suggest that the ratio of window openings to wall area should not be too great when glazing of average quality is used, and should not exceed 45 per cent of the total building surface when standard glazing is employed. If this percentage is surpassed, a better quality of glazing should be used to diminish heat loss in winter. To gain energy through transparent openings, one needs to select glazing with excellent insulating values and good light and thermal transmission values. Glazing facing the sun, where the radiation is captured in the interior through the well-documented greenhouse effect – UV-radiation is transformed into IR thermal radiation as it passes through the glazing and falls onto surfaces – is more or less efficient, depending on the type. Frames are a weak point in window construction. The insulating qualities of frames are generally lower than those of the glazing – despite profiles with thermal separation and other specialized construction characteristics. Window frames with good insulation values are elaborate in design and can often appear cumbersome – much work remains to be done in this area. One alternative is to do without frames altogether, as long as this approach is compatible with the structural and ventilation concept and with the use of the building: fairly large window formats combined with few openable elements arranged in an optimal fashion for ventilation. An often-overlooked option is the selection of suitable doors, and for this reason, doors are often weak

points in terms of energy efficiency. Poorly insulated doors opening to the outside or onto unheated rooms also warp as a result of the contrast in temperatures to which the two sides are exposed – they no longer close properly and mechanical problems are the consequence. A windscreen can solve the problem, provided it is possible and desirable in terms of the available space. The requirements for openings are not static. As the interface between indoor and outdoor climate they should be able to take in or repel light, air and energy, depending on exterior conditions and internal requirements. The flexible building skin, capable of adapting to changing conditions and requirements, is therefore the focus of architectural development.

Glazed Buffer Zones – Winter gardens
Glazed buffer zones or winter gardens make sense from the perspective of energy efficiency if they are unheated and are not intended for everyday use. When used as intermediate temperature zones or simple warm-air collectors, the pre-warmed air in this area can be distributed throughout the building with the help of gravitational ventilation or mechanical systems. The alternating effects between interior and exterior in different weather conditions are very attractive, not only in residential construction. Roof glazing plays an important role in how we experience a space; in terms of energy efficiency, however, it poses disadvantages such as rapid cooling at night and overheating when the sun is high in the sky in summer. The spatial qualities of such buffer zones can tempt one to transform them after the fact into an additional living space that has to be heated. This is in conflict with the function of buffer zones, however, because the large glazed surfaces and the low glazing qualities (preferable single glazing) nullify any energy-related advantage created at the outset. Sliding balcony doors can achieve similar effects as a winter garden. This type of temporary winter garden is especially popular in Scandinavian countries.

Transparent Insulating Materials (TIM)
The expression transparent insulating materials is a misnomer because the insulation is generally translucent, rather than transparent. It is available in a variety of materials – as translucent materials, embedded between glass panes, or as light-transporting and diffracting synthetics integrated into equally translucent rendering, the so-called aero gels, which are quasi homogeneous in structure and available in the form of lamina or beads (Fig. 2.10, 2.11). Transparent insulating materials are installed on an absorbent external wall; the wall heats up as a result of the sunlight that is allowed to pass through the materials. With the appropriate structural design, these materials become, in effect, a solar wall heating system, especially in winter and in the transitional seasons (Fig. 2.15).

If the wall has good thermal storage capacity, comfort can be maintained even on cold nights and overcast days. In summer, on the other hand, the TIM must be effectively

2.12

2.10 Aerogel granules
2.11 Aerogel granules; Aerogels (Basogel ®)
2.12 Technical College, Kufstein (2000), Henke and Schreieck. Daylighting in classroom with PC workstations; shading via louvred blinds in the double facade.

shaded to avoid overheating. This increases the effort and makes the entire system more prone to repairs. TIM can also be employed in the form of light-scattering glass, particularly in skylights. This ensures that light is evenly distributed in the interior, which can be advantageous especially in workshops or exhibition spaces with great room depths. It is important to note that TIM embedded into glazing generally results in a far greater installation depth and higher costs than with spectrally selective, or gas-filled windows. Fritted, sand-blasted or printed glazing with comparable light-scattering effect are more common.

Storage Masses
Storage masses stabilize the temperature inside the building despite fluctuations in the outdoor climate, insolation and internal heat sources. They maintain a constant indoor climate and can thus contribute toward the efficient use of energy.

Massive Storage Components
The solar utilization of massive building components, or components with good storage capacity, is both simple and efficient. Thermal storage capacity is facilitated by a large surface, the high thermal capacity of the material and direct insolation. Exposed massive building components such as walls and ceilings have these characteristics. Hollow floors and suspended ceilings, on the other hand, reduce the storage capacity considerably, and solar energy can then be utilized only to a limited extent, for when there is no stabilizing effect, indoor temperatures rise during the warm season and active systems for cooling are required. Liquid storage components can be used instead; they have the advantage, for example, when water is used as the storage medium, of providing a much higher storage capacity per unit of volume. Large liquid storage can be used as long-term storage units (seasonal storage) and the solar energy stored in summer is then used for heating in winter (cf. pp. 43ff). However, this requires very large storage volumes, roughly 50 m³ for a single-family house. Consequently liquid storage units are economically efficient when they are used for larger applications, in particular, for solar district heating in housing developments. Several pilot projects are in operation; they all employ large underground storage units, where the A/V-ratio is much better than in smaller units attached to a house.[11] Liquid storage units always require additional active components, like pumps, to integrate them into the heating system. The same is true for so-called energy piles. In this application, the high storage capacity of the foundation concrete is utilized in combination with the relatively stable temperatures in the soil to store solar heat in summer and utilize it in winter via heat pumps. Conversely, the low temperature in the soil can be used to cool the building in summer.

Latent Thermal Storage
Latent thermal storage utilizes phase transition in materials – predominantly from liquid to solid state – for material-efficient thermal storage with a correspondingly high storage capacity. When heat is stored the material begins to melt but does not increase in temperature until it is completely melted. Because no noticeable temperature increase occurs despite the heat transfer, the heat that is stored during phase transition is also referred to being "hidden" or latent. Paraffin is a possible storage medium: its thermal capacity is ten times

2.13

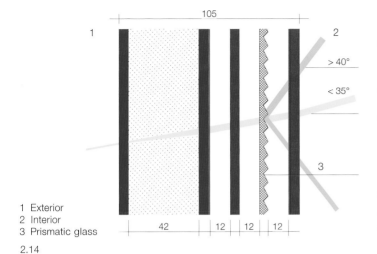

105

1

2

> 40°

< 35°

3

42 | 12 | 12 | 12

1 Exterior
2 Interior
3 Prismatic glass

2.14

higher than concrete. A 3-cm-thick dry wall with paraffin additive achieves the same storage capacity as a 40-cm-thick concrete wall. When it is integrated into glazing, paraffin can be very attractive. The interaction with the outside world is experienced in the interior through the brightness of the wall. In summer, it appears opaque in the interior. In winter, it brightens on sunny days because the paraffin has melted. When the weather turns cold, it is once again obscured because the paraffin freezes as it releases energy to the interior.[12]

On the Road to Smart Solar Architecture

The last example is the first step on the road toward interactive comprehensive systems. Additional approaches and technologies are currently in development and even in use (cf. pp. 38ff, pp. 56ff).

• Ground Ducts for Pre-warming and Cooling:
Earth ducts utilize the constant temperature levels in the soil. As heat exchangers they are located in the frost-free layer. As it passes through the length of the duct, suctioned in fresh air is pre-warmed to the soil temperature (approx. 8°C all year long). During the cold season, the earth duct pre-heats the supply air required for the building, and cools the air in summer.

• Adiabatic Cooling:
Adiabatic cooling functions according to the fountain principle that was used in antiquity. As water evaporates, it humidifies the surrounding air and cools it by a few degrees. Although this process has physical limitations, free adiabatic cooling and its atmospheric qualities can greatly contribute to the comfort of users. The disadvantage of the increase in relative humidity combined with decreased temperature can be regulated in mechanical ventilation systems with the help of a heat exchanger.

• Free Night Cooling:
Free cooling is no more and no less than window or gap ventilation. Combined with thermal storage masses, however, it can be very effective in balancing summer temperatures: heat stored in building components over the course of a day, thereby preventing temperature peaks, can be released at night through open windows or gaps. The dimension and construction of these openings is designed to prevent break-ins, to keep insects out and to avoid excessive air velocities. They can be controlled manually or mechanically. By the time morning arrives, even well-insulated volumes are effectively cooled by this means.

• Light-directing elements:
Light-directing elements guide daylight deep into rooms and reduce the need for artificial light. They come in the form of reflecting louvres or light shelves, light-scattering panes, light-deflecting prisms or holographic-optical elements. They should be designed to optimize daylight supply by means of

2.13 Residential building, Argau (1997), Theresia Schreiber. Exterior wall with cardboard honeycomb insulation behind a single layer of toughened glass to dynamically improve the U-value.

2.15 Residential building, Ebnat-Kappel (2000), Dietrich Schwarz. Schematic section of wall construction with paraffin latent storage.

minimized cross-sections, without greatly increasing heat loads as a result of incident sun.

• Switchable Glass:
Glass technology is progressing at a rapid pace. Switchable glass is of particular interest in the area of building. They are charged with current or injected with gases and transformed into various states, for example, from transparent to translucent. Depending on the incident light or temperature, they may even change automatically and thus, for example, provide shading. This type of glass is very complex; but it will no doubt be introduced in practice in the coming years.

• Switchable Film/Film Cushions:
New types of synthetic materials offer light-weight solutions. ETFE-film results in very light building components, usually in the form of dimensionally stable pneumatic cushions. Printed inserted layers and evacuating the air from interstitial layers are used to create facades, which can respond to temperatures, light incidence and user requirements.

• Vacuum Insulating Panels:
Until now, the so-called "VIPs" were primarily used for refrigerating appliances. They function in accordance with the principle of a thermos. They consist of insulating materials, for example, compacted silicic acid, which are vacuum packaged in a plastic film. Two-cm-thick panels insulate as efficiently as 20 cm of mineral fibre. This opens up new design possibilities both for renovations and for new constructions: the thickness of wall- and roof structures can be drastically reduced.

These and many other developments combine what are usually referred to as passive elements with active components, which are generally independently "intelligent." They are smart, meaning they are able to react to changing climate conditions and fluctuations in solar radiation. This increases their material and energy efficiency. And this will be the path to sustainable, energy-efficient solar architecture. It begins with passive solar use, is easy to implement and is reliable and efficient thanks to materials, which respond appropriately to solar radiation – smart materials. It is controllable through intelligent, self-regulating control technologies – smart control. Finally, it combines passive and active solar systems: direct, passive utilization of solar energy will create synergies with active utilization of solar radiation. Keywords in this field are hybrid solar systems, micro-climatic building skins and self-regulating facades. The development of smart solar architecture will give rise to new technologies, and to an eagerly anticipated new architecture.

Notes

1   At the beginning of 2003, the European Union created the international commission on "Sustainable Construction Methods and Technologies (SCMT)" under the auspices of the Architects Council of Europe (ACE) with the goal of studying the theme of sustainability in building for future legislation.
2   Lotter, Wolf (Text); Kimmerle, Julia (Timeline); Kochs, Monika (Drawings). "Trägheit. Ein kompakter Überblick über unverstandene Worte wie Nachhaltigkeit, Grüne, Gentechnik und Inertia, übersetzt: Trägheit." brand eins, 9/2002
3   The UN-expert commission chaired by former Norwegian prime minister Gro Harlem Brundtland formulated the principal thesis, the so-called Brundtland formula: "Sustainability is development that meets the needs of the current generation without influencing the opportunities of future generations." brand eins, 9/2002
4   Federal German Statistics Agency www.destatis.de
5   Circa 400 AD, Socrates called for cone-shaped, south-facing solar houses and designed the archetype of a passive house, the Megaron House.
6   Wagner, Martin. "Das wachsende Haus: Ein Beitrag zur Lösung der städtischen Wohnungsfrage." Leipzig, 1932
7   The report "Limits to Growth" was published in 1972. It was compiled on the initiative of the Club of Rome and is based on the model of "dynamic of complex systems" in a homogeneous world. The report takes into consideration the interactions between population density, food resources, energy, material and capital, environmental destruction, land use, etc. www.clubofrome.org
8   Heating demand according to location: in cold-air pressure regions 125 per cent; in shaded, densely wooded areas 110 per cent, in exposed, elevated locations 110 per cent, in wind-sheltered flat locations 85 per cent, in exposed south-facing locations on a slope 85 per cent, in wind-sheltered, sunny south orientations 60-70 per cent. From: Sabady, Biologischer Sonnenhausbau, 1980
9   The Energy Savings Regulation (EnEV) was enacted as law on February 1, 2002, in Germany. It amalgamates the previous heat protection and heating system regulations and applies to all heated buildings, including existing buildings; the energy savings potential mentioned here is expressly noted in the new regulation. www.bmvbw.de
10   Pfeifer, Günter: "Vernetzte Systeme" and "Das kybernetische Prinzip." Der Architekt, 11/2002
11   For example, the solar housing development in Hanover Kronsberg, or the urban district Wiggenhausen-South in Friedrichshafen.
12   The melting temperature of paraffin is dependent on the number of its atoms; special paraffins can melt and freeze at room temperature.

2.15   Studio, Munich (1994), Thomas Herzog. First construction of facade structure with aerogel granules.

2.15

Solar Technology – From Innovative Building Skin to Energy-Efficient Renovation

Roland Krippner

The first solar collectors were installed on rooftops in the mid-1970s, followed nearly a decade later by the first integrated photovoltaic system. Now that the initial problems, such as system glitches and economic hurdles, have been overcome, active solar technology has gained a solid position in the construction market. Indeed, it is a routine component of many building concepts, and not only of those with innovative energy strategies. In the field of solar architecture, the so-called indirect systems play a special role. The collector installations and photovoltaic modules integrated into the building skin are far more present, visually speaking, than direct measures such as compactness, high-performance glazing, intelligent insulation or efficient building systems. In addition to the functional tasks – heating domestic water, complementary space heating and power generation – the introduction of these components also translates into a considerable semantic expansion of the technological repertory of building.

A key characteristic of integrated solar technology is the visible installation of the components on roofs or facades, which function as the required interfaces between solar radiation and the building system. It is the building skin that allows us to experience architecture and architectural design in the public space – in the street, square or urban quarter. The question arises, however, whether and to what extent, solar systems engender novel building solutions, and what their contribution might be to the cultural quality of architecture.

The Search for Quality in Architecture

The lack of quality in architecture has been noted for some time, both professionally and politically. If German architectural culture seems to suffer from neglect in general, what is the status of so-called solar architecture in particular? Even after nearly three decades of intensive focus in this field, solar architecture – as pars pro toto of architecture in general – continues to reflect a certain "randomness and lack of style"[1] and 'solar' buildings are criticized for their lack of architectural quality. On the one hand, many architects still refuse to address the topic and leave the issue in the hands of engineers and builders; on the other hand, it seems even more difficult to define what constitutes quality given the complexity of the requirements and the abundance of system choices.

When we take a look at quality in architecture, two phenomena are immediately apparent: first, the difference in opinion between experts and laypeople, and second, the view that architectural quality is simply a matter of aesthetics. It is true that the rigour of a solution, including the appropriateness of the means and the logic of the expression, is strongly defined by aesthetic criteria both in terms of its integration into the urban context and the building concept itself, but limiting quality in architecture to these criteria is simply too restrictive. This is because architecture is closely linked to utility and stability, and is determined by functional and structural characteristics of quality as well. Defining these characteristics is difficult enough owing to the wide range of requirements and poorly defined criteria. The question of aesthetic quality – of what makes a building beautiful and conclusive in terms of spatiality, scale, proportion, colour and surface treatment – poses an even greater challenge because the criteria on which assessment is based in this instance are even less definitive due to different depths of knowledge and personal preferences. The use of solar technology places new demands on the complex construct of the envelope – for example, to act as an information carrier between climate modulator and media screen. This does not mean, however, that established modes of evaluation have become superfluous. Ultimately, architectural quality can only flourish through the interplay and interaction of architectonic categories in the Vitruvian sense.

Intelligent Building Skins

In the context of re-defining the building skin, that is to say, its transition from monofunctional protective roles to polyvalent control functions, much ado is made of synergetic effects, and the expression "intelligent building skin" is frequently mentioned. If "responding to new situations with problem-solving behaviour"[2] constitutes a criterion of intelligence, then the technological advances and new facade elements can justifiably be referred to as exhibiting "intelligent behaviour."

In addition to a multitude of window systems for the direct utilization of solar energy, including natural ventilation, so-called manipulators for shading and heat protection, and daylight deflection, solar components play an impor-

3.1 Archeological Museum, Herne (2003), by von Busse Klapp Brüning. The rooftop photovoltaic system feeds 100 kW/h into the municipal power grid of Herne.

tant role in intelligent or innovative building skins. The technology they introduce (and their link to an electronic network system), enables the facade and the roof to respond flexibly to changing external conditions. The result is a lasting effect on essential room or building characteristics, in other words, on user comfort.[3] The product spectrum is vast and the rate of innovation truly stunning; photovoltaics are gaining in importance as power generators for the necessary control technologies and as manipulators suitable for many applications. Technology is vital for creating architecture that is both physically and aesthetically satisfying, and for establishing a more humane and intelligent approach to building.[4]

But intelligent building is not necessarily just a matter of technical systems. The tremendous variety in regional approaches to building exemplifies what intelligent, that is, efficient, use of material and energy can be, because they combine rational thinking and craftsmanship with conclusive forms of expression. More technology is, clearly, not the only answer. Avoiding unnecessary technology, especially when it becomes an end in itself, can be just as innovative and intelligent.

Solar Technology

The technical and economic potential of solar technology is continually being questioned. Recently, however, the systems have improved tremendously. The amortization periods for the investment costs have diminished considerably in some cases, even when primary energy is taken into account. Nevertheless, the original principle still applies: collectors and photovoltaic installations can only make a noticeable contribution toward replacing fossil fuels and reducing CO_2 emissions if the direct measures – the basic strategies relating to the building's energy consumption and indoor climate and above all the building skin – are extensively utilized. This can lead to concepts for energy surplus buildings, which generate more energy per year than they consume.

A fundamental differentiation is made between two different types of indirect utilization of solar energy: thermal use of solar energy and photovoltaics (PV). In thermal use of solar energy, collectors transform solar radiation into heat, whereas PV-cells generate power out of solar radiation. The energy yield of these systems is influenced by conditions at the site and can vary greatly depending on geographical location.[5] The energy yield is also determined by the incline and orientation of the installed components, although these factors influence thermal solar and photovoltaic systems to varying degrees. When collectors are employed, the placement is also influenced by the use to which they are put. Thus, installations designed for heating domestic water should be oriented toward the higher solar altitude in the summer season, while installations for supplementary space heating should target the lower solar altitude in winter. South-facing collectors should therefore be installed on a shallow incline of 20° for domestic water systems and a steeper incline of 60° should be used for systems designed to supplement space heating. Rigid PV-generators with southern orientation achieve the greatest annual yield in Germany when they are installed at a 30° angle to the horizontal plane. In simplified terms, a south-east/south-west orientation

3.2

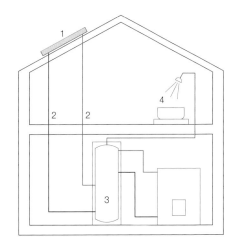

1 Collector
2 Solar cycle
3 Storage tanks
4 Warm water

3.3

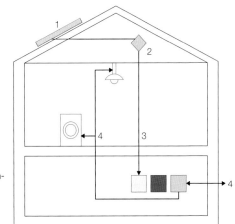

1 Solar generator on mounting
2 Connection solar generator
3 Direct current
4 Consumer circuit (alternating current)

and roof incline up to 45° yields optimum results with only negligible deviations; conversely, insolation is drastically reduced on vertical facade surfaces.[6]

Solar Systems for Thermal Use
Air- and warm-water collectors (flat plate and evacuated tube collectors) are chiefly used to preheat supply air, to heat domestic water and to supplement other heating systems.

Flat plate collectors generally consist of a solid metal absorber set into a rectangular frame. The absorber is covered by a glass pane on top, is insulated on the underside and is equipped with lateral connections to the heat carrier medium. By its very function, that of absorbing energy, it is the most important component of a collector: its absorptive and emissive power determines the collector's efficiency. Simple, black coatings are rarely used today and have been largely replaced by more efficient solutions. New, highly selective absorber coatings, which deliver a high ratio of absorptance (95 per cent) and drastically reduce reflectance in the infrared region of the spectrum, further increase the annual energy yield. Moreover, changes to the surface structure can be used to create coatings ranging from blue-black to blue-grey instead of the previously monotonous black coatings, thereby expanding the design options.

In evacuated tube collectors, glass tubes with built-in absorbers are bundled in a collecting pipe. The glass tubes serve simultaneously as a transparent cover and a housing. Since heat losses are virtually eliminated as a result of the vacuum in the individual tubes, operating temperatures of up to 120°C can be achieved. However, the increased performance of evacuated tube collectors (up to one third higher) is linked to a doubling of costs. Evacuated tube collectors are manufactured in a variety of system designs, although most are "open systems", meaning they do not form a water-bearing layer and must therefore be mounted on roof supports or suspended in front of the facade. In the meantime, first attempts have been made towards integrated installations, which make evacuated tube collectors a more interesting option for facade applications as well, although the additional effort required for insulation must be taken into consideration.

Collector systems for water heating are generally sized to deliver roughly 50 to 80 per cent of the average annual requirement; while nearly 100 per cent coverage can be achieved in summer, the output dips to approximately 50 to 60 per cent in winter as a result of heat losses and diminished insolation. For single-family and duplex houses, the standard calculation is based on 1.2 to 1.5 m² flat plate collector area and a storage volume of 80 to 100 litres per person.

Standard solar systems designed to supplement the heating requirements, called combination systems, are sized according to the heating load. A rule of thumb, roughly 1 m² of collector area per kW, results in common system dimensions of 8 to 16 m² collector area – an area of roughly 10 m² is

3.4

3.2   Functional diagram of thermal use of solar energy
3.3   Functional diagram of photovoltaic system
3.4   Multi-family house in Zurich (2001), architect: Beat Kämpfen.
      The balcony balustrade is composed of evacuated tube collectors.

3.7

sion of a transparent cell. Thin-film technology has tremendous technical and aesthetic potential.[9] These cell types are economic in terms of material consumption – layers of no more than a few micrometres (1-6 μm) are sufficient for absorption – and are also energy efficient, because the manufacturing temperatures of 200 to 700 °C are 25 per cent less than those required for crystalline cells. A high level of automation in the production is another source of potential savings.

Thin-film solar cells offer many advantages in terms of dependency on solar incidence and temperature; they are also more tolerant to shading. Diffuse and weak light is utilized to a greater degree and the output losses as a result of temperature increases in the cell are diminished, while the long strips ensure that single cells are never fully shaded. Another advantage of thin-film technology is its variability in shape. Since these modules are not tied to standardized wafer dimensions, as is the case with crystalline cells, they can be shaped into a variety of geometrical shapes and can also be mounted on curved and flexible carrier materials such as sheet metal or plastic foils. This cell type is especially suited for integration into building sections where sufficient rear ventilation is not guaranteed or where shading may occur. In the continued research and development of thin-film cells in the 1990s, several semiconductors were tested in addition to amorphous silicon, among others copper-indium-diselenide (CIS) and cadmium-telluride (CdTe). In the area of thin-film technology, CIS-technology currently delivers the highest efficiency (14 per cent). The overall efficiency has been improved with the development of so-called stacked cells, in which two or three layers are mounted on top of each other (tandem or triple cell). To further optimize the output of such stacked cells, each of the films in the triple cells, for example, is designed to respond to a different spectral range (short-, medium- or long-wave radiation). The appearance of a thin-film PV module is characterized by homogeneous surfaces structured by extremely narrow and transparent separating cuts. These are the result of the production process, that is, the electronic separation and connection of the individual cell layers. Variations in width or additional horizontal separating cuts can also be employed as design elements. Whereas polycrystalline cells are becoming available in an ever-increasing range of colours, dark hues continue to dominate in the area of thin-film technology, ranging from black to reddish brown or dark green.

Integration

Manufacturers are constantly improving the parameters for the structural integration of solar systems into roofs and walls, especially with regard to fastening methods and sealing along the sides. New frame sections facilitate the assembly of the individual elements and installation; they also minimize profile heights and projection widths. The many options available today allow for a fairly flexible integration of solar systems in the building skin. There are a growing number of fully integrated solutions that facilitate combinations of thermal solar and photovoltaic systems and the combination of these systems with other elements in the envelope. The key is the integration of collectors and PV modules with the building systems. Depending on the system design, a variety of wiring arrangements and additional equipment technology is required to this end – a factor that must be taken into consideration especially for external wall and facade structures. Photovoltaic systems are ideally suited for integration, owing to the slender dimensions of the mounted components and flexible power cables with small diameters. The diameter of pipes for water collectors is considerably larger; provisions must also be made for these installations to ensure that the pipes and connections are sealed and frost resistant.

With regard to formal aesthetic criteria, solar systems offer a wide range of design options. Manufacturers try to respond to nearly all of the wishes expressed by architects. The maximum range of colours is frequently cited as a special advantage of photovoltaics. Naturally, the appearance of the installations is influenced by the colour variation in the absorber surfaces and the multitude of section designs[10] as well as the lateral connecting elements at roof or facade level. It is important, however, to carefully assess the introduction of additional colours and shapes to the building skin. Yet architectural integration of solar systems into the building skin is more far reaching, because each element that is included in the wall or the roof also assumes functional and structural tasks as a component thereof. It is important to establish an overall harmony between the requirements and characteristics of the physical structure and the aesthetic and functional criteria of the energy system.[11]

Additive versus Integrated Installation?
Collectors and PV modules on the roof or the facade, retrofitted in some case, are often perceived as visually unpleasant. Even in the early years, raised installations, that is, additive measures, were seen as the "main evil". Little has changed in this perception to this day. Integrated roof installations, conversely, are thought of as inherently inconspicuous and even elegant solutions. Retrospectively, the first integrated roof installation of a collector system (1976) was praised as a "successful architectural solution."[12] This is a serious misunderstanding that has prevailed ever since. The result, in the aforementioned case, may well have been innovative and correct in terms of function, i.e. energy-efficiency, but it would be wrong to speak of an integrated design in the existing roof surface.

The discomfort with systems that are "planted" on top of the existing surface has little do to with the structural solution itself. Regardless of whether the system is mounted or integrated into the roof skin or the facade, the key parameters of an aesthetically satisfying solution are the module dimensions, the proportions of the element as a whole and its internal divisions, and, above all, the arrangement within the given area. There are many built examples, which demonstrate that concepts where solar systems are mounted either on the roof or on the facade can be highly integrated from an architectural perspective. In these projects, the collectors or the PV modules are interpreted as an additional functional level, which is separate from the water-bearing layer. Rea-

3.8

3.7   Single-family house in Öhling, Austria (1999), architects: Poppe Prehal.
3.8   Low-energy house in Bregenz (2001), Daniel Sauter. The PV system is structurally and aesthetically integrated into the facade.

3.9

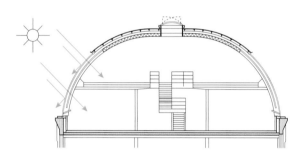

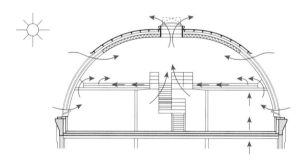

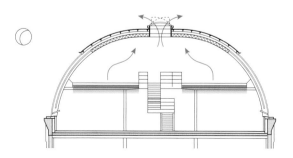

3.10

sons for this choice may relate to construction sequence, but also to utilization considerations, such as sufficient rear ventilation, sheltered maintenance areas, etc. Structural and energy considerations aside, the most important aspect of architectural integration is to fit the elements harmoniously into an overarching visual concept; the question of additive versus integrated installation is secondary.

Existing Buildings
Many debates on solar architecture have raised the question about whether it is sensible, ecologically speaking, to create energy-efficient single-family houses on open land. The argument that resource-conserving measures are ultimately only feasible on existing buildings is often emphasized.[13] Moreover, there is little demand for new construction, and forecasts indicate that the annual renewal rate of existing buildings will be roughly 1 per cent in coming years and is likely to decrease. A tremendous potential has been identified, on the other hand, in converting, retrofitting and architecturally upgrading existing housing as well as industrial and commercial developments.

Given the fact that 40 per cent of the total energy consumption in Europe continues to be expended for the construction and operation of buildings, and that the major developments dating from the 1950s, 60s and 70s are particularly lacking in terms of insulation, the energy-efficient optimization of existing buildings takes on a high priority. For architects and engineers, the tasks of the future will be the maintenance, conversion and adaptation of existing buildings as well as new construction in the form of additions.

The decision in favour of a solar thermal system is also closely linked to the lifespan of existing heating systems: In Germany, estimates anticipate that more than four million old heating systems will be renewed or upgraded in the coming five years. Based on 5 m^2 of collector area per renovation, this forecast would translate into roughly 1 million m^2 of collector area for single- and duplex-homes alone.[14]

Area estimates reveal a tremendous potential for the application of solar technology. A study of selected residential buildings from different periods in Bavaria revealed that there is an abundance of available area for solar use, especially on the facades. Individualized studies, on the other hand, showed that considerable limitations were further exacerbated in some cases by heritage protection orders.[15] The facades of existing buildings are therefore not as viable an option as one might think. Roofs, conversely, provide opportunities for architecturally harmonious and energy-efficient solutions; this is due to the exposure and incline and also to the option of continuous installations across a large area.

Solar Technology and Heritage Protection
With the growing use of regenerative energies for building operation, heritage protection must increasingly take the wish for solar technology on monuments or ensembles – such as entire street fronts, squares and urban quarters – into account. The question of whether and how heritage protection and solar technology are compatible is a delicate one, since the preservation of monuments is often linked to strict design guidelines and high requirements for interventions into the existing substance.

The principal criterion for assessing the structural integration of solar systems into heritage-protected buildings is visibility. This means that installations on the facade and, in some cases, even on steep roofs, are deemed problematic because they are visible from an elevated standpoint or from the street. If installation on the facade or the roof is limited or not allowed, there are still other alternative locations close to the buildings that are worth exploring, for example, balcony, garage, carport, pergola or greenhouse. Material(s) and construction methods are also very important issues because any change is always a kind of intervention into the existing substance and, hence, a potential risk for subsequent damage.

In addition to building codes, the architect's copyright, which is inherited and can, in general, apply to every building, must also be taken into consideration and this may lead to further restrictions. The integration of solar systems into the roof and/or facade of monuments must always be analyzed in each individual case, although a solution can usually be found through constructive dialogue. Although these problems are only relevant to a small percentage of existing buildings, the outstanding architectural quality of such buildings tends to heighten public awareness and to invest them with symbolic value.

The use of solar technology invariably translates into a new image for the building skin, a change that must be carefully planned in each instance. While more than 90 per cent of all existing buildings do not fall into the category of heritage protection, these 'ordinary' buildings also require individual solutions that are in harmony with the conditions at the site in order to achieve conclusive results in terms of energy efficiency and architectural aesthetics.

"Solar Scouts"
A 2002 study[16] on the solar heating market in Germany revealed that 71 per cent of homeowners have a positive attitude towards solar energy. Five out of ten respondents expressed a strong to very strong interest in solar thermal installations.[17] The new solar energy campaign launched by the German Energy Agency (dena) stresses that contractors play a "key role in implementing the initiative for thermal use of solar power." Today, master craftsmen run so-called solar checks or make the rounds in residential areas as voluntary "solar scouts" to test which homes are suited for the installation of collectors or PV modules. Most homeowners decide to purchase and install a solar system on the basis of the contractor's sales pitch and negotiation skills, not least of all because permits are rarely required for this type of work. This illustrates who the real decision makers are in single-family housing, since building service engineers and architects – probably in this sequence – are only consulted for larger solar installations.[18] However, there is one aspect of the clients' attitude towards solar energy that comes as a surprise. While the widespread, generally positive assessment is hardly surprising, the reason given for it is: The focus, it seems, is not on climate and environmental protection but on the desire for new, innovative technology, which often even "supersedes" the cost argument. In other words, solar installations have become status symbols. It is "chic" to install collectors on the roof or the facade;[19] the method and manner of installation seem to be of secondary importance. This describes the current situation because one important problem of solar design in everyday architecture is that the solar technology is often cloaked in a very "plain dress."[20] Considering the enormous potential of roof and facade areas, the consequence may well be that an important opportunity – in the sense of a culture of sustainable building – is not being realized, particularly in single-family and duplex houses.[21] The integration of solar systems in the building skin requires consideration of structural and aesthetic aspects with the goal of developing an optimized overall solution. This is primarily a task for an architect, with the participation of experts in the field, that is, manufacturers and contractors, engineers and conservationists.

Conclusion
Collectors and PV modules are important elements of solar architecture. In the future, they will be standard components of innovative building skins and building blocks of energy-efficient renovations. Today, the active use of solar energy can already make an important contribution to a sustainable supply. However, efficiency and a high ratio of solar utilization remain linked to the sufficient use of fundamental passive strategies. Solar technology must be integrated into a comprehensive concept that takes the spatial organization, the formal appearance of a building as well as the material and primary energy flows into consideration for new constructions and existing buildings. As numerous design awards demonstrate, the systems available on the market stand for both efficiency and elegance. Today, clients and architects regard these systems as innovative products and to some degree they have become symbols of technological progress. Despite all this, solar technology still seems to have an image problem because performance and improved product design are arguments that are not powerful enough in their own right to lead to a breakthrough in the market. Without "additional emotional benefits such as freedom, flexibility and prestige"[22] there seems to be no widespread acceptance among the population.

Solar systems must meet specific requirements and require innovative solutions, especially for complex building tasks and demanding indoor climate concepts. Building with systems is once again topical, if the different protective and control functions of the envelope – from insulation and daylight deflection to power generation – are integrated into prefabricated and recyclable building components. Whether facades and roofs are "more intelligent" as a result is another issue. What is clear, however, is that the transformation of the building skin into a climate modulator and polyvalent membrane enables it to react to changing weather conditions with increasing flexibility.

Interesting and striking treatments of the topic are notably found in a growing number of major building projects. It is important, however, that the popularity and expanded semantic content of solar technology produce more than merely symbolic monuments or spectacular office buildings. The task now is to develop equally distinctive solutions for

3.9   Renovated multi-storey factory in Berlin-Oberschöneweide (2000), architect: Frank Augustin
3.10 Multi-storey factory, Berlin-Oberschöneweide. Climate concept barrel roof: shading, ventilation and thermal storage mass.

3.11

the energy-efficient modernization of existing buildings in order to tap into the potential of solar technology in a far more challenging field. Herein lies a true opportunity to enhance the value of large and small housing developments and commercial agglomerations, in terms of energy efficiency and architecture. This improvement, however, must go beyond mere facade decoration. In view of the manifold tasks, the goal must be to achieve the highest possible level of architectural quality in the built environment. Thermal solar systems and photovoltaics have opened up a multitude of options for application and offer high-quality products. Indirect solar systems have considerably broadened the technical repertory of building. This must now be translated into architectural concepts. When one considers the search for quality criteria and competent decision makers, the need for architects, who can create groundbreaking examples that bridge the gap between technologically perfected systems and mediocrity in everyday applications and act "multipliers" in the interest of solar technology, is abundantly clear.

3.11 Studio in Dresden-Hellerau (2003), architects: Haller/Morgenstern/ Quincke. Photovoltaic modules and transparent elements alternate in the roof area.
3.12 Flat plate collectors integrated into the facades of a terraced housing development in Batschuns, Vorarlberg, Austria (1997), Walter Unterrainer

Notes:
1   Rau, Johannes: "Die große Ratlosigkeit. Was ist Baukultur?" Süddeutsche Zeitung, April 5/6, 2003, p.14
2   Meyers Großes Taschenlexikon in 24 volumes, volume 10, Mannheim/Vienna/Zurich 1987, pp. 264ff
3   This must not lead to the use of technology in order to compensate, or completely nullify, dysfunctional patterns of behaviour.
    Herzog, Thomas: "Wohltemperierte Bunker. Über ökologisches Bauen und intelligente Gebäude." Deutsches Architektenblatt, 5/1998, pp. 592–594
4   Aicher, Otl: die welt als entwurf, Berlin 1991, p.141 and pp.150ff
5   In Germany the sum of annual global radiation ranged from 913 kWh/m² in Hamburg to 1183 kWh/m² in Munich. Sonnenenergie, May 2003, p. 64
6   Krippner, Roland: "Die Gebäudehülle als Wärmeerzeuger und Stromgenerator." Schittich, Christian (ed.): Building Skins, Basel/Boston/Berlin 2001, pp. 51–55
7   Berner, Joachim: "Sommersonne für den Winter.Langzeit-Wärmespeicher haben ihre Tauglichkeit bewiesen." Sonnenenergie, November 2001, pp.16–19
8   Eicker, Ursula: "Entwicklungstendenzen solarthermischer Kühlverfahren." Bauphysik, 5/2002, pp. 300–303
9   Haselhuhn, Ralf: "Dickes Ende für die dünnen Zellen?" Sonnenenergie, March 2003, pp.26–29; ibid.: "Warten auf den Marktdurchbruch. Schlanke Zellen, große Erträge, Teil 2." Sonnenenergie, May 2003, pp. 35–37
10 The fact that 92 per cent of respondents to a survey of architects on the topic in Austria mentioned the lack of visually attractive covering strips for the facade area as the principal deficit seems to reveal a strong reduction in quality requirements.
    Knackfuß, Günter: "Das gewisse Etwas.Vom Schutzdach zum Nutzdach: Integration von Sonnenkollektoren." Solares Bauen, special edition of the journal Sonnenenergie, October 2002, p. 40
11 Krippner, Roland: "Architektonische Aspekte solarer Energietechnik. Studien zur baulichen Integration und architektonischen Einbindung solartechnischer Systeme in die Gebäudehülle." 9th Symposium on Thermal Solar Energy (Proceedings), Regensburg 1999, p. 237

12 Auer, Falk: "25 Jahre 'Sonnenenergie'. Ein Rückblick auf die ersten drei Ausgaben des DGS-Mitteilungsblatts." Sonnenenergie, January 2001, p.16
13 Moewes, Günther: "Solar, defensiv oder beides?" Detail, 3/1997, pp. 292–296
14 Kohler, Stephan: "Start der 'Initiative Solarwärme plus'. Ohne Reue stundenlang Duschen." (Interview) Sonnenenergie, May 2003, p. 24
15 Krippner, Roland: "Building Typology and Monumental Protection. Studies on the Architectural Integration of PV-Systems as Part of the Existing Building Skin." PV in Europe. From PV Technology to Energy Solutions (Proceedings), Munich/Florence, 2002, pp. 962–966
16 Sunrise 2002: "Die europäischen Märkte für Solarthermie und Photovoltaik;" market study. www.deutsche-energie-agentur.de
17 Stryi-Hipp, Gerhard: "Gute Vorzeichen." Sonnenenergie, May 2003
18 Hackstock, Roger: "Austria aktuell. Was tut sich Neues in Österreich?" Sonnenenergie, May 2003, p.10
19 Kohler, Stephan: "Start der 'Initiative Solarwärme plus'. "Ohne Reue stundenlang Duschen." (Interview). Sonnenenergie, May 2003, pp. 23ff
20 Bauwelt, 33/1999, p.1818
21 Helmut Gebhard already remarked upon the lack of architectural quality in the built environment in the early 1980s. At the time, Gebhard deplored the fact that the plethora of new building materials and building components – that is, the abundance of choices with all the concomitant risks of incompatible combinations for technical construction and design, [...] – was contrasted by a "lack of competent decision makers."
    Gebhard, Helmut: "Architekturdiskussion und Alltagsarchitektur." Willkür oder neuer Konsens? Zur Situation des Bauens. Six lectures. Munich 1984, p. 84
22 Hübner, Gundula: "Wir brauchen ein Image für die Solarenergie." (Interview). Sonnenenergie, January 2002, p. 69

3.12

Solar Concepts for Building

Michael Kuehn, Dirk Mattner

Humans have influenced the climate ever since they first inhabited the Earth. First, through the clear cutting of forests, followed by the increasing growth of settlements and cities and the sealing of the earth's surface that went with it. Accompanying the reduction of natural resources, population growth has led to an enormous rise in energy consumption. There are many theories on the effects and consequences, but these are not the subject of this work. The fact remains, however, that people in industrial nations, in particular, are destroying their own foundations for life and that of other species in a short-sighted and arrogant manner. The content of CO_2 and other trace gases such as chlorofluorocarbons (CFCs), in the ozone layer (Earth's atmosphere) is growing rapidly. Steadily increasing carbon dioxide emissions and the anthropogenic transformation of the earth's atmosphere alter not only the chemical, but also the physical characteristics of the climate systems. Fossil fuels for power and heat generation are, unfortunately, the principal source of air pollution and they have a negative impact on the environment, our health and our quality of life. Despite an awareness of the problem, the global political community is completely at a loss in the face of this catastrophic development, which is only too evident in their compliance, or rather non-compliance, with the Kioto Protocol.[1]

However, we can make a difference on a small scale. Humans erect buildings to seek shelter from the elements and should utilize natural resources to do so in order to protect the environment. Adopting this alternative means building solar architecture. This chapter serves as a guideline for conceptual approaches to integrating solar systems with building systems. The solar building blocks, which can act in concert with other systems, will be presented and explained. The chosen examples illustrate approaches that usefully combine comfort and efficiency, as well as aesthetic options for designing with these technologies. Energy conservation, in combination with the improved efficiency of technical systems, can be advantage for clients, hired consultants and executing firms. Architects and engineers are in an ideal position to offer advice in this area and to influence the design and implementation of these building systems. In doing so, they can play a more active role in the preservation of our environment, as well as our health and overall well-being.

Solar Architecture

Most people in developed countries live in latitudes where heating demands play a major role. Roughly 30 per cent of annual total energy consumption is used to meet these demands. As recently as 50 years ago, most buildings had little insulation. Windows and facades were leaky and high ventilation heat losses were the consequence. Thanks to tremendous improvements in this area, including facade constructions with thermal transmittance coefficients (U-value) of less than 1.2 W/m²K, consumption per area has been reduced by more than 80 per cent.

This has, however, led to a shift in some of the problems. In administrative buildings, in particular, the internal heat loads caused by electricity and occupants, led to excessive room temperatures in summer. These internal loads must, in turn, be reduced with the help of mechanical ventilation systems in order to maintain comfortable working conditions inside the building. Energy demands are once gain rising steeply. Electrical energy is required not only for air circulation, but also for the generation of cold water for cooling. This is one starting point for conceptual approaches to solar architecture. The goal is to create optimum comfort in the building, in summer and in winter, with as little energy consumption as possible and, in consideration of environmental factors, through the use of natural resources.

Utilization Potential

"Environmental building blocks", which take climatic and energy-related influences into account, can be conceived in reference to the demands of the environment. However, in order to optimize the utilization of the available options for energy reduction, different technical systems should act in unison. The most interesting building blocks at the current time are:
• heat recovery in housing construction
• building core activation
• seasonal energy storage
• sorption technology
• geothermal heating/cooling
• power-heat coupling
• intelligent controls and regulation.

4.1   Swiss Re headquarters in London (2003), Foster and Partners

4. 2

The following technical solutions represent possibilities that, with the help of natural resources, can provide a comfortable indoor environment that is fit for human occupation.

Heat Recovery in Housing Construction

The demand for heating energy in housing is mainly influenced by its use, the climate conditions at the site and the building form. High energy consumption is the result of heat transmission and ventilation heat losses via openings (i.e., doors and windows). While the U-values of windows have been reduced over the past years – from roughly 3 W/m^{2}K to less than 1.2 W/m^{2}K – ventilation heat losses are dependent on the frequency of ventilation and, hence, on user behaviour. The heating demand linked to ventilation is generally higher than 60 per cent. Even opening windows for short periods can result in uncontrolled natural ventilation. The logical conclusion is to employ the mechanical ventilation systems developed for administrative and commercial buildings to housing developments. This makes it possible to drastically reduce heat losses while maintaining a constant indoor air quality. To ensure the constancy of air quality indoors, the necessary volume of fresh air – 40-60 m^3/h per person for hygienic reasons – can be supplied even when windows are closed. Fresh air supplies that fall below these values means that there is insufficient ventilation, which could cause the formation of mould fungus as a result of humidity, or diminished air quality as a result of allergens such as ornamental plants, dust mites and pets. The heating demand of a low-energy house with excellent insulation and active solar components can be roughly 50 kWh/m^2 per annum in accordance with the EnEV. This corresponds to an equivalent of approximately 5 l/m^2 heating oil per year. The heat losses are divided into transmission losses of roughly 20 kWh/m^2 per year and ventilation heat losses of roughly 30 kWh/m^2 per year. If air change is achieved exclusively by means of mechanical ventilation, and if windows are kept closed when outside temperatures are low, the heating demand can be reduced by a further 50 per cent to approximately 25 kWh/m^2 per year (passive house standard). In combination with passive measures, a solar installation is sufficient to meet this demand and to create comfortable room temperatures. However, this low energy consumption is only achieved if the mechanical ventilation system is equipped with a heat exchanger. Supply air and exhaust air from the living space are transported via a plate heat exchanger. The two air streams never come into direct contact in this process; instead, they are transported in a counter-current. The heat from the escaping air is transferred to the incoming air supply in the heat exchanger via extremely thin walls. Depending on the device, the potential efficiency of heat transfer ranges between 50 and 75 per cent. A system of air ducts distributes the pre-warmed fresh air supply to the rooms. A second duct system extracts air from the space. Hence two ventilating fans are required for the mechanical air supply and extraction.

The architectural firm of Johannes Kaufmann has realized a passive housing development in Dornbirn, Vorarlberg (Austria), which features this type of ventilation for the apartments (cf. pp 72ff). The housing development consists of nine units with 86 m^2 of usable area each. The passive construction employed in this example achieves energy savings of roughly 80 per cent in comparison with conventional apartment buildings. Heating is provided with the help of a controlled mechanical supply air and ventilation system. The residual required heat is generated by means of wood pellet combustion. The resulting energy consumption is both exemplary and cost-effective.

Building Core Activation

Building core activation is an innovative system of thermally activating concrete floors for heating and cooling. The building components are heated or cooled via the floors or ceilings incorporating water-carrying serpentine pipes. The temperatures of the carrier medium are close to the room temperature. For heating, up to 28 °C is required, while up to 18 °C is required for cooling. This so-called thermoactive ceiling differs from all conventional heating and cooling systems in that it possesses a far greater storage capacity. This results in increased inertia and precludes the option for rapid load changes, meaning the system can only react to new conditions with a time lag of several hours. This is not necessarily a disadvantage. As the natural temperature fluctuations are diminished, the resulting room temperatures reflect the changes in the exterior. In summer, concrete floors and ceilings absorb the excess heat from solar radiation and internal loads. The limit for maximum room temperatures in buildings with HVAC-systems (in Germany, according to DIN 1947, Part 2) can generally only be maintained with a thermoactive ceiling when external influences are minimized with the help of an effective external shading system. When these provisions are in place, the system can maintain indoor temperatures well below the outdoor temperatures, thereby ensuring comfortable conditions. In winter, the heating output of the thermoactive ceiling is sufficient to cover the transmission heat demand of buildings according to EnEV and to meet the comfort requirements, (i.e., a glass-covered area at a maximum of 70 per cent).

The following aspects must be taken into consideration for building core activation utilizing thermoactive ceilings:
• Room temperatures of up to 27 °C can be achieved, considering that perceived temperatures are lower as a result of radiant coolness.
• Rapid temperature adjustments are not possible.
• An upper limit in room temperature cannot be maintained without additional measures.
• The influence of external factors on the thermal demands must be diminished with the help of optimized heat protection in winter and in summer.
• Additional heating units are not required when a complementary ventilation system is installed.
• Detailed analysis of the heating operation is required for rooms with window ventilation.
• The sizing of the glass areas, U-values and storage mass must be harmonized.
• Suspended ceilings, false and double floors must be avoided.

4.3

4.2 Row housing and office building, Rosenheim (2002), Hirner & Riehl, Peter Kunze
4.3 Administration building in Creuzburg (2001), Seelinger and Vogels, concrete component cooling

4.4

• Energy consumption can only be calculated on the basis of area.

System advantages:
• Low initial investment.
• Primary energy consumption is drastically lower than for conventional systems.
• Heating- and cooling output (peak loads) are reduced as a result of the storage capacity of the concrete masses.
• Existing cooling supply systems can be utilized for over-night storage operation.
• The pronounced differences in system temperatures open up possibilities of harnessing energy resources in the environment: for cooling (e.g., ground water utilization), cool outside air can be utilized overnight via re-cooling plants; for heating, solar collectors with heat pumps can be used.

Comfort limitations:
• Maximum room temperatures of 26–27 °C in summer can only be achieved with an effective shading system.
• Individual temperature control per room during the heating period is not possible.

The limitations of the building core activation lie in the output, and, in particular, in the sluggish response to sudden changes in cooling or heating requirements. A high heating requirement exists, for example, when windows need to be opened to flush out the air in an office space. For without a fresh air supply, the indoor air quality suffers as a result of exhalation, etc., which can lead to illness (e.g., Sick Building Syndrome). However, intensive window ventilation is only possible for roughly 50 per cent of the working hours with satisfactory results. When windows are tilted open and outside temperatures are below 7 °C, cold air streams into the room and cools the floor to less than 18 °C depending on the duration for which the window is kept open. This creates high and uncomfortable air velocities of over 0.25 m/s along the floor (draught). The effect is particularly uncomfortable near windows and strongly compromises comfort, although this discomfort decreases with greater distance from the external wall. Short bursts of window ventilation do not offer a satisfying solution, nor do supplementary measures such as under floor convectors, which would, moreover, represent a system change to the building core activation (i.e., considerably higher feed temperatures). The following concept is an alternative that can be employed in combination with building core activation: incoming fresh air is warmed directly at the window to at least 10 °C by mixing it with warm room air. This diminishes cold air influx and achieves draught-free flushing of the air in the room. The basic heating requirement of the offices is covered by activating the concrete core. The admixture of warm room air and cold fresh air directly at the window is achieved by means of small air inlets in the facade posts (Fig. 4.5). A miniature fan in the false floor suctions room air into the system at floor level, whereby heat is transmitted to the concrete ceiling, and then transports it, via a heating profile integrated into the double floor, to the facade posts. As the air temperature rises, air is released evenly into the room via the small inlets in the facade posts, mixing directly with incoming fresh air and thus preventing cold air from entering into the space through the windows. The rel-

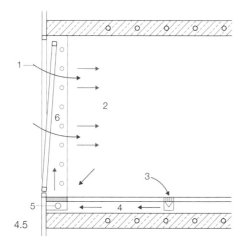

4.5

1 Fresh air, cold
2 Supply air, pre-warmed
3 Floor air inlet with air filter
4 Air return in double floor
5 Small fan
6 Air-conducting facade post

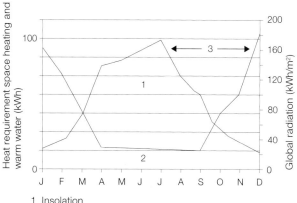

1 Insolation
2 Space heating
4.6   3 Seasonal asynchronicity

evant thermal and hygienic requirements for HVAC systems must be taken into consideration. In Germany, these requirements are outlined in DIN 1946 and in the VDI-guideline 6022, in the case of air movement via double floors without air ducts.
The concept offers the following advantages:
• year-round window ventilation without draught
• sufficient "flushing" with air all the way to the core zones
• comfortable floor surface temperature

Seasonal Energy Storage/Long-term Storage
In addition to passive energy concepts, where a building is supplied with the help of deliberate measures such as window ventilation, thermal storage masses or heating and water temperatures adjusted to a low-energy level, active solar measures, such as collector installations, can also be integrated; the excess heat of which, in summer, is stored for heating in winter (Fig. 4.6). The area of installed solar thermal collectors has increased rapidly since the early 1990s. While there were roughly 450,000 m² of collector areas in 1990, the number had risen to roughly 3 million m² for short-term storage collectors in 2000, which provide warm water with temperatures below 100 °C for daily use. Currently, they still play a greater role than long-term storage (cf. pp 26ff). However, the development of district-heating concepts for the supply of entire residential districts and small industrial parks is accelerating. The goal is to increase the percentage of requirements covered by solar power and to make better use of the seasonal asynchronicity between available solar energy and heating demands. Constructed earth reservoirs, large storage tanks and bore holes are suitable options (cf. p. 30), although area requirements are high because of the dimensions of the storage units.

Sorption Technology
The principle of cooling by evaporation offers an alternative to cooling outside air in summer by means of conventional, power-operated chillers. It is called "Desiccant and Evaporative Cooling" or DEC (Fig.4.7). Dessicants, which extract humidity from the air, are stored in a rotary heat exchanger. Cooling and dehumidification of fresh air supplies in summer is regulated by adding heat to the exhaust air. The dryer the exhaust air, the greater the percentage of humidity the exchanger extracts from the outside air. If the exhaust air is heated to about 80 °C, the extracted percentage of humidity is especially high. On overcast summer days, the heat required for this process is generally provided by district heat. On clear days with high solar radiation, high-performance solar collectors can be used for this purpose (Fig. 4.8). Once the outside air has been dried with the help of the sorption generator and the connected heat recovery plant, the air is cooled to the desired supply temperature by means of evaporation humidifiers. In other

Fresh air
(supply) ——
Exhaust
air   - - - -

4.7

1 Outside air dehumidification
2 Pre-cooling (heat recovery, HR)
3 Cooling (adiabatic)
4 Warming (waste heat from supply air fan)
5 Room air cooling (adiabatic)
6 Warming (HR)
7 Re-heating
8 Desorption

4.4   Installation of cooling pipes in reinforcement
4.5   Concrete core activation and window ventilation via air-conducting columns, pre-warming via small fan
4.6   Available solar radiation and total heating requirement of a low-energy row house
4.7   h,x diagram; percentages of changes as a result of sorptive dehumidification and adiabatic cooling

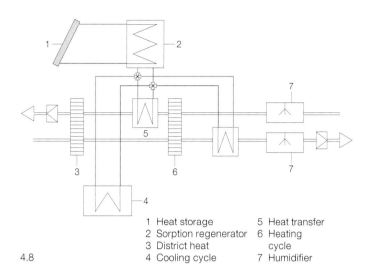

4.8

1 Heat storage
2 Sorption regenerator
3 District heat
4 Cooling cycle
5 Heat transfer
6 Heating cycle
7 Humidifier

words, this is a cooling energy process based on air desiccation followed by evaporative cooling, in which water replaces the CFC- or FC-containing refrigerants in conventional chillers. Since the warm and humid outside air must be cooled even on overcast days, or, conversely, the cold outside air heated in winter, a conventional heating system is essential for this system. The advantage of foregoing the use of an electrically powered chiller lies in the savings, that is, the reduction of electrical energy, which can be replaced with district or solar heat. An approximate average of 300–400 full operating hours is required to cool the outside air in summer. The heating requirement should be largely met with solar heat at supply temperatures of 80 °C; the remainder is covered with district heating. In summer, in particular, this heat is the product of rational energy use in the form of heat waste from power stations. The advantage of DEC-systems, compared to systems with conventional cooling energy production, lies in the low electrical connect load (because there is no chiller), and the resulting low annual consumption of power and water (because there is no need to re-cool a chiller).

Geothermal Heating/Cooling
The increased use heating/cooling ceilings, concrete core activation and the simultaneous improvement of insulating standards promote the use of geothermal energy[2]. In contrast to nearly all other regenerative energies, geothermal energy is not dependent on incident solar radiation, except in the surface layers. The topic of geothermal energy near the ground surface is discussed in the section on heat pumps. The majority of geothermal systems derive the required heat from layers in the earth ranging in depth from 0–40 m. As a source of heat and cold energy for earth-coupled heating and air-conditioning systems, permission is easily obtainable in Germany for depths up to 99 m. Earth or groundwater temperatures, which are more or less constant year round, offer ideal prerequisites for generating energy for heating or cooling buildings with the help of a variety of systems. One of the most advantageous for office and administration buildings is the combination of so-called energy piles, change-over heat pumps, as well as area heating and cooling systems such as radiant heating/cooling ceilings and concrete core activation (Fig. 4.9). The low operating temperatures of such systems in conjunction with the relevant harmonization of the three individual measures mentioned above and favourable geological conditions, create an ideal scenario for energy- and cost-saving building operation. In Germany, the amalgamation of regulations for heating systems and insulation into a single energy savings regulation (EnEV) has further improved the parameters for implementing integrated solutions of this kind.

Heat-Power Coupling
Conventional power generation in condensating power plants and heat in boilers is inefficient because the majority of energy required to generate power is lost in the form of wasted heat. In a combined heat and power plant (CHP), on the other hand, up to 34 per cent of the primary energy is transformed into power and up to roughly 53 per cent is transformed into heat (Fig. 4.10), which translates into an overall efficiency rate of 90 per cent. Conversely, the overall efficiency of separate heat and power generation lies

4.9

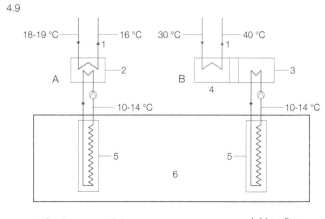

A Cooling
B Heating
1 to consumer
2 Water-heat exchanger unit
3 Heat pump
4 Liquefier
5 Energy pile
6 Soil

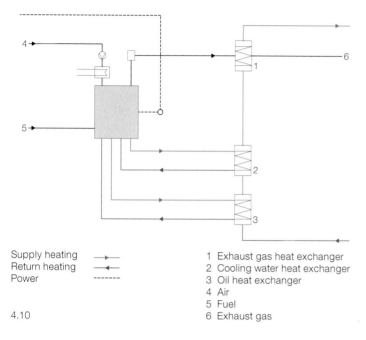

Supply heating   →
Return heating   ←
Power   -------

4.10

1 Exhaust gas heat exchanger
2 Cooling water heat exchanger
3 Oil heat exchanger
4 Air
5 Fuel
6 Exhaust gas

below 60 per cent. CHPs therefore generate energy and emission savings of roughly 30 per cent. Several parameters should be taken into consideration for the efficient application of CHPs because the initial investment costs and the operating costs are higher. Since power fed into the grid is still remunerated at a much lower rate than is charged to consumers, the goal should be to achieve direct consumption of as much of the generated power and heat as possible. The efficient sizing of the plant is therefore based on a basic output demand; the remainder is supplied by conventional means. Depending on the heating demand, the operating time of the CHP and the output it delivers can be estimated as follows:
• For space heating only:
recommended CHP output 10–15 per cent of total required output, operating time from 4.500 h/a
• For space and warm water heating:
recommended CHP output 10–15 per cent of total required output, operating time from 5.500 h/a

To assess the economic viability of a CHP, one must compare the costs against the financial benefit gained through energy savings. Boiler systems and CHPs must be compared in consideration of investment, maintenance and fuel costs. For smaller systems (approximately100 kW el), the total costs for CHP and boiler are roughly twice as high as those for a conventional boiler system. CHPs also require high repair and maintenance costs. To avoid downtimes, an additional module should always be included as a backup system when maintenance is being carried out. Considering the power savings and the national environmental tax credit[3] in Germany, for example, such systems can be economically viable and efficient when power rates are higher than 6 cents/kWh. However, owing to the wide range of additional parameters, the economic viability of employing a CHP must be analyzed for each individual case.

Intelligent Controls and Regulation
Energy conservation or solar building also means using efficient systems and intelligent control technology, which can implement the relevant option (e.g., night cooling) in a practical manner. This can translate into an energy savings potential of, for example, as much as 15–30 per cent for ventilation and air-conditioning systems (VAC). The use of intelligent building systems that respond to fluctuating conditions also ensures the smooth and energy-saving operation of the installation. BAS (building automation systems) are divided into three areas: management, automation, and application. Intelligent regulation is largely enabled by so-called bus systems[4], which make it possible to implement integrated concepts for monitoring, controlling, regulating and managing the technical building systems of a given property. Such integrated concepts facilitate communication between all automated components whose data can be digitally recorded, such as boilers, pumps, chillers, water processors, room automation (individual room con-

4.8 Diagram sorption technology (dessicative and evaporative cooling and absorption system)
4.9 Building core conditioning via energy piles in the soil
4.10 Functional diagram of CHP (natural gas)

trols), lighting controls, shading systems and the primary components of the HVC systems – both with each other (component to component) and with the corresponding operator. To this end, all automated, communication-capable system components provided by one manufacturer must be connected as simply and cost-efficiently as possible with the system provided by another manufacturer. Communication protocols for bus systems and BAS networks are becoming increasingly important. Open, fabrication-independent communication protocols have become the dominant platform for the areas defined above (management, automation and field application). The marketplace also offers a wide variety of specific, product-dependent bus systems. A detailed cost-benefit analysis can, in individual cases, reveal that a product-specific system bus is more economical. In each instance, the prerequisite for making the right choice is project-specific, innovative planning, which also takes the future use of innovative systems that are still beyond the scope of the current technology, into account.

Comfort and Efficiency

All supply systems employed in office and administrative buildings serve to ensure the comfort and well-being of the users in order to promote maximum performance in the workplace. This can only be achieved by meeting physiological and hygienic parameters, among which air quality, temperature and air velocity in the room play a key role. However the perception and experience of thermal comfort is also influenced by individual factors (Fig. 4.12). Room temperatures that are comfortable for humans are based on a body temperature of 36.6 °C and are created when there is a balanced equilibrium between heat losses, heat generated by the users themselves and ambient temperature. Physical comfort is also influenced by perspiration. Air humidity and air movement, therefore, play important roles. Whereas people experience moderate to strong air movement as perfectly comfortable outdoors, provided they are wearing appropriate clothing, any kind of draught is experienced as uncomfortable indoors. This is especially true for sedentary work in offices where maximum air velocities of 0.15– 0.2 m/s are recommended to avoid the effects of draught.[5] Air movement on the outside is assessed according to Beaufort's scale of wind force (also known as Beaufort force).[6] According to this scale, wind force up to 0.2 m/s denotes calm. Wind force 1 (0.3–1.5 m/s) is described as light air, where wind is only visible through smoke, and wind force 2 (1.6–3.3 m/s) constitutes a light breeze. In interiors, air that flows predominantly from one direction and is cooler than the room air results in draught.[7] For high outside temperatures of approximately 32 °C, operative temperatures of 26–27 °C are acceptable indoors. Naturally these temperatures have a direct influence on the performance capacity of humans, which is highest for temperatures between 20 and 25 °C, and decreases as temperatures rise. At over 35 °C (50 per cent relative humidity) performance is at 80 per cent on average. In addition to room air temperature, the ambient temperature is a particularly important and oft-overlooked criterion for comfort. Ambient temperature is the mean of room air and surface temperature. Wall temperatures can be increased in winter with the help of radiant heating units. Heated facades, which diminish cold airdrops and

4.11

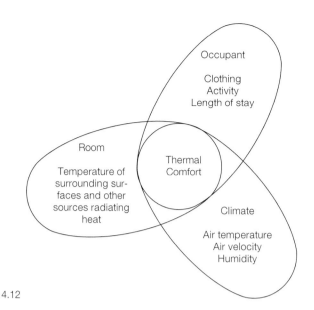

4.12

reduce draught on tall facades, are also advantageous. Even the addition of a single pane can lead to an improvement. Recent developments in thermopane glazing take this phenomenon into account. In combination with the low thermal transmission values of the glass, surface temperatures do not fall below 18 °C even on cold winter days. There are various options for arranging the so-called low-E layer (cf. pp. 56ff). Indoor air quality is another comfort requirement. Ventilation and air-conditioning systems should create a physiologically favourable indoor climate of impeccable hygienic air quality. To fulfil this task, a series of measures are required during the planning, design, construction and operation of the building. In Germany, 30–40 m³/h of fresh air is generally deemed sufficient for every workstation. This corresponds to an air change of 2 ac/h. If smoking is allowed, the fresh air rate must be increased to 60 m³/h. However, in order to adequately exhaust other loads, for example, exhalations and odours – from humans, materials, carpeting – up to 80 m³/h of fresh air should be supplied per person.[7] In buildings with natural ventilation (window ventilation), air change cannot be defined with precision; it depends on wind pressure and external temperatures. The type of window opening – its design as tilt-and-turn window, sliding window with synchronized horizontal openings at top and bottom, or sliding window with vertical openings – is also important in practice. The differing designs and concepts (simple or cross-ventilation) result in very different air change rates and perceived indoor air comfort.

Efficiency

The demand for flexible and innovative spatial organizations, and for savings in operating costs, has resulted in planning and design concepts that are comprehensive. Aside from the understandable demand for comfort, the issue of efficiency is becoming more important. Ultimately, decisions are based on the financing of a new construction and the anticipated operating costs. Although the tasks of building systems have become more complex in recent years and can only be solved in an interdisciplinary manner, only some 5 per cent of total budgets are dedicated to planning and designing these systems. The production costs are in the region of 25 per cent and 70 per cent are dedicated to operation. These numbers should illustrate the focus of clients and/or investors and the areas in which they should invest. In the past, buildings were often thoughtlessly equipped with technology; facades were poorly insulated and left without shading systems or with systems that were inefficient . Energy consumption was, and continues to be, correspondingly high. Low efficiency coefficients and oversized heat-generating systems exacerbated the wasteful management. The annual energy requirement of roughly 900 kWh/m² in the mid-1960s was reduced to 400 kWh/m² by the early 1990s (Fig. 4.13). Today, an administrative building with an energy coefficient of roughly 150–170 kWh/m² in terms of primary energy

4.11 "Westhafen-Tower" in Frankfurt/Main (2002), Schneider + Schumacher, prefabricated facade system, air-water cooling ceilings, river water cooling.
4.12 Comfort criteria

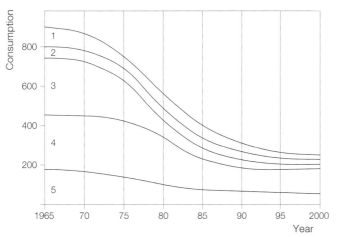

Consumption in kWh/m²/a:
1 – 3 Air-conditioning system (1 fans/blowers, 2 cold air supply, 3 warm air supply)
4   Facade
5   Lighting

4.13

requirements is classified as a low-energy building in Germany. However, old buildings, in particular, are still being operated with outdated building systems. In other words, energy consumption continues to rise because the building skin has deteriorated over time through exposure to the elements and systems can no longer achieve acceptable efficiency, despite regular maintenance. The lifespan of a building, especially of the structure, is two to three times longer than the lifespan of the technical equipment. Changes in communications technology are further decreasing the life cycles of technical building equipment. The evolution of PCs and information technology has brought about inevitable changes in building use. These changes, along with new technical systems, translate into necessary adaptations. The acceleration in changes to building systems will increase, albeit not automatically or necessarily, with each innovation in the effectiveness and functions of electronic data processing and information technology, which will, in turn, increase the energy efficiency of the building systems. Different potentials for solar building can be harnessed depending on building type and requirements. The topic has sparked many debates, but it is only in recent times that new supply concepts have been developed. The advantages of the new developments are particularly evident when compared to the old systems. To illustrate the potential of technical solutions, three renovation projects have been chosen in which comfort was increased and energy requirements were reduced (including, CO_2 emissions).

The examples are:
• BMW headquarters in Munich
• Former Chamber of Deputies high-rise "Langer Eugen" in Bonn
• Former Reichstag in Berlin

Each of these buildings is known beyond the borders of Germany and they are considered icons of timeless architecture. The authors were directly involved in the technical upgrades of the two high-rises in the form of project studies carried out over several years. The Reichstag renovation, on the other hand, was planned and executed as an exemplary model of solar building. The key aspects, which led to the improved comfort conditions and reduced energy consumption, are discussed for each of these examples.

BMW Headquarters in Munich
The Viennese architect Karl Schwanzer completed the BMW headquarters building between 1968 and 1972. The shape and unique proportions of the high-rise became a symbol and an urban link to the grounds of the Olympic Games, which were held in Munich in 1972, the same year the building was completed. The building's unique plan made it possible to create a variable and flexible office structure. Each workstation was assigned an area of 10.25 m² at the time, which resulted in a ratio of 73 per cent usable area to 27 per cent circulation area. The division of the usable area into four sections grouped around the building's core resulted in work areas with a more or less equal share of daylight (Fig. 4.14). The BMW high-rise was the first example in Europe of a facade structure where breast wall, intrados and lintels were composed of a single

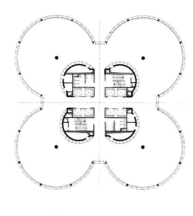

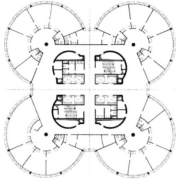

4.14

4.15

element. The facade design is particularly noticeable. Each element consists of a trapezoid, a roughly 2 m²-large pane of antisun glass, which is tilted outward by an angle approximately 9° (Fig. 4.15, 4.17). This ensures that sound is not reflected directly into the room through the facade, but redirected via the ceiling. Another advantage, albeit not deliberately planned, is the diminished angle of solar incidence. Compared to the real altitude, the sun always seems to be 9° higher in the sky. The insolated glass areas – and hence the external cooling loads – are reduced. This prefabricated facade is also called an alcast-facade (alcast = aluminium-cast).[8] The offices in the high-rise are supplied via so-called two-duct, high-velocity air-conditioning systems, a concept that was popular and technically excellent at the time. The VAC equipment was housed in the basement and on the 15th and 23rd floors. Air was transported vertically in the building core to the individual floors. Horizontal floor distribution to the individual office areas was effected via air ducts suspended from the ceiling. Fire-protection registers in the shaft separated the fire compartments. Cold and warm air were mixed in variable air volume boxes according to the set values for room temperatures and injected into the rooms at a constant volume flow. The air was injected into the room from the variable air system via air inlets and the suspended ceiling from above; spent air was similarly suctioned off through outlets. Tremendous air volumes were required to extract the heat loads in the offices. Air change was $ac = 7$ h^{-1} in the outer area of the cylinder, and $ac = 10h^{-1}$ in the inner area. This meant that an average of 24 m³/h of air had to be injected for each square metre (Fig. 4.16). Requirements had changed after more than 25 years of operation: computer had replaced typewriters, the number of workstations had increased and so had the cooling loads in summer. Problems also became evident on the facade: the sealant was porous. Thermal bridges began to form between sections and the facade was no longer airtight. In 1997, the company was inspired by these visible signs of wear and tear, and by design/construction errors, to consider renovating the high-rise. A competition was held and the first commission issued for an analysis of necessary renovations on the administrative building. The results of the study led to a proposal for executing a renewal of the facade in conjunction with the implementation of a completely new air-conditioning concept – taking current requirements for workplace conditions and communications technology into consideration. It was suggested that the air-only system should be replaced by mechanical and natural fresh air ventilation in combination with a water-cooled system in the form of a cooling ceiling. The original fresh air rate of 24 m³/h per square metre was reduced to a mere 6 m³/h per square metre with the proposed displacement ventilation system, which ensures draught-free, flexible and efficient ventilation. The radiant cooling from the cooling ceiling creates a comfortable indoor climate. With the existing variable air volume system, air was injected into the rooms in a

4.13 Trend in energy consumption in Germany
4.14 BMW high-rise, Munich (1972), Karl Schwanzer, Vienna, room division on standard floors
4.15 BMW high-rise Munich, assembly of prefabricated facade elements

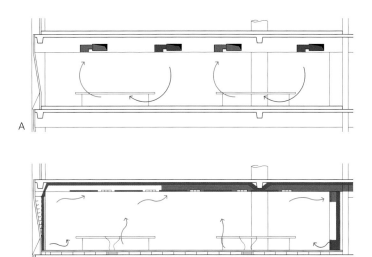

A

B

4.16

4.17

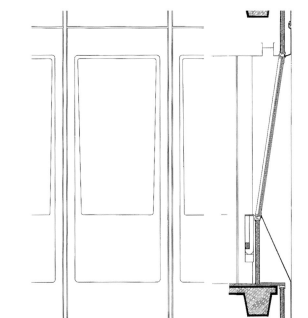

fairly turbulent manner and with relatively high velocity. The resulting eddies flushed the rooms with air. The vertical air jets reached nearly all utilized areas. In the proposed displacement ventilation system, the pre-processed fresh air is injected noiselessly into the room across a large area. Due to the cooler temperature of this air, it sinks to the floor and forms a kind of "sea" of cold air. It rises along warm bodies – occupants and computers – bringing fresh air directly into the space and distributing it around the room. Noiseless and draught-free, it absorbs heat and is extracted at the top (Fig. 4.16). Up to 70 per cent of internal and external loads are utilized via heat recovery systems to pre-warm the fresh air in winter, or to pre-cool it in summer. Another advantage of this system is the modest installation height required in the ceiling area.

The proposed technical upgrades not only radically reduce energy consumption, they also cut operating costs for repair and maintenance in half:
• replacement of facade insulation
• improvement of shading from g=44 per cent to g=12 per cent (approximately) with the help of 30°daylight-directing louvers
• 75 per cent reduction of required air volume
• air supply temperature raised from previously 17 °C to 20 °C in summer through displacement ventilation
• increase in the energy recovery coefficient to roughly 70 per cent as a result of new systems and equipment

Former Chamber of Deputies High-rise "Langer Eugen" in Bonn
The former Chamber of Deputies high-rise for the German Bundestag has been in operation for over 30 years. The innovative design and concept for the landmark, erected between 1966 and 1969, were created by Egon Eiermann. Today, the building houses various UN institutions (Fig. 4.19). The building is divided into five zones: entrance, deputy offices, restaurant/café and kitchen as well as equipment floors. It consists of a circulation and a supply core constructed with in-situ concrete, the load-bearing steel skeleton structure and the prefabricated concrete floor slabs. The column grid on the two lower floors is 7.50 × 7.50 m, decreasing to 3.75 × 3.75 m on the floors above (Fig. 4.18). The shading system is fixed rigidly in place. It consists of glass-fibre reinforced polyester louvers screw-fastened to the vertical beams (square sections) of the facade. The distance between louvers and outer building edge is roughly 1.2 m (Figs. 4.21, 4.22). The advantage of this design is the passive use it makes of solar radiation. The angle of incidence changes as a result of the projection depending on the season, and in summer the system provides effective shading for the offices. Without diminishing visual contact with the outside, the shallow winter sun also leads to heat gains. The offices are supplied with air via induction units mounted below the windowsills on the inside. Fresh-air is pre-warmed (or pre-cooled) in the centralized plant on the equipment floor and transported to the induction units via the support columns for the steel girders. Every second column conducts air and cold or warm water. The induction units extract spent air at floor level and inject fresh air into the room at ceiling level (Fig. 4.20). Depending on the cooling loads, this leads to variable and high air velocities (draught) and loud flow noises. From the

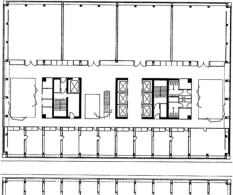

4.18

4.19

areas near the core, spent air flows from the offices into the hallways and anterooms. This system no longer meets current fire-safety standards. The goal of the study was to adapt the building to current office building standards, while preserving the external form. The proposed upgrade for the climate concept is based on newly developed induction technology.

The old units were to be replaced with new displacement air induction units. This system reverses the airflow direction. Air is suctioned off above the window and fresh air is injected into the room horizontally and with low velocity. A water-cooled system (cooling convector/ceiling) covers the remaining cooling demands, although the output was sized exclusively for the offices. The areas near the core are supplied from a separate central ventilation system. The diminished output of the latter means that the ducts can be smaller, which adds 20 cm to the clear room height. The main advantages of the proposed displacement ventilation system are:

• guaranteed continuous air exchange
• the reduction of draught
• diminished energy consumption (Fig. 4.20).

Reichstag Conversion in Berlin
The conversion of the Reichstag Building into the German Bundestag in Berlin (1996-1997) introduced changes to the spatial programme and, at the same time, symbolized the new parliamentary use of the building. Remarkably, the clients also wanted to create an ecological symbol and decided that this would be the principal criterion for awarding first prize. The winning design has met these requirements in an exceptional fashion. It has not only made the building accessible to the public all day long – a solution that is unique in the world for this type of building – but also implemented an extremely advanced ecological concept that was equally unique at the time. The existing building had been fundamentally restructured in the interior after the Second World War and was equipped with building systems dating from the 1960s. Nevertheless, the Reichstag – planned and realized over a century ago by the architect Paul Wallot in collaboration with engineer David Grove (1884-94) – was nothing short of a technical marvel in its original form. The concept corresponded largely to contemporary standards. The seat of the German Bundestag was conceived to not only ensure efficient operation with minimal energy consumption, but also to act as a symbol of a "democratic and transparent parliament, a model of ecology" (cf. pp 148ff). Since the building substance was largely preserved, the conversion could be based on the advanced heating and ventilation system developed by

4.16 BMW high-rise, Munich, existing mixed ventilation system (A), proposed system of air injection at floor level/displacement ventilation system with cooling canvas (B)
4.17 BMW high-rise, Munich, facade section. The facade is joint-fastened to the concrete slab, U-beams ensure lateral stability.
4.18 Chamber of Deputies high-rise, Bonn (1969), Egon Eiermann; standard floor plan with offices and conference halls
4.19 Chamber of Deputies high-rise, Bonn, facade image in 1969

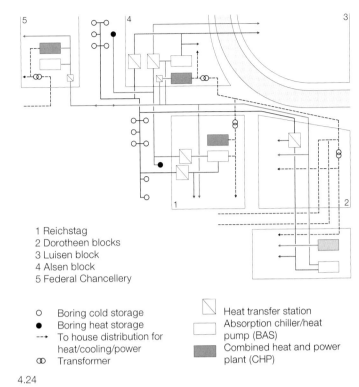

1 Reichstag
2 Dorotheen blocks
3 Luisen block
4 Alsen block
5 Federal Chancellery

○   Boring cold storage
●   Boring heat storage
--→   To house distribution for
       heat/cooling/power
⊙⊙   Transformer

◻   Heat transfer station
▭   Absorption chiller/heat
      pump (BAS)
▬   Combined heat and power
      plant (CHP)

4.24

CO_2 emissions. In the Reichstag, the goal was to achieve economically efficient and ecologically sustainable autonomous supply. In addition to efficiency, the symbolic character of this building designed for reduced energy consumption also played an important role. A photovoltaic system was therefore installed on the roof as an additional solar component, which enables nearly emission-free solar power generation.

Energy Savings
The building is run in stand-by operation (large storage mass and short-term occupation periods). Floor heating covers most of the heating demand in winter, maintaining a low temperature level and preserving a steady state in the building through constant heat supply. This prevents a decrease in internal wall temperatures. The advantage of this operating method is that the peak heating loads are reduced by roughly 30 per cent. While Grove was unable to precisely determine the constant fluctuation in heating demands in the Reichstag, dynamic building simulation programmes make it possible today to calculate hourly heating loads. In summer, cooling ceilings continually extract heat from the building with little effort in terms of energy consumption. A mechanical ventilation system is activated only when internal loads rise rapidly because there are more occupants (peak load). This system design drastically reduces the power demand for the fans, because their use is limited to very short periods of time. Moreover, the varying demand for heating, cooling and power in the parliamentary power grid ensures excellent utilization of the CHPs. The utility supplier BEWAG supplies peak load and stand-by power if the capacity limit is exceeded. A dual and spatially independent 10-kV supply ensures that the grid is supplied with power (Fig. 4.24). The ducts and pipes (also for heating/cooling and the aquifers) are laid in underground tunnels between the buildings. This complex power generation and supply system requires an overarching energy management, which uses prognoses processes to ensure that energy supply is optimized at all times.

Efficient Building – Standardized Building
A variety of methods and tools are required to reduce the energy consumption of building even during the planning and construction phase and to ensure comfort even when economic resources are scarce. These include simulation calculations and numeric modelling, employed to determine parameters such as temperature conditions and room quality. From both the economical and the ecological perspective, the quality of the systems installation work and of the building's structure should also be monitored and harmonized at the earliest possible stage. Optimization has long become a standard in industrial manufacturing processes, (e.g. automobile manufacture); this aspect still seems to be neglected in building processes. The current research into "systems engineering" aims to develop a methodical approach to organizing complex building projects, which makes it possible to also standardize the technical requirements that change from project to project in architecture. Fully prefabricated solar building components are transformed into coherent building modules. Given the same construction costs, this leads to greatly improved quality in execution, shorter assembly and instal-

lation times and also provides a solid foundation for facility management (roughly 75 per cent of the total cost required to operate a building for 30 years). Planning and building processes can only be optimized if architects and engineers adopt a new way of thinking: they must approach tasks from a systemic and not only a systematic perspective. What we need are systems of measuring, databases, industrial prefabrication as well as intelligent controls and comprehensive electronic data management. New ideas, designs and building methods can raise the always anticipated, albeit rarely delivered, quality in craftsmanship to industrial standards. Complex building processes become manageable through planning projections, and thus, efficient – a foundation for solar, that is, sustainable building.

4.24 Reichstag, Berlin, parliamentary power grid, diagram of energy supply concept
4.25 Administration building, Munich (2001), von Seidlein, prefabricated facade, natural ventilation, regulation/control via Bus system, building component cooling

4.25

Notes:
1 The Kioto Protocol (ratified in 1997) – the United Nations agreement on climate change – contains the contractual commitment of the signatory states to gradually reduce emissions in order to counteract global warming. www.unfccc.int/resource/docs/convkp/kpeng.html
2 According to VDI guideline 4640 in Germany
3 The bill on the preservation, modernization and expansion of power-heat coupling (power-heat co-generation bill) came into effect on April 1, 2002. Operators of eligible CHP installations will receive estimated subsidies of € 4,448 billion by 2010. Operators of newly created small CHPs of up to 50 KW and of fuel-cell installations enjoy the greatest benefit. www.bmwi.de
4 The bus constitutes a common link between several communicating systems (participants) – e.g., building systems, alarm systems or computers. This connection is the basis for building automation. Every participant preparing to access the bus, verifies whether the bus is currently transmitting data. The rules for data transmission are referred to as the protocol.
5 The maximum velocities for offices are set at 0.15–0.2 m/s to prevent draught (DIN 1946).
6 The British Admiral Sir Francis Beaufort (1774–1857) developed the Beaufort scale named after him in 1806. It is used to estimate wind force based the effects of wind according to a given definition. The scale ranges from wind force 0 (calm) to wind force 12.
7 In Germany, the range of comfortable room air temperatures is defined in DIN 1946.
8 Alcast-facade construction: Alcast element: approx. 2m2 antisun trapezoidal glazing; Type: Auresin 66/44 with air cavity; Structure: 8 mm +12 mm, +6 mm SZR, no thermal separation from frame; internal shading: vertical louvers, U-value of 1.8 W/m2 K, 44 per cent transmission coefficient
9 Axial fans transport air in the direction of the propeller shaft. This produces high volume flow with very little power consumption. This method is very suitable for short routes with low counter pressure.
10 Adiabatic cooling (→ evaporative cooling)
11 Aquifer reservoirs are large natural, underground reservoirs for seasonal storage, which utilize water-filled porous layers in the earth.
12 Sorption technology (sorptive conditioning) describes the combination of desiccation, evaporative cooling and heat recovery (→ sorption technology).

Utilizing Daylight

Helmut F.O.Müller and Heide G.Schuster

The Task

From simple weather protection to multifunctional building skin
"Care must be taken with all buildings, [to ensure] that they are bright […]."[1]

The first windows were conceived less for utilizing daylight than for ventilating rooms. The house itself was intended to provide protection against extreme weather conditions and to offer safety. Historically, buildings have always been planned in an integrated manner based on necessity: the characteristics and effects of daylight were well-known because no other medium could provide adequate illumination. It was only after the invention of electrical light and its widespread use that architects and planners began to lose their knowledge of daylight. This, and the division of planning into design, building physics, building systems and load-bearing systems, obviated the integrated interpretation of space and light, which was superseded by a purely physical approach to technical solutions. Artificial light was seen as indisputable progress because it allowed for the creation of windowless rooms and enormous room depths. But the industrial revolution also made it possible to realize larger openings in the building skin with the help of glass and iron. Load-bearing, solid walls were eliminated; entire roofs could be covered in glass. The evolution of the curtain wall allowed for the creation of glass-steel facades that were independent of the load-bearing structure, and the invention of air-conditioning systems made it possible to compensate for the overheating in buildings resulting from the large glazed surfaces.
The interior of a building could thus be cooled and illuminated independent of climate and weather conditions. After several generations of architects were no longer compelled to design with daylight in mind, there was a noticeable lack of training and expertise in this area.
Today, we have access to technological options, which can minimize many of the problems associated with glass facades in the past. Nevertheless, there is a growing interest in daylighting, inspired, on the one hand, by lower costs for lighting and cooling and, on the other hand, by user comfort. The influence of daylight on humans and the significance of daylight quality are generally underestimated. For the lux value alone is a poor indicator of the physiological and psychological effect of the surroundings. As the number of available types of glass and materials increases, simulation tools, which facilitate in the planning and design of complex systems, will gain in importance.

Designing Architectural Space with Light
"More and more, so it seems to me, light is the beautifier of the building."[2]

Master architects have always worked with light and its effects in interiors. Light is the prerequisite for architecture, for architecture cannot be perceived without light. Light is alive, varied and changes nearly every second. Intelligent use of daylight can achieve a powerful intensity in the spatial effect and awaken emotions in the observer. The architect can manipulate light in terms of colour and intensity, utilize it directly or indirectly, or employ it in its natural state. Openings can blur the transition from the interior space to the exterior or deliberately "frame" the exterior space.

It is important to distinguish between ambient lighting designed to achieve a specific effect – for example, a mystical spatial effect in churches – and the utility lighting that is essential for the use of a building, for example, office buildings. The rule of thumb for the latter is: the more daylight is used, the more comfortable is the user.

Changing priorities over time wrought the aforementioned changes in architecture. In the past, the imperative was to adapt to the regional climate, today, artificial lighting and heating or cooling make it possible to design architecture independent of climate conditions – with global rather than regional characteristics. Today, the language of architecture is more or less the same worldwide, regardless of where a building is located. But energy consumption – particularly in lighting – is strongly dependent on the local climate, cultural environment and building form. A German engineer recently made a memorable statement: "The best and most effective form of energy efficiency is thinking."[3]

Visual Perception and Visual Tasks
The sensitivity to light of the human eye ranges from 380–760 nanometers (nm) and is optimally adapted to solar radiation: the greatest sensitivity lies in the range of

5.1   Airport Munich, Terminal 2 (2003), Koch +Partners;
      Check-in hall, direct and indirect utilization of daylight.

5.2

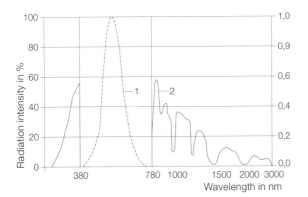

5.3

5.4

1 Visible range of light/light sensitivity of the human eye
2 Global radiation

the maximum radiation intensity at 550 nm (yellow), diminishing as it reaches the short- and long-wave radiation spectrum. The retina of the human eye has different types of receptors: approximately 5–6 million cones for colour perception in daylight and over 100 million rods, which are sensitive to light and react to low light intensity (night vision). A third type of receptors that influence the circadian behaviour of humans (i.e., for the biological inner clock) was only discovered in recent years.

The light sensitivity of the eye dependent on the wavelength is the reference for the photometric units, which are employed to measure and calculate lighting designs (official SI-units[4]):
• Luminous flux (Φ): total light output of a luminous source; unit: lumen (lm).
• Luminous intensity (I): luminous flux in solid angle of 1 steradian (lm/sr); unit: candela (cd).
• Illuminance (E): luminous flux/area (lm/m^2); unit: lux (lx).
• Luminance (L): impression of brightness emanating from a light source or illuminated surface, given as luminous intensity per area (cd/m^2).

The bandwidth of the brightness, that is, luminance, perceptible by the human eye covers an astonishing range: in nocturnal situations with rod vision from 106 to 100 cd/m^2 and in diurnal situations with cone vision from 100 to 104 cd/m^2. Adaptation is achieved through adjustment in the pupil and biochemical processes in the retina. This process takes time, particularly in the case of adaptation from very high to very low luminances, a familiar experience with glare when driving at night (up to 30 minutes for adaptation from a bright to a dark environment, approximately 3 minutes for the reverse). Although less noticeable, extreme contrast in luminance in the visual field of perception is just as uncomfortable because the eye attempts to simultaneously adapt to the bright and the dark areas. Exposure to contrast glare over long periods, especially in the workplace, causes fatigue and discomfort. Very high luminances present, for example, when direct sunlight falls onto reflecting surfaces, also result in uncomfortable glare effects, which must be avoided at workstations.[5]

Aside from glare prevention, there are additional requirements that must be considered when daylighting interiors, such as contact with the exterior, brightness, colour neutrality and detail resolution. Visual contact with the outside through windows is a basic requirement; its importance to room quality has been proven in many user surveys.[6]

Brightness is essential both for the perception of the interior space and for the effort- and errorless execution of certain visual tasks. Default standard illuminances[7] for certain types of room use should be understood as minimum values (e.g., 500–1000 lx for offices); higher values result in better visual performance.[8] The same applies to the lower boundary value of the daylight factor (ratio of horizontal illuminance in the interior to the horizontal illuminance on the exterior under overcast sky) according to DIN 5034: the factor 0.9 per cent for living areas lit from one side represents the absolute minimum, whereas good daylighting requires considerably higher factors of 5 per cent or more depending on room use. Given a mean exterior illuminance of 10 000 lx under overcast sky, for example, the latter would translate into a minimum illuminance of 500 lx for the interior. However, it is often insufficient to limit brightness in interior lighting to horizontal illuminance (at a working plane of 85 cm above floor level), for vertical illuminance, in particular, is significant with regard to the biological effect of light and for specific visual tasks, for example, looking at exhibits in a museum setting. The user's visual impression of a room is, however, not influenced by illuminance, but by luminance.

The spectral composition of daylight should remain unaltered by the glass or shading device of the window because it is the prerequisite for correct colour rendition in the room (colour neutrality). Detail perception is extremely important for many visual tasks; differences exist for office work, precision mechanical work and textile work. As brightness increases, so does the resolution capacity (perception of details), although a minimal contrast, for example, through cast shadows, is required. To summarize: the efficiency of visual performance increases as illuminance increases.

Physiological and Psychological Effects of Light
"Lighting is not an exact science, but also an art that affects objects and humans."[9]
Natural light with cast shadows, fluctuations and colour rendition is the yardstick by which humans assess light quality, and is in part related to cultural background, climate and location. Personal experience also plays a role. People are influenced by the prevailing light conditions. Their biorhythm is based on the natural change from day to night, the duration and intensity of sunshine, and the spectral composition of light. When we consider that humans did not originally inhabit enclosed space, we can easily understand how working exclusively under artificial lighting conditions can lead to illness. In some latitudes, (e.g., Central Europe), there is a risk of insufficient exposure to daylight especially in winter, which may cause the well-documented winter depression (Seasonal Affective Disorder). We now know that exposure of the eye over several hours per day to a vertical illuminance of at least 2500 lx is required to synchronize the internal clock.[10, 11] The stipulated minimum illuminance in offices, on the other hand, is only designed for visual performance, not for the circadian system, that is, the system which influences the biorhythm. The called-for 500 lx in the workplace (horizontal measurement) is far too low in this regard.[12] If one were to provide the amount of light necessary for the biorhythm solely with the help of artificial light, the result would be a drastic jump in the average amount of energy that is consumed and a corresponding increase in cooling loads. Moreover, light quality is much diminished by the use of artificial light, because the latter only renders parts of the spectrum and distorts the appearance of colours in the interior.

5.5

5.2   Light effect as a result of dust in an Asian temple.
5.3   The photometric units: luminous flux (Φ), illuminance (E) and luminance (L)
5.4   Sensitivity of the human eye to brightness in dependence of wavelength
5.5   Church St. Thomas Aquinus, Berlin (1999), Höger Hare Architects

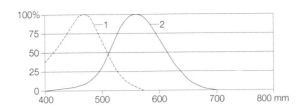

5.6

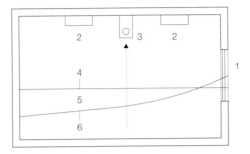

1 Daylight, exterior   4 Illuminance (nominal value)
2 Luminaire   5 Artificial light component
3 Light sensor   6 Daylight component

5.7

Colour temperature in the short-wave range has a positive influence on hormone production and seasonal changes in light have a positive effect on mood. Given the same illuminance, daylight has twice the influence on the circadian system than an incandescent lamp.[13] It is the only available and, moreover, free source for a higher and more effective level of illumination. A positive psychological effect of light is achieved when a room appears bright and open. There is a close correlation with the room-enclosing surfaces. Thus, a room that is predominantly black has an entirely different effect on people than a room with light surfaces and identical illuminance. The guidelines for building planning include a statement that windows should offer an unobstructed view. This is vital, because the information, which the user in the interior gathers from looking through a window, (e.g., pertaining to season and weather), is essential for his or her comfort. Daylight makes it possible to create an environment, the brightness of which would be perceived as uncomfortable if it were created with artificial light. In other words: the reliability of visual performance, which artificial light offers in theory, is outweighed by the increased readiness for greater performance in daylit rooms. Psychological glare is a subjective impediment, which differs for daylight and artificial light under identical objective conditions (contrast and luminance). The cause for this differing evaluation has not been fully explained scientifically. [14] Recently, experiments have been undertaken with variations in artificial light in the workplace. But even in this case, daylight is preferable over artificial light, because the changes in daylight are unpredictable and hence more interesting to people.

Balancing Daylight and Artificial Light
Daylight differs qualitatively and quantitatively from artificial light in many different aspects, for example, in spectral composition and brightness as well as in fluctuation over the course of a day. This is why daylight cannot be replaced by artificial light. Human beings need daylight because it satisfies two basic needs: illumination of the room and the biological stimulation of the psychological and physical sense of well-being. It is generally agreed that working in daylight causes less stress and discomfort than long-term working in artificial light, and that the latter can even have a negative impact on health.[15] For this reason, interiors designed for daytime use and occupation are preferably lit with daylight, restricting the use of artificial light, whenever possible, to those times when daylight is unavailable. Economic and ecological arguments also support the minimized use of artificial light. While daylight is freely available in the form of solar energy, artificial light consumes electricity and is thus a major contributor to the operating costs of buildings and to the stress on the environment. Sunlight is not only free, with a luminous power of roughly 110 lm/W, it is also far more efficient than artificial sources (e.g., incandescent lamp 12 lm/W, fluorescent lamp 80 lm/W). At the same time, artificial light, and the tremendous wasted energy which is radiated as heat, contributes a great deal to room temperatures in summer, that is, to cooling loads.

A prerequisite for saving energy consumed for lighting is to provide automatic control of the artificial lighting system in dependence of daylight. The required use of artificial light in addition to daylight can be quantified with the help of calculating the daylight autonomy (percentage of annual work hours with daylighting) or utility lighting (percentage of annual lighting available through daylight).[16] The term lumination, introduced by Aydinli[17], takes not only the daylight-dependent use of artificial lighting into account, but also a quantification of daylight use when the artificial lighting is dimmed. Various processes are used to calculate annual power consumption (i.e., energy costs for artificial lighting). A standardized analysis process is anticipated when the German Institute for Standardization implements the EU-guideline on the "total energy efficiency of buildings." Monitoring of case studies of the IEA[18] reveals clear differences in energy consumption for artificial lighting in dependence of daylight utilization.

Basics of Daylighting

Daylight Availability under Overcast and Clear Sky
Daylight availability, solar altitude and sunshine hours are strongly dependent on the location of the site. A climate analysis is therefore absolutely essential in the planning of building designs and particularly in daylighting design. The daylight availability in the exterior space is many times greater than in the interior of a building. Thus, an overcast sky provides an average of approximately 10 000 lx, which can be utilized for lighting in the interior. In summer, this value rises up to 100 000 lx under clear skies. We differentiate between direct and diffuse radiation. The latter is largely non-directional and is the product of scattering of solar radiation in the atmosphere. Direct radiation, on the other hand, is directional depending on the solar azimuth. In Germany, an annual average of 37 per cent[19] of direct radiation are incident on a vertical facade with southern exposure, dropping to roughly half that value for east- and west-facing facades. Direct radiation is dependent on the degree of cloudiness and is subject to strong variation depending on weather conditions. Daylighting design is based on an evenly overcast sky (e.g., daylight factor). In reality, however, the luminance varies according to solar azimuth and building orientation. It is greatest, for example, when the azimuth is at its highest, in which case it would make sense to deflect the zenith light into the interior.

Design Parameters: Investing Space with Light …
"Architecture is the sage and correct play of the bodies in light."[20]

Urban Planning
In addition to the climate conditions, the location of a building in its immediate environment plays an important role. Shading from neighbouring buildings or trees as well as orientation influence the incidence of daylight into the interior to a considerable degree. These parameters must be taken into consideration from the very beginning in the initial sketches of a design, because they have the strongest

5.8

5.6   Influence of daylight on biorhythm (1) and eye sensitivity (2).
5.7   Daylight-dependent control of artificial lighting.
5.8   Urban district in Shenzhen, China (2001)

5.9

impact on the subsequent energy consumption in a building. A downtown district in the Chinese city of Shenzhen (Fig. 5.8) is a negative example. The distance between the apartment blocks is extremely small. As a result, there is no more than a minimum of air movement and no light penetrates into the spaces. This is exacerbated by another major problem arising from the large glass and metal surfaces on the facades: the reflection from these facades can lead to pronounced reflected glare even in north-facing rooms. This parameter must also be taken into consideration in the building design. The shape of the building dictates the orientation and depths of rooms, which play an important role later on for the design of the building skin and the need for artificial lighting. In high-rises, room depth and height, planned courtyards, atria or light wells as well as terracing or recesses, which are intended to allow daylight to penetrate from the top down to the ground floor, are important parameters.

Building Skin
The building skin creates the transition from interior to exterior and vice versa. Designs may vary between perforated facades (fenestration) or fully glazed facades. The building skin forms a membrane, which regulates the quality of interior lighting in conjunction with use and ensures the exchange of light, air and heat. At the same time, it provides weather protection, influences the appearance of a building, creates a sphere of privacy and sometimes even serves as an advertising platform.

Interior
The interior is only perceived as a result of light. Key planning and design parameters are the surface structure of the space-enclosing surfaces, the position of the workstation in relation to the window and the arrangement of the furnishings. Bright surfaces are generally preferable over dark surfaces because they reflect more light, and matte surfaces are preferable to glossy surfaces.

Shading and Glare Protection
"A glass house without shading is like a Porsche without breaks."[21]

An effective shading system prevents overheating in a building's interior and adapts to different weather and light conditions. The aim is to reduce energy consumption for cooling and lighting – which constitute a large percentage of the total energy consumption in office buildings – and to provide a glare-free work environment. Generally speaking, it is easiest to provide shading for south-facing facades because of the high solar altitude, which facilitates light deflection. East- and west-facing facades, on the other hand, must contend with stronger incident solar radiation as a result of lower solar altitudes. Shading and light deflection are difficult to realize in these conditions. A possible solution is to replace the more common horizontal shading elements with vertical elements to better reflect solar incidence from shallow angles. Accordingly, the shading system determines the look of a facade in a building depending on orientation. The system may be hidden unobtrusively in the facade cavity or serve as an expressive design element. Many moveable shading systems are equipped with automated controls for optimum efficiency.

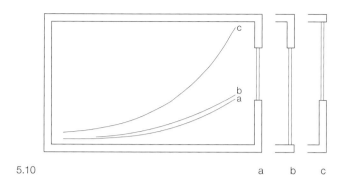

5.10

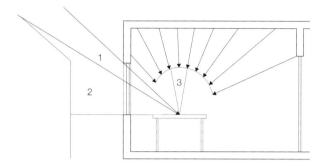

$D = Ds + Db + Di$
1 = Sky factor (Ds)
2 = Built-environment reflection (Db)
3 = Interior reflection (Di)
5.11

5.12

Such automated systems respond to the current incidence of solar radiation and are usually coupled with the building automation system. The clear advantage is that such systems prevent overheating in the interior as a result of errors in manual operation or when users are absent. At the same time, they monitor the interactions between heating, cooling, ventilation, shading and glare protection in a centralized fashion, ensuring optimum adjustment and harmonization. The disadvantage is chiefly experienced by the user, whose freedom of choice is limited and who may experience a constantly adjusting shading system as an unwelcome distraction. Complementing automatic controls with manual options is a good solution because it enables the user to adjust lighting conditions on an individual basis. When this option is not provided, experience has shown that users try to manipulate the system or even switch off the controls.

Basics of Calculation: Drawing Light – Calculating Light – Simulating Light
"Shadows have always been the brushwork of the traditional architect."[22]

Architectural drawings have always used light and shadow to render facades, for example, in a more plastic fashion. Geometry is the basis according to which shadows are drawn, making it possible to determine the precise perspective of shadows depending on the time of day and the orientation and location of the building.

Daylighting is planned on the basis of standardized guidelines.[23] In Germany, DIN standards for window dimensions are mainly based on visual contact with the outside world, and less on the daylight quality in the interior. Daylight is measured with the daylight factor, that is, the ratio of interior to exterior illuminance under an overcast sky (the mathematical mean at a height of 85 cm above floor level). However, the daylight factor does not indicate the quality of daylighting in interiors; it is only helpful in rapidly assessing the minimum requirements for wall openings.

According to the daylight factor, the values in rooms located on the north and south side of a building are similar, even though the light conditions are clearly different in reality. Other important planning and design parameters are, for example, the interior illuminance for open or closed shading and glare protection, as well as the distribution of light in the room for direct solar incidence and the resulting luminance, which is an important factor in terms of glare. Additional factors in this case are the direct incidence from the visible portion of the sky, external reflection onto buildings on the opposite side and onto the ground as well as reflecting surfaces in the room.

5.9   Pool, Bad Elster (1999), Behnisch and Partners. The screen-printed, pivoting glass louvres provide shade and glare protection.
5.10 Comparison in interior illuminance according to window position.
5.11 Sky factor; external and internal reflection
5.12 Public library, Landau (1998), Lamott Architects. Rigid wooden louvers mounted in front of the glass facade provide shading.

Today, the realistic rendition of architectural scenes is no longer a problem thanks to advanced CAD technology. Excellent visual renditions of this kind are usually created for competitions or presentations to good effect. Things are more complicated, however, if the aim is to "cast scenes in the appropriate light," that is, when the rendition is to be accurate from the perspective of lighting engineering.

The current marketplace offers a variety of software for daylight simulation. There are simple programmes, which are usually capable of calculating both artificial light and daylight;[24] they also provide data on the overcast sky, the daylight factor and the resulting distribution of illuminance and luminance in the room. These programmes are mainly used to establish minimum window dimensions and minimum brightness ratios for daylight and artificial light. They are less helpful, however, in assessing the quality of light. They are easy to operate and can be used to rapidly establish basic results with regard to the size and position of openings during the design process. Other programmes take the clear, sunny sky into consideration and are therefore capable of providing realistic and physiologically correct calculations. These programmes import CAD files and utilize them for the simulation. In addition to illuminance and luminance, they also provide accurate data on materials, with the option to modify individual characteristics. For the calculation of diffusing, defracting or directing characteristics, however, it is frequently necessary to consult additional programmes that are customized for the specific case. The complex nature of these programmes requires a great amount of training and the relevant expertise for reliable interpretation.

Daylighting Design Principles

Skylights
Lighting from above – through openings in the roof – is far more efficient than lighting from the side – through openings in the walls – because the entire hemisphere is available as a light source. Windows set into walls, on the other hand, can only tap into half of the hemisphere as a light source and thus achieve only one fifth of the illuminance given with skylights of the same size. A second reason, why windows are less effective, is the distribution of brightness under an overcast sky, which diminishes by approximately one third from the zenith to the horizon. Another key advantage of skylights is that they allow light to penetrate into floors of any depth. As little as 20 per cent of skylight area per floor area can achieve comfortable daylight factors of roughly 5 per cent. It is important, moreover, to consider the solar heat gains in conjunction with daylighting. The incline of skylights in relation to the sun is, therefore, an important factor in the optimized use of solar energy for lighting and heating/cooling. Passive solar heat gains are desirable for heating applications; they are undesirable, however, with regard to cooling applications, which are of prime importance in work environments, where solutions, which allow only diffuse light to penetrate and deflect direct sunlight, are preferred. In the case of hall roofs, this is often achieved by means of transparent north sheds with an incline of 60°, which do not allow direct light to penetrate, even though they create fewer advantageous lighting conditions than horizontal windows. The large roof area of

5.13

5.14

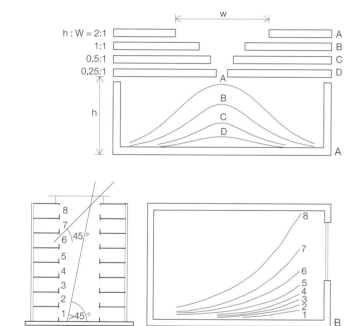

5.15

5.16

shed roofs, moreover, often results in considerably higher heating energy consumption than horizontal roofs without raised inclines. Skylights with vertical glass areas are the least effective solution from a lighting perspective.

The horizontal glass roof at the University of Bremen exemplifies the effective realization of shading and daylighting with the help of customized glass (Fig. 5.13): a colour screen print provides sun and glare protection; evenly distributed lighting in the entrance lobby from direct sunlight in daytime supplemented by artificial light at night (radiant luminaires above the roof) is provided with the help of individual glass elements with light-directing holograms.

Light Shafts and Atria

Light shafts and atria are architectural means of introducing daylight into compact buildings with deep floors, which would be difficult to light via the external facades. Offices adjacent to such light shafts or atria, even those located in the least advantageous position, must satisfy all the requirements for daylighting, meaning, the minimum daylight factor and, above all, visual contact with the outside. A survey carried out by Hans Jürgen Schmitz[25] indicated that visual contact with the outside through an atrium has a significant influence on user acceptance. This means that atria with full-time workstations should not be fully enclosed; in other words, a glass roof alone is not sufficient and should be complemented by a glass facade to the exterior. Sufficient daylighting for workstations on the lowest level is ensured if the angle of light incidence does not surpass roughly 45° across the entire height of the atrium, as demonstrated in computer simulations and measurements. Terraced floors or cone-shaped courtyards are additional architectural tools used to realize high user density in combination with good daylight conditions. Narrow atria and courtyards can be realized when there are no full-time workstations on the lower levels. Narrow courtyards or shafts can considerably augment measures for directing sunlight at the roof level, especially on sunny days.

Windows

The arrangement, size and division of windows play an important role in daylighting. Thus, floor-to-ceiling windows allow daylight to penetrate deeper into the space, whereas a glass breast wall has virtually no advantageous effect for the interior. To ensure sufficient illumination in side-lit rooms, the room depths must not exceed 2.5 times the window height. Light-directing measures must be implemented for rooms with openings on one side and greater depths. In these cases, a horizontal division of the opening areas is recommended to provide areas with views of the

5.13 Entrance lobby, University of Bremen (2001), Jan Störmer Architects. Light-directing holograms are integrated into the roof (cf. Fig. 5.25).
5.14 R & D centre, Meiningen (2002), Kauffmann, Theilig and Partners. Light-directing systems bring daylight into the offices.
5.15 Daylight availability under overcast sky: for different roof openings (A), and for rooms adjacent to an atrium according to floor level. The angle of incident light for the lowest level should not fall short of 45° (B).
5.16 Principle of sunlight deflection in atrium in comparison to conventional solution without light deflection.

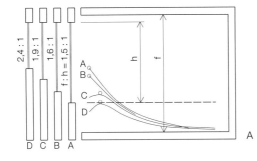

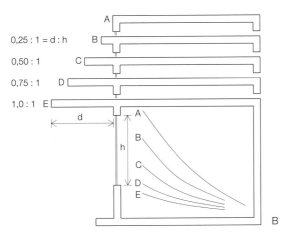

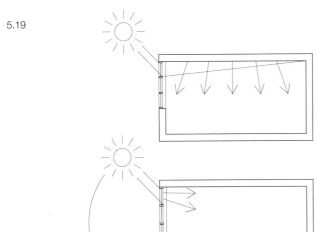

Section
Plan

outside and with shading as well as for daylight incidence and light direction. The new office building for Deloitte & Touche in Düsseldorf (Fig. 5.17) is a good example. The following basic principle applies: the taller the window, the better the resulting daylight utilization. Other factors, such as shading projections, can have a negative influence because they reduce not only direct radiation but also the percentage of diffuse light under an overcast sky – an effect, which is not as advantageous in Germany as it is in other countries with more solar radiation. In terms of office building interiors, a facade system can be said to be well-designed if it allows diffuse light to penetrate into the room, but deflects direct light in order to avoid excessive solar gains and, above all, to provide a glare-free work environment. Reflected glare on monitors can occur even in north-facing rooms or under overcast skies; the same is true for direct glare when looking out of a window. Glare protection is required in the last case; it should be adjustable independent of the shading system and, ideally, still allow for visual contact with the outside.

Light-directing, Glare- and Sun-protection Systems
The design of transparent building components and windows is, on the one hand, defined by the primary function of light penetration and visual transparency. On the other hand, these elements fulfil an important control function with regard to strongly fluctuating radiation intensities and are also relevant for aspects of lighting and heating/cooling. The primary function is fulfilled in the arrangement and orientation of the building, the sizing and placement of windows, and the selection of the most transparent glazing for the least favourable conditions, (e.g., an overcast sky). To some degree, interior lighting can also be improved with the help of light-directing systems.[26] These systems make it possible to light very deep rooms through windows or very tall and narrow rooms through skylights. Deflection of diffuse light from the bright zenith range of the overcast sky, frequently employed for window installations, has proven elaborate and inefficient because of the moderate availability of light. There is, however, no viable alternative for north-facing rooms. A far more effective approach is to redirect direct sun radiation, especially in combination with shading measures, for example, rigid, horizontal louvres in the upper half of the window, frequently referred to as light shelves. There is a risk of glare, however, when the sun is low in the sky, unless a moveable shading system is provided. The House of Commons in London (Fig. 5.29) is a successful example of integrating light-directing and ventilation functions in the facade. The rigid, internal and external horizontal louvres serve to redirect diffuse light, distribute artificial light and provide shading. Moveable light-directing louvres in the top half of the window can reflect direct sunlight into the depth of a room. So-called light-deflecting glass has been available in the marketplace for some years. It allows for glare-free distribution of sunlight in the depth of a room without the need for additional flexible components. The system effects vertical and horizontal deflection of direct radiation, creating even and glare-free lighting up to a room depth of 10 m. Glare protection, that is, protection against direct sun incidence in the occupied area or high luminance near windows, should be flexible and user-operated.

66

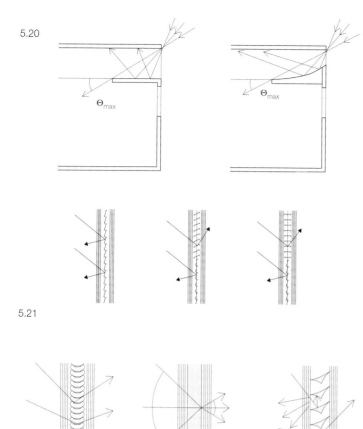

5.20

5.21

5.22

5.23

Relevant installations such as roller blinds or Venetian blinds need not be identical with thermal sun protection; they can also be mounted separately and on the inside of the window. This also provides additional passive solar heating in the cold season. The thermal sun protection should not interfere with daylighting and visual contact with the outside, a stipulation that is not so easy to fulfil if one takes a look at standard blinds. Artificial light is frequently required in interiors when the shading system is activated. Many different solutions can be categorized according to the following, simplified, criteria:

Flexibility:
• constantly in effect (e.g., anti-sun glass)
• effective depending on solar altitude, rigid (e.g., roof overhang, rigid louvre)
• flexible according to user manipulation (moveable installations such as blinds, Venetian blinds, awnings, horizontal and vertical louvres, switchable glass[27])

Reduction of radiation transmission:
• undifferentiated reduction of global radiation (direct and diffuse, from all directions)
• selective spectral reduction of the infrared range of solar radiation (not visible)
• selective directional reduction of direct solar radiation (transparent for diffuse radiation)

Placement:
• external, in front of glazing
• internal, behind glazing
• internal, on room side of glazing

Flexible solutions are extremely advantageous for daylighting. Conversely, constant reduction of transmission as well as rigid shading depending on solar altitude are particularly disadvantageous for natural light in a room especially under an overcast sky.

Daylighting is influenced by the different options for reducing the transmission of solar radiation: undifferentiated reduction without consideration for direction, spectral range and radiation intensity, (e.g., in the case of standard anti-sun glass), also limits light transmission, which is a disadvantage especially on overcast days. Selective spectral anti-sun glass has high light transmission and low infrared

5.17 Office building, Düsseldorf (2003), Deilmann, Koch and Partners Light-directing glass in the facade enable daylighting of a second workstation even when the shading system is in use. (cf. Fig. 5.26)
5.18 Daylight availability under overcast sky: for side-lit room with varying window-sill heights (A), for side-lit room with different roof overhangs (B).
5.19 Light distribution with light-directing elements in the facade and reflection off the ceiling.
5.20 Shading and light direction with light shelves, functional diagram for New House of Commons, Westminster, London. Daylighting design: Michael Hopkins & Partners
5.21 Flexible shading system in the form of louvred blinds; the louvres can be utilized in part for redirecting sunlight.
5.22 Functional principle of light-deflecting glass
5.23 Administration building in Wiesbaden, Herzog and Partners Light shelves in the shape of scoops re-direct the direct sunlight.

Projects

Active measures	Supplementary heating	Heating energy demand	Primary structure
collectors for warm water	Pellets-supplementary heating	end house: 19 kWh/m²a row house: 12 kWh/m²a	prefabricated timber components
collectors for warm water	district heating	29 kWh/ m²a	brick walls
collectors for warm water 5 m²/house; photovoltaic connections	district heating	12.5 kWh/m²a	prefabricated timber components; sandlime blocks
collectors for warm water 140 –190 m²/building	gasheater	20 kWh/m²a	reinforced concrete slabs
collectors for warm water	electric heating	34.5 kWh/m²a	timber skeleton construction
collectors for warm water	exist. oil heating	4.11 kWh/m²a	timber skeleton construction
Photovoltaics collector connections	wood chip combustion	15 kWh/m²a	prefabricated timber components
collectors photovoltaics	heat and power plant	28 kWh/m²a	timber skeleton construction
–	gas boiler	50 kWh/m²a	steel structure
–	–	–	reinforced concrete
–	gasheater	–	reinforced concrete
collectors for warm water	heat and power plant	35 kWh/m²a	steel skeleton construction
collectors/photovoltaics	CHP rapeseed oil	27 kWh/m²a	light-weight timber construction, reinforced concrete
photovoltaics 9300 m²/roof 800 m²/south-west facade *integrated solar power plant	CHP gas	< 50 kWh/m²a detached houses	timber skeleton construction
photovoltaics 300 m²	MHKV rapeseed oil	–	existing structure: solid construction dome: steel construction

Passive-Energy Terraced Housing in Dornbirn

Architect: Johannes Kaufmann, Dornbirn
Energy consultants: E-Plus, Ralf Lenninger, Egg

Enjoying a view to the Bregenz Forest, this row of nine terraced houses with a communal unit at the end is situated on
the outskirts of Dornbirn in Vorarlberg, Austria. A group of
clients, including the architect himself, joined forces to realize
this scheme. The dwellings form the first stage of a mixed
development. Further housing strips and a commercial unit are
also planned. The use of prefabricated timber elements
helped to ensure low production costs and a short construction period. The individual two-storey houses, each with a floor
area of roughly 80 m², allow a flexible use of the internal
spaces. The only fixed elements are the ground floor kitchen,
laid out along the western party wall of each house, and the
WCs and bathroom on the ground and first floors. From the
open kitchen and living area, a single-flight staircase, with
storage space beneath, leads to the upper level. Here, there
are two rooms, with the bathroom in the middle and a separate
WC. In the entrance hall of each dwelling, a trap door in the
floor provides access to a small cellar space containing
mechanical services, which comprise a combination of individual and communal systems.
The high density of the development means that the site has
been exploited with great economy. It was nevertheless possible to create a small open space with a timber patio on the
south side of every house. Pivoting shutters provide visual
screening to the balconies and the private points of access on
the garden side. A small porch-like structure, consisting of a
landing with a side wall and roof in fibre-cement sheeting,
forms a sculptural element on the north face of each house.
The porches afford protection against the weather and also
define the entrance situation. Parking spaces will be provided
later in the form of an underground garage.
The consortium of clients received a grant from the state of
Vorarlberg from funds to support environmentally friendly housing in the region. The level of financial support was calculated
according to a points system based on a comprehensive list of
criteria. These included the use of ecological building materials
and forms of construction, and other measures designed to
promote passive low-energy housing. The system provides
support for individual building concepts drawn up for specific
situations. The scheme was planned and executed in such a
way that it would achieve the maximum possible subsidy under
this assessment system. With this low-cost development, the
architect and other clients have managed to reconcile the
needs of qualitative design with high environmental standards.

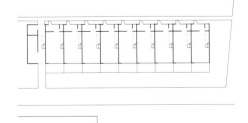

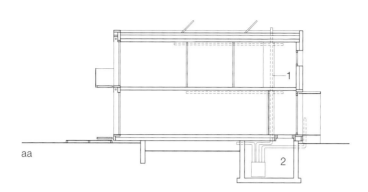

aa

Site plan
scale 1:1000
Section
Ground and
first floor plans
scale 1:200

1 Ventilation and
  heating runs
2 Basement space
3 Kitchen/Living room
4 Room
5 Bathroom
6 WC

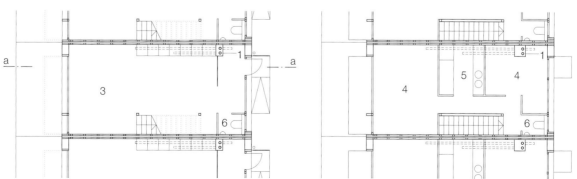

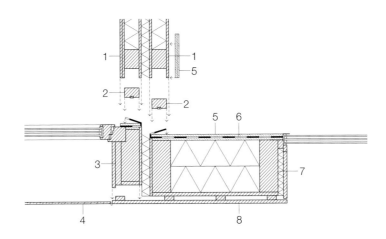

Construction

The ten terraced units were erected in a dry form of construction with prefabricated, multilayer timber elements. An amend-
ment of the state building laws in Vorarlberg allowed the party
walls to be built in timber. Executed in a two-leaf form of construction for sound-insulating purposes, they provide a certi-
fied one-hour fire resistance. Only one cross-wall, between
houses 5 and 6, had to be built in reinforced concrete as an
additional means of fire protection. It acts as a rigid slab that
also serves to brace the row in the longitudinal direction. The
ground floor slab, consisting of softwood box elements filled
with insulation, is borne by the concrete basement units on the
north side of the houses and a strip foundation along the south
side. The upper floor construction consists of prefabricated,
five-ply, solid laminated-timber elements spanned between
the party walls of the houses. There are no further finishings on
top: the smooth softwood surface forms the actual flooring. It
was also possible to do without impact-sound insulation within
the individual dwellings. The soffit is finished with a suspended layer of larch boarding, with electrical runs laid in the
intermediate cavity. A prefabricated, solid laminated-timber
construction was also used for the flat roof. The outer walls
consist of insulated timber box elements, complete with the
necessary door and window openings. Work executed on site
included the triple glazing, the external horizontal larch boarding, the roof insulation and finishings, and the gypsum fibreboard linings to the internal walls.

Horizontal section through
south facade
on ground floor;
joint between construction
elements;
assembly sequence
scale 1:20

1 internal wall elements
2 85/50 mm timber
  stud with sealing strip
3 external wall element 2
  (window)
4 hinged shutter
5 internal wall lining
6 vapour barrier folded
  back at edge
7 external wall element 1
8 external cladding

Passive-energy standard
The passive-energy standard was achieved here by using highly insulated external construction elements, with triple insulated glazing and controlled air-supply and extract systems; and by ensuring that the building skin is otherwise airtight. The primary-energy needs are 60–80 per cent lower than for conventional buildings of this kind. The compact volumetric form and the broad areas of glazing to the south faces of the houses also contribute to energy savings.
The individual dwelling units have their own heating and ventilation plant. Vertical and horizontal ducts for heating and ventilation and the water supply are located on the western side of the houses along the party walls. In the living rooms and bedrooms, fresh air is blown in from above.

Vitiated air is sucked out in the kitchens and bathrooms. The ventilation plant draws in fresh air via a heat-exchange unit, heats it further over a heating grid if necessary, and then feeds it into the rooms. The heat-exchange unit exploits waste heat from the kitchens and bathrooms. The heating grid is fed with hot water from a solar combination tank.
The towel-rail radiators in the bathrooms are supplied with hot water from a central source. The communal hot-water supply, also using rainwater, is heated by solar collectors.
In the event of an energy shortfall, a pellet-fired boiler is available as well. This supplementary source of heating and the solar combination hot-water tank are situated in the basement of the communal unit.

Diagram of heating system
1 Solar collectors on roof of houses 1–3
2 Pellet-fired boiler in basement of communal unit to supplement heating supply at times of peak demand
3 Solar combination tank (2,000 l) in basement of communal unit
4 Heating supply connection to communal unit
5 Heating and ventilation connection to individual houses
6 Radiators in bathrooms and in communal unit
7 Ventilation plant in basements of houses with water/air heating grid for additional heating supply at times of peak demand; and air/air heat exchange for normal demand
8 Recirculated water draw-off points for individual houses

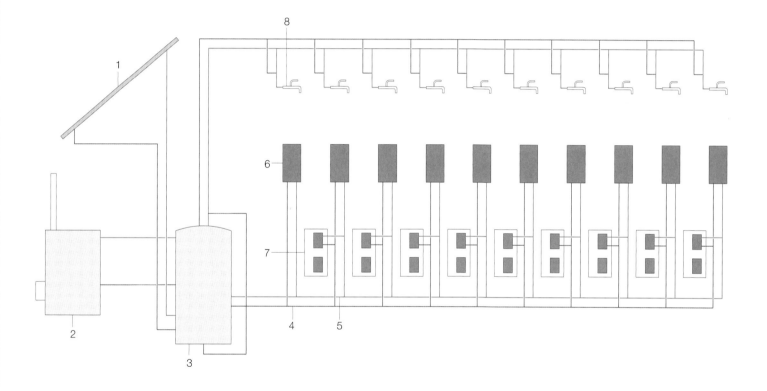

Housing Estate in Kolding

Architects: 3XNielsen, Århus
Lars Frank Nielsen, Kim Herforth Nielsen

Site plan
scale 1:2500

This Danish development, comprising 59 terraced houses and a building with communal facilities, was the outcome of a competition for environmentally friendly construction. To achieve a maximum exploitation of solar energy, the houses are turned at an angle of 15° to the north-south axis, thereby ensuring the ideal orientation for buildings at this latitude. The north-facing external walls are in a well-insulated multilayer form of construction. The south faces, in contrast, are fully glazed. Integrated in the glazing of every house is a vertical solar wall element between 6.00 and 8.40 m² in area. Behind the double glazing in these strips is a black, perforated sheet-steel panel, with a cavity and a layer of insulation to the rear. When exposed to solar radiation, the steel panel heats up and warms the air in the cavity. The system is used as a supplementary form of heating, complementing the central heating supply from the community building.

The solar walls are divided into two sections. The lower part serves to preheat the fresh-air intake, while the heat gains in the upper part are stored in the 290 mm concrete party walls between the houses. If the temperature within the solar wall rises above 30 °C during the heating period, a fan is switched on which blows the heated air into the storage walls. These, in turn, yield their heat at night to the dwellings. At the top of the solar walls are ventilation flaps. In summer, when the fans are turned off and heating is not required, the flaps can be opened to allow warm air to escape, thus avoiding overheating of the wall.

Two different types of prefabricated thermal storage walls were developed. The system for the party walls consists of concrete units with built-in heating tubes with hot-air circulation. For the outer walls to the end houses of each row, hollow cellular concrete elements were manufactured with an integral layer of broken stone.

On completion of the work, test measurements were made in two representative houses to determine the thermal behaviour of the solar walls and the storage mass. Parallel to this, a survey was carried out among the residents. The wall systems have proved effective, and the users are satisfied with the system. In the case of the solar wall strips, the costs were 7 per cent higher than for conventional forms of construction (i.e. a standard glazed facade). The costs for the storage wall were 45 per cent higher than for a normal brick wall. The energy savings achieved with this system (115–125 kWh/m²a) compensate for the greater outlay, however[1].

1 1 kWh in Denmark costs €0.06 (figures for 2000 = year of measurement).

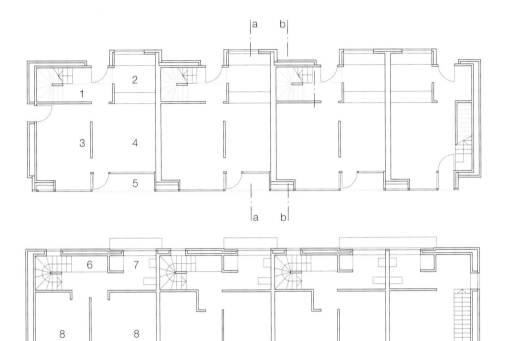

Floor plans · Section
scale 1:200

1 Hall
2 Kitchen
3 Living room
4 Dining room
5 Terrace
6 Void
7 Bathroom
8 Bedroom
9 Balcony

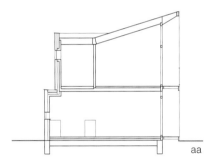

aa

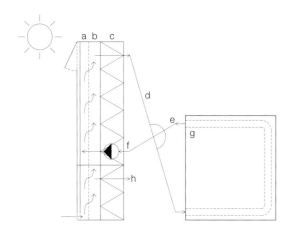

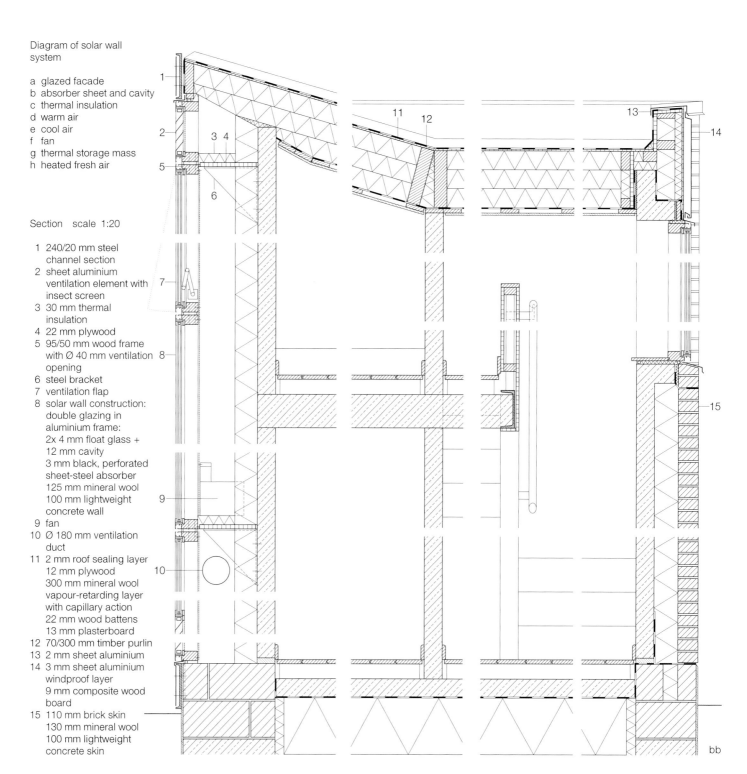

A End wall system
Hollow concrete elements with an integral layer of stone chippings. Fresh air enters in the lower part of the wall and rises through the stones to the top. Heat is absorbed in the concrete, and the cooled air returns through ducts to the base. Every house has a glazed solar wall with an effective area of 5.20 m², of which 4.20 m² are used for the thermal storage system.

B Party wall system
Concrete dividing wall with heating tubes laid out in circular form in the core. Heated air is fed into the storage element at floor level. It flows through the circular arrangement of tubes and heats the concrete.
Each of the thermal storage elements in the concrete walls has an area of 7.40 m², of which 6 m² are actually used for storage purposes.

Diagram of solar wall system

a glazed facade
b absorber sheet and cavity
c thermal insulation
d warm air
e cool air
f fan
g thermal storage mass
h heated fresh air

Section   scale 1:20

1 240/20 mm steel channel section
2 sheet aluminium ventilation element with insect screen
3 30 mm thermal insulation
4 22 mm plywood
5 95/50 mm wood frame with Ø 40 mm ventilation opening
6 steel bracket
7 ventilation flap
8 solar wall construction: double glazing in aluminium frame:
   2x 4 mm float glass + 12 mm cavity
   3 mm black, perforated sheet-steel absorber
   125 mm mineral wool
   100 mm lightweight concrete wall
9 fan
10 Ø 180 mm ventilation duct
11 2 mm roof sealing layer
   12 mm plywood
   300 mm mineral wool
   vapour-retarding layer with capillary action
   22 mm wood battens
   13 mm plasterboard
12 70/300 mm timber purlin
13 2 mm sheet aluminium
14 3 mm sheet aluminium windproof layer
   9 mm composite wood board
15 110 mm brick skin
   130 mm mineral wool
   100 mm lightweight concrete skin

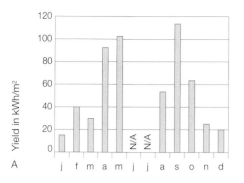

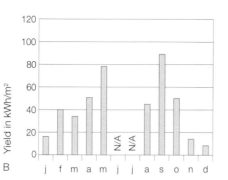

Thermal behaviour of solar walls and storage elements

The graphs show that the system functions well in practice. Although the solar walls are not in use in summer, they can be activated whenever needed. The yield is approx. 114 kWh/m² (air ducts) and approx. 124 kWh/m² (stone layer), taking account of heat-transmission losses. Measurements of solar radiation show that partial shading caused by neighbouring buildings and the growth of vegetation have reduced the effectiveness of the system. Without shading losses, the energy yield would be roughly 25 per cent higher – between 150 and 160 kWh/m²a.

A External wall system
B Party wall system

Passive-Energy Terraced Housing in Ulm

Architect: Johannes Brucker, Stuttgart
Mechanical services: ebök, Tübingen

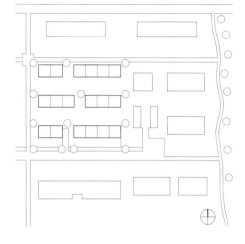

Site plan
scale 1:2500

Restrained in its design and economical in its use of resources, this development in Ulm, Germany, comprises 18 passive-energy houses laid out in three stepped tiers. Despite the high density of the estate, which was dictated by cost factors, the different levels of the housing strips mean that every dwelling enjoys panoramic views and a great deal of sunlight from the south. The architects chose a mixed form of construction: the south facades consist of large, prefabricated timber elements, while the external walls on the north side and the load-bearing party walls were constructed with large sandlime blocks. The use of reinforced concrete floor slabs allowed the creation of three column-free storeys that the occupants can lay out according to personal needs and which can be restructured at a later date. In addition, it is possible to divide the houses into two independent units or to install an office.

The individual dwellings do not have their own separate heating systems. Uncontrolled heat losses are avoided by means of tightly sealed joints in the outer enclosure as well as a high standard of thermal insulation: 40 cm in the roof, 30 cm in the outer walls and 20 cm beneath the base slab. The balconies and porches are discrete constructional elements set in front of the facades to avoid creating thermal bridges. In addition, all windows are triple glazed. The ventilation plant not only heats the intake of fresh air; through heat recovery and a process of geothermal heat exchange, it ensures an agreeable indoor climate and good air quality. If the energy from these sources plus that derived from insolation is not adequate in cold weather, a back-up system is available: residual heat can be drawn from the return flow of a district-heating service to a conventionally built block of flats nearby. The hot-water supply is provided by solar collectors concealed in the planted roof. A photovoltaic plant for the generation of electricity can be added if required. The requisite connections have already been installed.

A Exploitation of
  solar energy, and
  daylighting system

1 hot-water collector
2 photovoltaic installa-
  tion (optional)
3 daylight deflection
  (optical system)
4 passive direct
  exploitation

B Thermal insulation
  and airtight skin

1 25–40 mm thermal
  insulation
2 peripheral airtight
  layer
3 non-bearing
  perimeter insulation
  with thermal
  bridges at point
  fixings

C Ventilation and heat
  recovery

1 ventilation plant with
  heat recovery
2 geothermal heat
  exchange

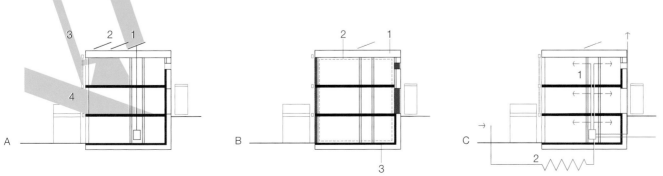

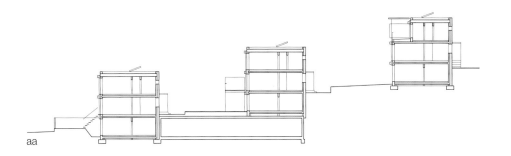

aa

a .... a

Ventilation
Every house has a mechanical air-supply and extract system with a heat-recovery facility. Fresh air is sucked in via a filter and can be preheated if required before being fed into the internal spaces. Conversely, exhaust air is sucked out and drawn over an air-to-air heat exchange unit before being emitted from the building. The volume of air and the air-change rate can be regulated by the occupants in a series of steps.

Hot-water supply
Part of the hot-water supply is provided by a thermal solar installation with a collector area of roughly 5 m² per house. The collectors are integrated in the extensively planted roof.
The requisite electrical connections and a control mechanism have been installed for a photovoltaic collector system to generate electricity. Scope is thus provided for the generation of additional power from solar energy.

Supplementary heating system
In the event of the heating supply proving inadequate in cold weather, a reserve source is available in the form of the municipal district-heating supply. The plant for the present estate is connected to the district-heating intake station in a neighbouring block of flats, whereby only the return flow is used.

Section
Ground floor layout
scale 1:500

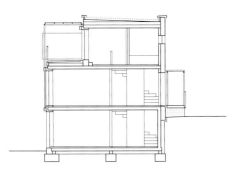

Section
scale 1:250
Sectional details
scale 1:20

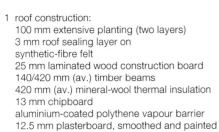

1 roof construction:
  100 mm extensive planting (two layers)
  3 mm roof sealing layer on
  synthetic-fibre felt
  25 mm laminated wood construction board
  140/420 mm (av.) timber beams
  420 mm (av.) mineral-wool thermal insulation
  13 mm chipboard
  aluminium-coated polythene vapour barrier
  12.5 mm plasterboard, smoothed and painted
2 wall construction:
  textured rendering with two coats of paint
  4 mm reinforcing layer
  300 mm rigid-foam thermal insulation
  150 mm sandlime block walling (large blocks)
  3 mm skim-coat of plaster
  woodchip paper, painted
3 plastic casement with triple glazing
4 floor construction:
  20 mm oak parquet
  45 mm screed on separating layer
  20 mm impact-sound insulation
5 wood front door with rigid-foam core
6 terrace construction:
  400/400/50 mm concrete paving slabs
  40 mm layer of gravel
  6 mm granular-rubber mat
  roof sealing layer
  30–80 mm rigid-foam insulation finished to falls
  200 mm rigid-foam thermal insulation
  vapour barrier
  200 mm reinforced concrete floor slab,
  smoothed and painted on underside
7 aluminium external sunblind

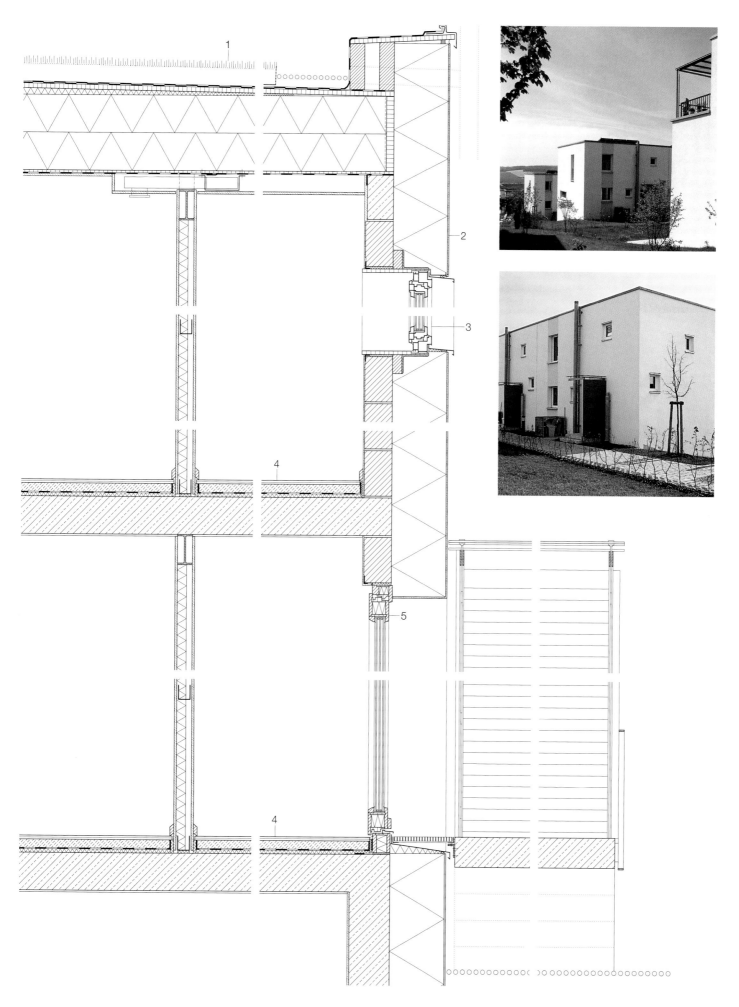

Point Blocks in Innsbruck

Architects: Baumschlager & Eberle, Lochau
Mechanical services: GMI Grasser & Messner, Dornbirn

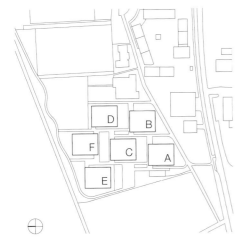

Innsbruck, the capital of Tyrol in Austria, lies surrounded by mountains in the broad valley of the River Inn. The Lohbach development, a publicly assisted housing estate, was erected in an attractive situation on the western outskirts of the city beneath the wooded foothills of a chain of mountains to the north. The six blocks of flats were constructed as low-energy buildings. They are laid out offset to each other in chequer-board fashion and stepped up the gently sloping site at various levels. As a result, the sun is able to penetrate deep into the courtyard spaces between the buildings. The layouts of the flats in blocks A and B and in blocks D and E are identical. The central building, block C, contains dwellings for senior citizens as well as communal spaces and care facilities. Continuous balconies around the outside of the blocks provide protected outdoor spaces, and there are surprising views to the surrounding landscape in all directions.

The compact volumes of the individual structures with their outer buffer zones were the starting point for the innovative energy concept. On the roof of every block, solar energy is harnessed by collectors and used to heat the hot-water supply and to preheat the fresh-air intake. Individual heating and ventilation needs are met by decentralized compact ventilation appliances in every dwelling. Prior to this scheme, the mechanical services concept had been tested in other developments that were much smaller in scale. The concept and the form of construction were coordinated to provide a high level of comfort for the 298 dwellings (with a total floor area of 21,500 m²), at the same time ensuring a low heating-energy factor of 20 kWh/m²a. That means a reduction of CO_2 emissions of 237 tonnes a year compared with the usual figure for new housing developments in Austria (60–80 kWh/m²a).

Site plan
scale 1:5000
First basement
garage level beneath
block C with solar
storage tanks (1)
scale 1:1500

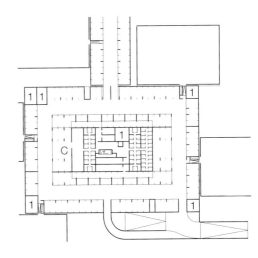

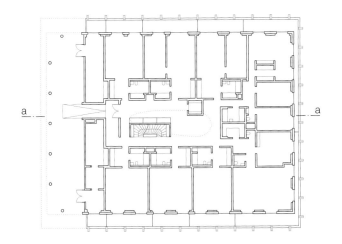

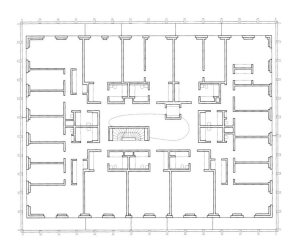

Ground floor plan
Standard floor plan
scale 1:500
Block C
Dwellings for senior
citizens
Section
scale 1:500

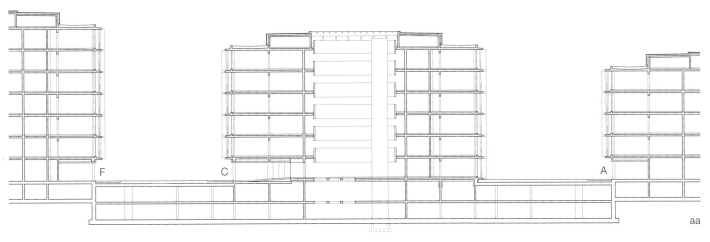

F   C   A

aa

89

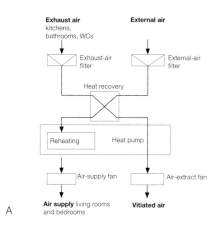

Exhaust air kitchens, bathrooms, WCs   **External air**

Exhaust-air filter   External-air filter

Heat recovery

Reheating   Heat pump

Air-supply fan   Air-extract fan

A   **Air supply** living rooms and bedrooms   **Vitiated air**

A Diagram of compact ventilation appliance with minimum-sized heat pump
B Part floor plan showing ventilation runs in diagrammatic form
C Section showing energy concept (without radiators)
  scale 1:200

The compact form of the blocks, with a good ratio between the footprint area and the volume (0.2), provides a sound basis for minimizing energy losses. The entrance halls act as buffer zones and reduce the problem posed by the front doors of the dwellings – normally the weakest point of the outer skin in terms of energy losses. The flats are heated largely via the ventilation system, with the use of minimally dimensioned heat pumps. In this system, fresh air has to be preheated to at least 5 °C, since the heat pump would no longer function efficiently at lower temperatures, and there would also be a danger of condensation freezing on the outgoing side of the heat-exchange unit. The large number of dwellings inevitably necessitates a greater volume of fresh air. Cost constraints and lack of space led to a decision to provide heating via water-filled solar storage elements rather than by means of an earth grid. On the roofs of the blocks, a mixture of glycol and water in the solar collectors is heated and pumped to the heat-exchange units in the solar storage elements. The heat from this medium fluid is transferred to the water in the storage tanks, and the cooled medium is then returned to the collectors. The tanks are situated in those corners of the basement garages that cannot be used as parking spaces. Solar storage elements have a further advantage over earth grids in that they allow temperatures to be controlled. They can also be used in summer to help heat the hot-water supply.

Decentralized compact ventilation appliances with flat heat-exchange elements and minimum-sized heat pumps have been installed in the bathroom of every dwelling behind room-height glass sliding doors. Regulated by pressing a simple set of buttons, the appliances can be operated at three different levels to meet individual heating and ventilating needs. The pretreated, filtered air supply is blown into the living spaces by rotary fans. Exhaust air is sucked out via disc valves in the sanitary and ancillary spaces. A special video film was produced and distributed to every household to instruct residents in the operation of the system. When the external temperature falls below 10 °C, a gas heater is automatically activated and supplies a conventional radiator installed in every flat. The radiator provides residents with an additional source of heating or a place to dry wet clothing. The outer skin of the building is so highly insulated that the internal temperature generated by secondary heat sources (people, appliances and lighting) would not fall below about 15 °C, even if both heating systems were out of action.

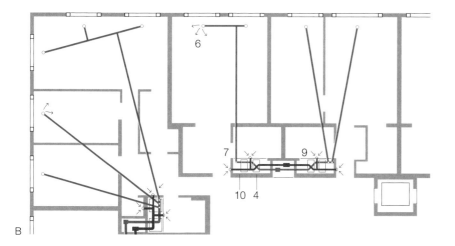

B

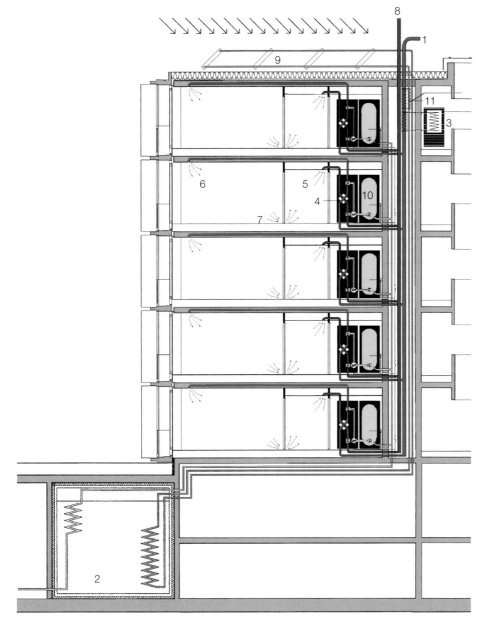

C

Heating and ventilation (diagrams B and C)

- Air is sucked in via the roof (1). In winter, cold external air is heated to a temperature of 0–10 °C by means of the solar storage unit (2). When no solar heating of the air intake occurs, this function is performed by a gas heater (3).
- In the ventilating appliances in the dwellings (4), the fresh-air intake is heated to 16–20 °C by heat extracted from exhaust air (5). In this process, 80 per cent of the thermal energy from the exhaust air (20–22 °C) is recovered without any contamination with vitiated air.
- In the event of no heating being necessary as a result of heat gains from people, lighting or insolation, the fresh-air intake is fed into the living rooms and bedrooms without being preheated. When heating is required, the fresh-air intake is heated to roughly 30–40 °C by a minimum-sized heat pump (4).
- Fresh air is conveyed to the ventilation inlets (6) in the living and sleeping areas via thermally insulated ducts in the concrete floor slabs.
- Vitiated air is removed from the kitchens, bathrooms and WCs by suction. The air from the living rooms and other spaces flows out through slits beneath the doors (7). Cooking fumes are extracted separately via activated carbon filters.
- Exhaust air passes through a heat-recovery plant in the ventilation installation (4) before being emitted at roof level (8).

Solar heating of hot water and preheating of air supply

Solar heating of the hot-water supply occurs by means of solar collectors (9) and central solar storage elements (2).

- When insolation occurs, the solar collectors, with an area of 140–190 m² per block, yield their heat to the central solar storage elements (80–105 m³ per block) situated in the corners of the basement garages.
- In summer, the requisite hot water is heated in the storage elements to a temperature of 40–60 °C and then fed into hot-water tanks in the individual dwellings (10), where it can be reheated by the heat pump; (roughly 65 per cent more efficient than an electric water heater).
- In winter, solar heat is used to warm the air supply (11). At this time of year, the storage temperature can sink to 5–15 °C. With temperatures around 20 °C, the collectors can yield solar heat. Using conventional collectors, therefore, very high yields of around 450 kWh per square metre of collector area can be achieved per annum.

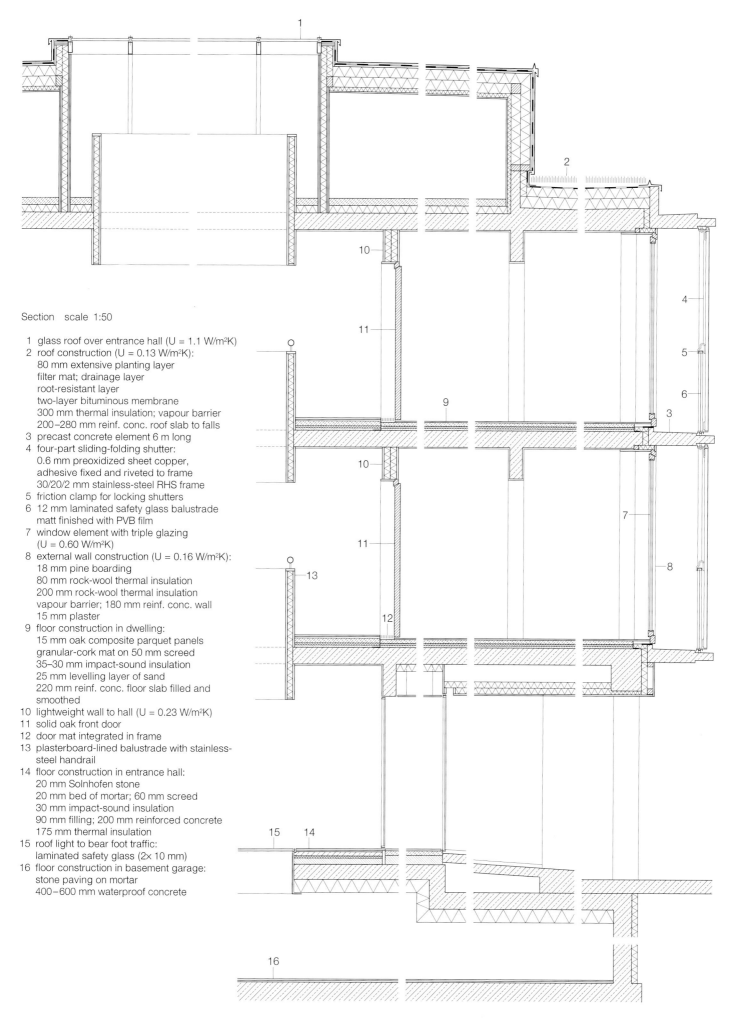

Section   scale 1:50

1 glass roof over entrance hall (U = 1.1 W/m²K)
2 roof construction (U = 0.13 W/m²K):
   80 mm extensive planting layer
   filter mat; drainage layer
   root-resistant layer
   two-layer bituminous membrane
   300 mm thermal insulation; vapour barrier
   200–280 mm reinf. conc. roof slab to falls
3 precast concrete element 6 m long
4 four-part sliding-folding shutter:
   0.6 mm preoxidized sheet copper,
   adhesive fixed and riveted to frame
   30/20/2 mm stainless-steel RHS frame
5 friction clamp for locking shutters
6 12 mm laminated safety glass balustrade
   matt finished with PVB film
7 window element with triple glazing
   (U = 0.60 W/m²K)
8 external wall construction (U = 0.16 W/m²K):
   18 mm pine boarding
   80 mm rock-wool thermal insulation
   200 mm rock-wool thermal insulation
   vapour barrier; 180 mm reinf. conc. wall
   15 mm plaster
9 floor construction in dwelling:
   15 mm oak composite parquet panels
   granular-cork mat on 50 mm screed
   35–30 mm impact-sound insulation
   25 mm levelling layer of sand
   220 mm reinf. conc. floor slab filled and
   smoothed
10 lightweight wall to hall (U = 0.23 W/m²K)
11 solid oak front door
12 door mat integrated in frame
13 plasterboard-lined balustrade with stainless-
   steel handrail
14 floor construction in entrance hall:
   20 mm Solnhofen stone
   20 mm bed of mortar; 60 mm screed
   30 mm impact-sound insulation
   90 mm filling; 200 mm reinforced concrete
   175 mm thermal insulation
15 roof light to bear foot traffic:
   laminated safety glass (2× 10 mm)
16 floor construction in basement garage:
   stone paving on mortar
   400–600 mm waterproof concrete

Lawyer's Practice in Röthis

Architect: Reinhard Drexel, Hohenems
Mechanical Services: Christof Drexel, Reinhard Weiss, Bregenz

Site plan
scale 1:2000

In the centre of Röthis, a small community in Vorarlberg, Austria, a cubic structure with shingle facades stands self-confidently between the old village church and a number of buildings of traditional construction. Having grown derelict over the years, this former agricultural outhouse was demolished down to the foundation walls and has now been rebuilt and converted into a legal practice for the client. A reinforced concrete skeleton-frame structure braced by a staircase was inserted within the existing refurbished walls, which now consist of stone and tamped concrete. The building has been raised in height, and the new concrete floors are supported on each storey by eight steel columns. A construction joint between the solid masonry plinth walls and the timber facade above marks the transition between old and new. The two parts are constructionally and thermally separated. The new external walls are in a three-layer lightweight stud construction with a high degree of thermal insulation (overall thickness 36 cm). Other aspects that support the passive-energy design are the compact cubic form of the building and the good ratio between the footprint area and the volume.

The facades are clad with a homogeneous skin of untreated Canadian larch shingles. The extensive areas of glazing are covered externally by bays of timber strip cladding. Above balustrade level, these sunshading strips are divided into top-hung pivoting elements in 80 × 2,000 cm specially manufactured bead-blasted aluminium frames. The elements, which can be manually operated by the staff to provide protection against insolation and glare, form an important part of the passive energy concept. Triple glazing was used throughout for the room-height windows behind the facade shading. While the large bays of fixed glazing consist of coated glass with an argon-filled cavity (U = 0.6 W/m²K), the glazing to the casement doors is filled with krypton (U = 0.7 W/m²K).

Internally, the building is distinguished by its meticulous detailing: exposed concrete surfaces with an oiled finish, which brings out the grain of the wood shuttering; black bituminous terrazzo; and perforated birch plywood to the ceilings. Instead of a conventional heating installation, a controlled air-supply and air-extract system were foreseen, with a minimally dimensioned heat pump and a heat-recovery facility. The external air is preheated by a roughly 50-metre-long geothermal collector. The fresh-air ducts are incorporated in the solid concrete floor slabs and function in the nature of a hypocaust system. A dynamic simulation program was used to test the energy concept at the planning stage, allowing any necessary constructional changes to be made in good time.

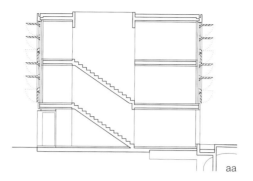

Section
scale 1:250

aa

Floor plans
scale 1:250

1 Lobby
2 Archive
3 Discussion room
4 Office

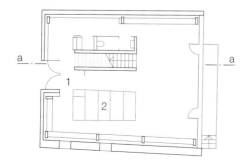

a

1

2

a

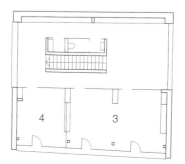

4

3

Sports Hall in Wängi

Architects: Fent Solar Architecture, Wil

In Wängi, Switzerland, the existing multi-purpose sports hall has now been extended by a new hall – the first minimum energy ("minergy") sports hall in that country. During the planning phase, heating-energy needs were calculated at 4.11 kWh/m²a. In other words, the energy consumption is 90 per cent below that of a conventional sports hall. The clear cubic volume of the new structure and its facades, consisting of prefabricated wood-and-glass elements, form a bold contrast to the existing brick building. A two-storey entrance tract between the halls links the two structures. On the ground floor is a large foyer for visitors. Access for pupils is at subfloor level. Internally, the finely articulated load-bearing structure is in native timber, which has been left exposed. To achieve the required minimum-energy standard, the building was constructed with a solar-active "Lucido" glass facade, a system developed by the architects themselves. Thick layers of insulation and an airtight skin also serve to reduce the heating needs. The thermal insulation in the east and west facades is 160 mm thick; in the north and south facades, it is 200 mm thick; and in the roof, 400 mm thick. Preheated air from the Lucido facades also flows into the cavity between the thermal insulation and the planted layer of the roof.

The Lucido facade functions as follows. Sunlight penetrates a single outer pane of toughened glass, and the solar energy is absorbed by a layer of wood louvres in the cavity to the rear. The air in the cavity is heated to a temperature of around 70 °C. This thermal energy is stored and released later into the interior. In view of the high temperatures involved and the thermal expansion they cause, the elements are point fixed with slotted openings at 1.25 m centres.

The system of fenestration for the hall consists of nine openable casement units within a larger area of fixed triple glazing (U ≤ 0.8 W/m²K). The post-and-rail construction was executed to passive solar-energy standards, one important criterion of which is that a building should have an airtight seal (n50 = 0.6 h⁻¹). In the present hall, a value of 0.2 h⁻¹ was achieved. The ventilation plant, with scope for heat-recovery, produces warm air via an air/water exchange system. The air is then blown into the hall. The energy needed for this process is provided by the heating plant in the existing hall. In the first year of operation, additional thermal energy was required from November onwards, but by the beginning of February, it was possible to heat the sports hall entirely from solar sources. In comparison with a conventional hall, the Wängi community saves roughly 14,750 litres of fuel oil a year, and carbon dioxide emissions are reduced by roughly 50 tonnes.

Site plan
scale 1:2000

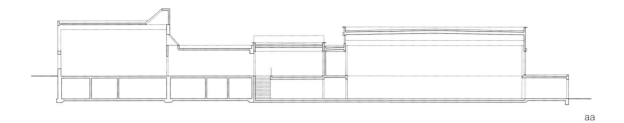

Section
scale 1:500

aa

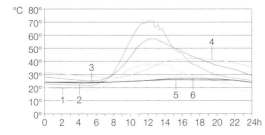

A Summer day: measurement period 0–24h;
for position of measurement points, see p. 100

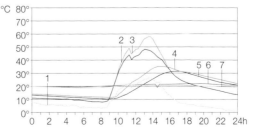

B Winter day: measurement period 0–24h;
for position of measurement points, see p. 100

Measurements made when hall in use:

1 External temperature
2 Temperature in space between glass and louvres
3 Temperature in spaces between wood louvres
4 Temperature of inner face of wood louvres
5 Temperature of Fermacell thermal storage element
6 Wall temperature internally
7 Internal air temperature

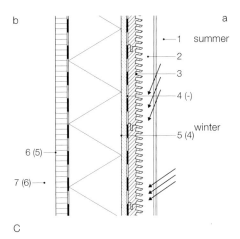

b   a

1 summer
2
3
4 (-)
5 (4) winter
6 (5)
7 (6)

C

Function of Lucido facade element
Fixed close behind a single pane of toughened glass, a wood louvre structure absorbs thermal energy. The prismatized single glazing facilitates the absorption of oblique rays of morning and evening light. Behind the louvres is a daytime thermal storage layer, consisting of plasterboard and softwood.
The wall system is a hybrid form of construction, in which solar energy is actively absorbed and stored. The conventional wall serves as a passive thermal storage element. The ventilated cavity between the glass and the louvres serves to control the heat balance. The absorption process is regulated in summer and winter in accordance with the angle of incidence of the sun and the cavity ventilation.

In summer, the rays of the sun fall on the facade at a steep angle and are largely reflected by the glass. Since the louvres provide mutual shading, high temperatures occur only at their tips. Convection currents in the cavity increase, and excess heat is borne off.
In winter, the sun's rays fall at a much lower angle of incidence. They penetrate the glass and warm the angled louvres. At lower temperatures, the convection process decreases. The cavity and the spaces between the louvres then function as a thermally insulating layer. The stored solar energy and the actual thermal insulation reduce heat losses to a minimum. In the sports hall, which has a volume of roughly 10,000 m³, there are virtually no fluctuations in temperature, and users enjoy an agreeable indoor climate.

Valuation after measurements made when hall in use:
Good energy efficiency in terms of heat storage and the reduction of heat losses in winter; good insulating properties in summer.

C Section through wall construction with heat-absorbent wood louvres
a external
b internal
Measurement in summer
(in brackets)

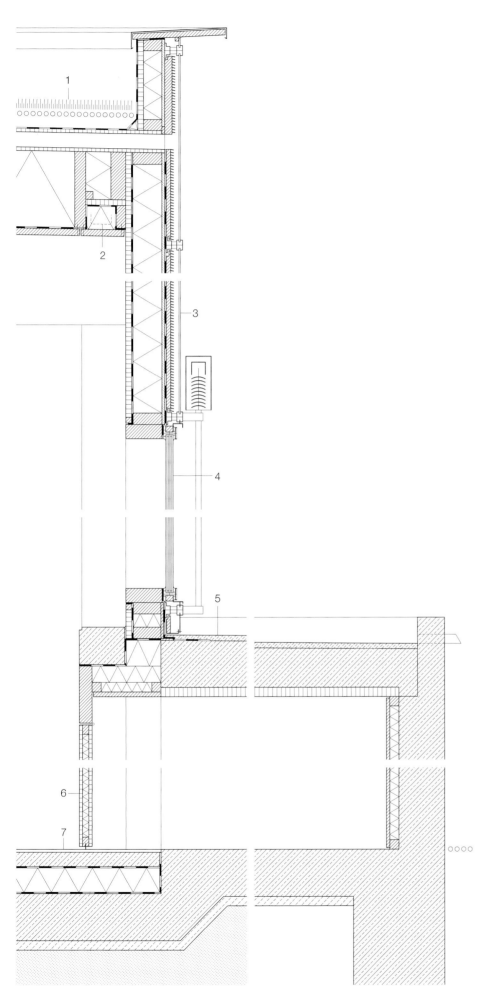

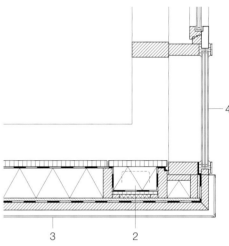

3   2

Sections through facade
scale 1:20

1 roof construction:
   80 mm substrate layer on roof sealing layer
   18 mm oriented-strand board
   80 mm cavity
   18 mm oriented-strand board
   400 mm cellulose thermal insulation
   vapour-retarding layer
   with black absorbent felt
   32 mm three-ply laminated softwood sheeting
2 insulated duct
3 wall construction:
   4 mm prismatic toughened solar glass
   30 mm cavity
   40 mm wood louvres
   windproof layer
   15 mm cellulose-bonded gypsum board
   160–200 mm cellulose thermal insulation
   sealing layer
   32 mm three-ply laminated softwood sheeting
4 triple glazing (U = 0.6 W/m²K)
5 flat roof construction:
   20 mm mastic asphalt
   250 mm reinforced concrete roof slab
   finished to falls
   50 mm cement-bonded lightweight
   wood-wool slabs
6 up-and-over door:
   composite wood board with insulation
7 floor construction in sports hall:
   15 mm poured polyurethane surface layer
   100 mm screed on separating layer
   160 mm polyurethane thermal insulation
   damp-proof membrane
   250 mm reinforced concrete floor slab
   50–100 mm lean concrete
   400 mm layer of broken glass

Secondary School in Klaus

Architects: Dietrich and Untertrifaller, Bregenz
Mechanical services: IGT Consulting & Engineering, Hohenems

Site plan
scale 1:3500

1 New school building
2 Sports hall tract
3 Former school building

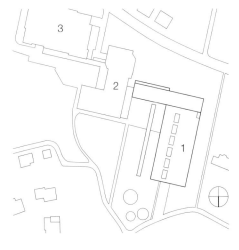

Vorarlberg, a small state in Austria, is known for the high architectural quality of its buildings. In the realm of environmental and solar construction, too, one finds pioneering projects such as the secondary school in Klaus, which was executed as a passive-energy structure. With a heating requirement of 15 kWh/m²a, a controlled air-supply and extract system combined with an air/earth heat-exchange grid, and the appropriate insulation values, the school complies with Vorarlberg standards for passive-energy buildings. This timber structure is thus a pilot scheme in the field of school construction.
On the basis of a study it had commissioned, the local authority decided to sell the old school building, for environmental and economic reasons, and to replace it with a new one. An existing sports hall tract has been retained and will be refurbished later in a second phase of construction. The school is situated directly on the road between the town of Klaus and a nearby industrial area. The clearly articulated volume of the three-storey building, together with a two-storey linking tract to the existing sports hall, screens the tree-lined playground from the road. The school provides teaching for 12 classes. The pupils come from Klaus and the two nearby communities of Weiler and Fraxern. At the head of the classroom tract is a two-storey entrance space, which is also used as an assembly hall. The upper floor of the linking tract accommodates a municipal library. Access to the two-bay teaching tract is via a long corridor illuminated by roof lights. WCs, ancillary spaces and mechanical services are housed in box-like structures inserted within the layout. Light wells extending over the full height of the building allow daylight to penetrate to the lower floors. The main classrooms on the ground and first floors of the eastern tract are connected by bridges to the corridors. Sunshading to the windows is provided by automatically controlled louvres, which can also be individually operated if required. The fully glazed south face of the assembly hall is protected against insolation in summer by a 30 per cent perforated sheet-copper screen fixed to a steel frame structure. The building consists entirely of prefabricated timber elements, with the exception of the staircase cores, which are in reinforced concrete. The school cost only 3 per cent more than a comparable building in a conventional, solid form of construction. From the outset, the architects and mechanical services engineers collaborated to achieve a school that would comply with passive-energy standards. A lot of persuasion was needed during preliminary discussions with local authority committees to ensure not only a high level of architecture, but the best and most efficient mechanical services for the situation.

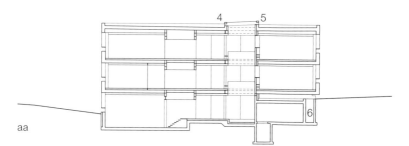

aa

Section
scale 1:500

4 Air intake
5 Vitiated air
6 Air intake via
earth grid

Cross-section through classroom tract
scale 1:20

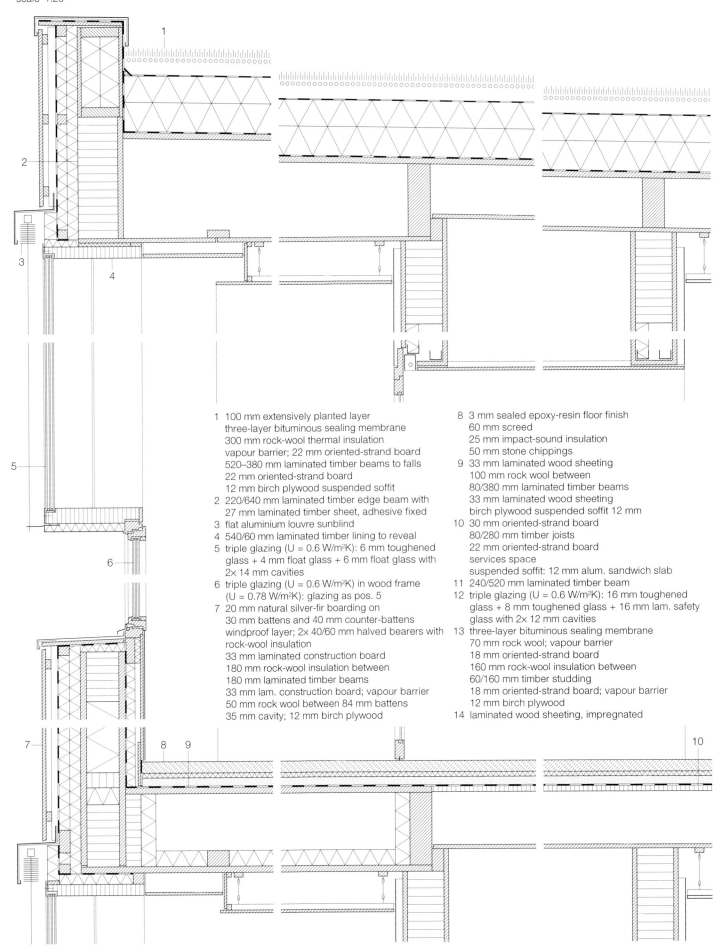

1 100 mm extensively planted layer
  three-layer bituminous sealing membrane
  300 mm rock-wool thermal insulation
  vapour barrier; 22 mm oriented-strand board
  520–380 mm laminated timber beams to falls
  22 mm oriented-strand board
  12 mm birch plywood suspended soffit
2 220/640 mm laminated timber edge beam with
  27 mm laminated timber sheet, adhesive fixed
3 flat aluminium louvre sunblind
4 540/60 mm laminated timber lining to reveal
5 triple glazing (U = 0.6 W/m²K): 6 mm toughened
  glass + 4 mm float glass + 6 mm float glass with
  2× 14 mm cavities
6 triple glazing (U = 0.6 W/m²K) in wood frame
  (U = 0.78 W/m²K): glazing as pos. 5
7 20 mm natural silver-fir boarding on
  30 mm battens and 40 mm counter-battens
  windproof layer; 2× 40/60 mm halved bearers with
  rock-wool insulation
  33 mm laminated construction board
  180 mm rock-wool insulation between
  180 mm laminated timber beams
  33 mm lam. construction board; vapour barrier
  50 mm rock wool between 84 mm battens
  35 mm cavity; 12 mm birch plywood

8 3 mm sealed epoxy-resin floor finish
  60 mm screed
  25 mm impact-sound insulation
  50 mm stone chippings
9 33 mm laminated wood sheeting
  100 mm rock wool between
  80/380 mm laminated timber beams
  33 mm laminated wood sheeting
  birch plywood suspended soffit 12 mm
10 30 mm oriented-strand board
  80/280 mm timber joists
  22 mm oriented-strand board
  services space
  suspended soffit: 12 mm alum. sandwich slab
11 240/520 mm laminated timber beam
12 triple glazing (U = 0.6 W/m²K): 16 mm toughened
  glass + 8 mm toughened glass + 16 mm lam. safety
  glass with 2× 12 mm cavities
13 three-layer bituminous sealing membrane
  70 mm rock wool; vapour barrier
  18 mm oriented-strand board
  160 mm rock-wool insulation between
  60/160 mm timber studding
  18 mm oriented-strand board; vapour barrier
  12 mm birch plywood
14 laminated wood sheeting, impregnated

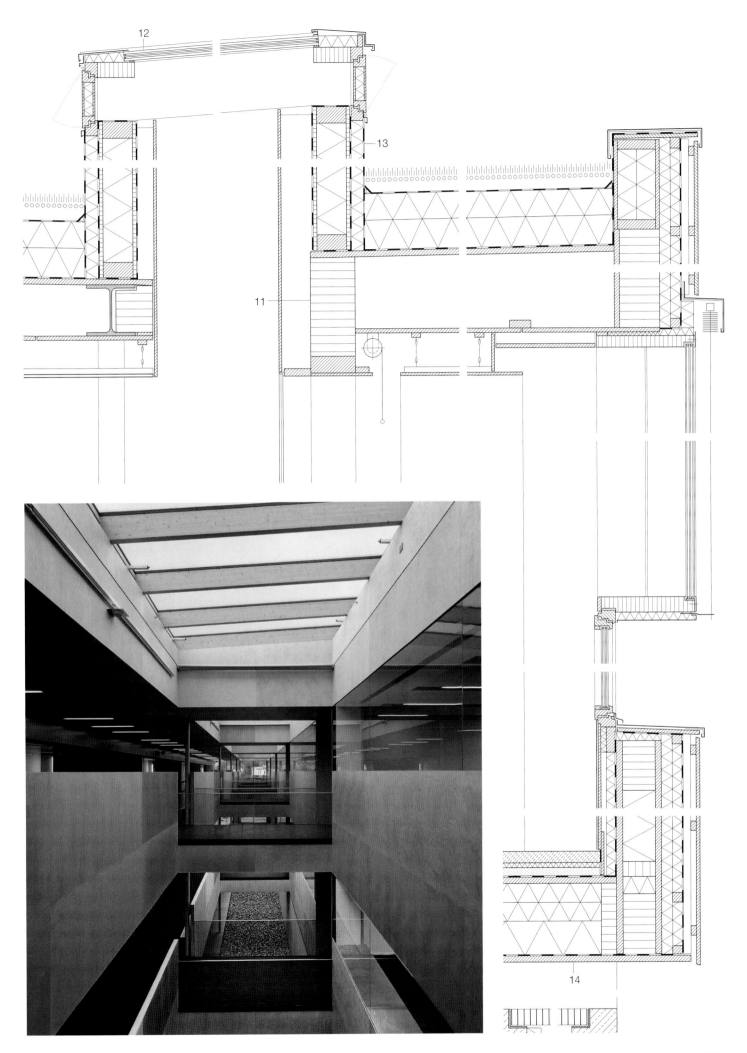

12

13

11

14

Conference and Exhibition Building in Osnabrück

Architects: Prof. Thomas Herzog +
Hanns Jörg Schrade, Munich
Mechanical services: NEK Ingenieurgruppe, Brunswick
Consultants for energy technology: ZAE Bayern e. V., Garching

Site plan
scale 1:4000
Floor plans
scale 1:1000

1 Foyer
2 Exhibition space
3 Conference space
4 Offices
5 Store
6 Cafeteria
7 Void

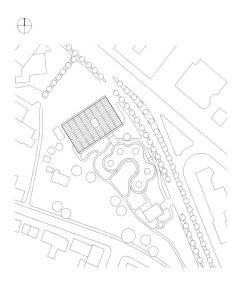

Designed for the German Federal Environmental Foundation in Osnabrück, Germany, this conference and exhibition centre was to provide ideal daylighting conditions combined with an efficient indoor-climate concept. In addition, the brief called for an extensive use of natural materials, functional flexibility, and the creation of close links with the adjoining park. The client also required an environmentally sustainable development that would conserve energy and natural resources without incurring additional construction costs. The building has a timber skeleton-frame structure and a height of 6.50 m. In the conference and exhibition areas, the full height was exploited to provide the appropriate spatial conditions. At other points, it was possible to create storage and office spaces on two levels. The structure is braced by a three-storey reinforced concrete core that houses sanitary and technical services. Set on top of this are a photovoltaic plant and vacuum-tube collectors.

The transparent, ventilated membrane roof forms the outer weatherproofing skin. The single-layer tensioned ETFE sheeting is fully recyclable, and its anti-adhesive properties mean that the surface is self-cleaning. A multilayer construction allows every bay of the roof to be adapted to the functional needs of the spaces below. Over the office and storage areas, for example, there is an opaque internal layer with a high degree of thermal and sound insulation. In contrast, a translucent form of construction was chosen for the roof over the conference and exhibition spaces. This allowed them to be illuminated by zenith light, which ensures a much higher radiant intensity than side-lighting. Pivoting louvres between the membrane skin and the glazing layer provide protection against insolation and control the ingress of daylight. On hot days, the louvre elements are computer operated to follow the course of the sun. It is also possible to darken the conference room completely.

The roof construction allows major savings to be made in the amount of electrical energy needed for lighting. In addition, direct insolation via the facades and roof results in a high passive thermal yield during the heating period. In summer, in contrast, effective sunshading helps to minimize cooling-energy needs. Special permission had to be obtained from the building authorities to realize this form of construction.

In winter, a cogenerating plant supplies heating energy to the new centre and the existing administration building. In summer, room temperatures can be lowered by a groundwater cooling system coupled with the underfloor heating installation. On hot days, a heat-exchange unit cools the intake of fresh air that flows through the ventilation plant, while in winter, the fresh air can be warmed.

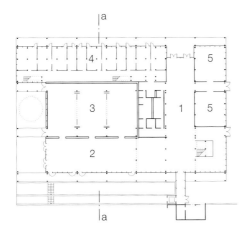

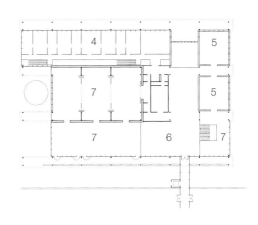

Section   scale 1:750
A Ventilation diagram
B Groundwater cooling diagram
Section through facade and roof   scale 1:20

1 single-layer ETFE membrane prestressed on
   four edges
2 120/80 mm galvanized steel RHS
3 aluminium pivoting louvres for sunshading/
   daylighting control/darkening space below
4 sheet-metal covering for blackout purposes
5 triple glazing: 6 mm toughened glass with
   low-E coating + 5 mm float glass + 10 mm
   lam. safety glass with low-E coating
   + 2× 12 mm cavities with argon filling
6 160 mm white-coated thermal insulation
   39 mm laminated timber sheeting
7 fly screen: white woven glass fabric
8 double glazing: 10 mm toughened glass +
   16 mm cavity with argon filling + 6 mm
   toughened glass with low-E coating
9 3 mm sheet aluminium fixed sunshading
   louvres bent to shape on
   Ø 8 mm stainless-steel cable

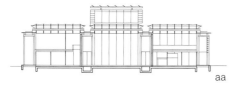

aa

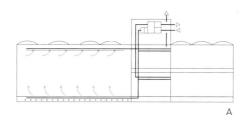

A

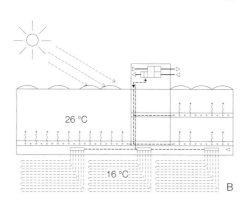

26 °C

16 °C

B

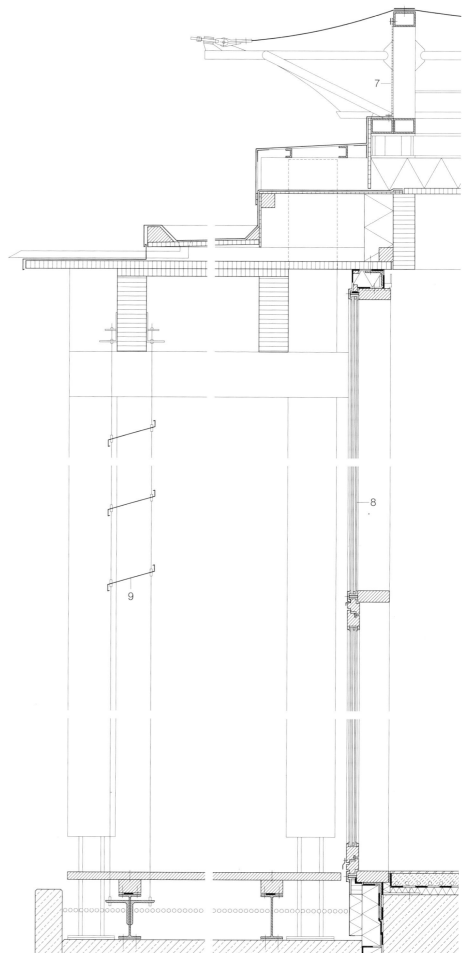

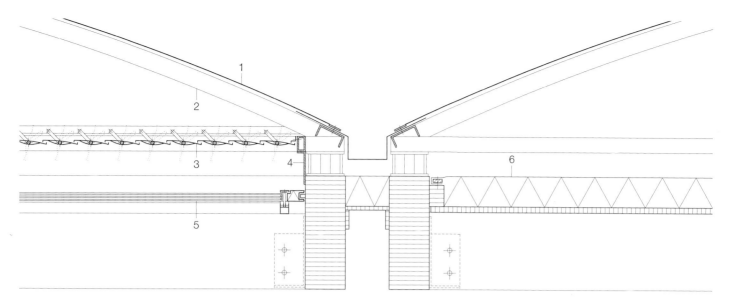

Ventilation

In addition to the scope provided for individual ventilation via the windows, a mechanical ventilation system was installed that serves the offices, and the conference and exhibition spaces. On hot days, the intake of external air is cooled to about 23 °C by a heat-exchange unit coupled with a groundwater cooling system. Over the year, the combined air-intake and extract duct achieves a heat-recovery rate of more than 80 per cent.

In the conference and exhibition spaces, the air supply is blown in at low speed from the bottom, so that there is always a layer of fresh air above floor level, and in summer it is relatively cool.

Warm, vitiated air rises to the ceiling, where it is sucked out. In other words, only the lower part of these large spaces has to be air conditioned. The installation also serves as a smoke-extract system in the event of fire.

The air supply rate is based on the volume of fresh air necessary to maintain hygienic conditions. The air intake is centrally filtered. There is no recirculation of air and no humidification or dehumidification. This means that the relative humidity internally is roughly the same as that of the extenal air: in winter, it is very low; in summer, relatively high. On the other hand, the technical resources are on a modest scale, and energy consumption is low.

Heating and cooling

The new and existing structures are heated by a cogenerating plant. Direct insolation via the facades, and especially via the roof, also yields considerable thermal gains. As a result of efficient sunshading and the groundwater cooling system, only minimal energy is needed for cooling in summer. Water is pumped through tubes beneath the foundation slab and cooled by groundwater before being circulated through the building via the underfloor heating system. With a temperature of approx. 20 °C, the water cools the internal spaces to about 26 °C. A far smaller airflow volume is required for the night-time removal of excess heat than for air cooling.

Office Building in Solihull

Architects: Arup Associates, London

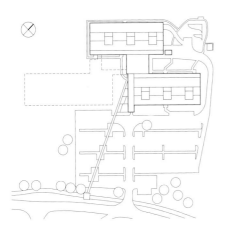

At first sight, the new Arup office in Solihull near Birmingham would seem to be a straightforward, pragmatic building in which the architects were able to perfect their strategies for energy-efficient construction. Special importance was attached to natural lighting and ventilation, which had a great influence on the form and construction of the building. The compact, deep wings contain more or less continuous open spaces that allow a flexible use of the structure and support the interdisciplinary collaboration that takes place within the planning teams. The two storeys in both of the linear tracts are linked by openings in the floor situated on the central axes. Carpeted floors and acoustic "wings" fixed to the ceiling lights provide the requisite sound insulation in these large spaces. Y-shaped steel columns support the striking structures that project above the roof. These solar stacks, which bring daylight into the office spaces and also serve to ventilate them, made it possible to design spaces with a depth of 24 m. Daylight is able to penetrate to the heart of the building via the north-facing angled glazing to the roof lights. Automatically controlled flaps on the opposite side, in conjunction with flaps in the facade, ensure a largely natural form of ventilation internally. Only the computer centre and the auditorium are air conditioned by means of a displacement system, in which external fresh air is used for most of the year. The different forms of facade construction and sunshading are an integral part of the energy concept, with fixed aluminium fins in front of the windows in the end facades, internal sunblinds to the glazing in the north-west face, and external wood shutters to the windows in the south-east face. The ventilation and sunshading are automatically controlled, whereas the sliding windows and wood shutters can be manually operated by the staff. Precast concrete hollow-plank floor and roof slabs with exposed soffits provide solid structural elements that can be thermally activated. In summer, they are cooled at night by air that flows in via automatically controlled flaps.

Up to now, the building has proved itself in use, even during the record heatwave of August 2003, when external temperatures rose to 35 °C. On cold winter days, the great temperature differences in the high spaces and cold-air drop on the inside of the facades can result in a certain loss of comfort. The running costs are far below those for conventionally air-conditioned office developments. Now that the building has been in operation for two and a half years, the practice expects a saving on energy costs amounting to £80,000, with a further £70,000 saving on maintenance costs.

Site plan
scale 1:3000

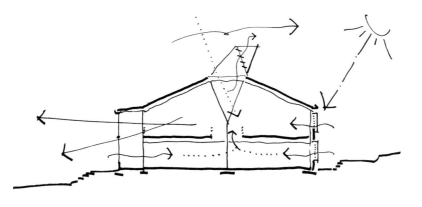

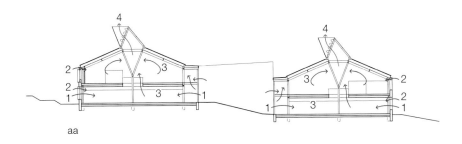

aa

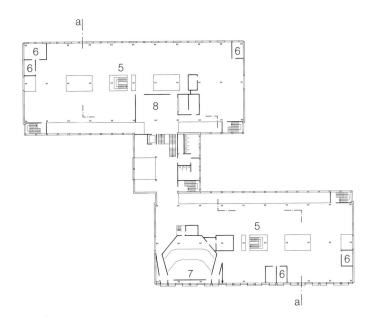

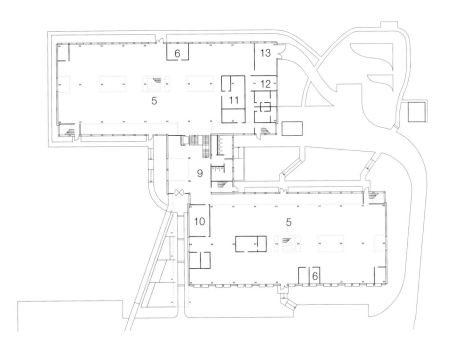

Section
scale 1:750

1 Air supply
2 Mechanical night-time/winter
   ventilation
3 Thermal storage mass
4 Air extract

Upper floor plan
Ground floor plan
scale 1:1000

5 Open-plan office
6 Cellular office
7 Auditorium
8 Café
9 Entrance hall
10 Conference room
11 Computer centre
12 Fitness room
13 Testing workshop

Section through south-east facade
scale 1:20

14 13 mm plywood surround with
   sheet-aluminium cladding
15 45 mm red cedar window shutter
16 mechanical operating gear
17 automatically operated insulated flap
   for night-time/winter ventilation
18 wall construction:
   20 mm red cedar boarding
   50 mm cavity
   breather membrane
   18 mm plywood
   120 mm mineral-wool insulation
   vapour barrier
   12 mm medium-density fibreboard

Passive energy concept with high
proportion of natural lighting,
effective sunshading,
natural ventilation,
compact building form

Automatically operated flaps in the solar
stacks on the roof serve to remove vitiated air
from the entire internal space (flue effect).
The north-facing sloping glazing in these roof
elements also allows daylight to penetrate to
the central office zones below, thus enabling
deep layouts and compact building volumes
to be created.

The facades and sunshading vary according
to the situation. The glazing in the north-west
face is shaded by internal blinds. On the
south-east face, there are external wood
shutters and automatically operated flaps for
night-time and winter ventilation. Fixed aluminium louvres provide shading to the windows in the end facades (north-east and
south-west). The ventilation and sunshading
systems are automatically controlled. The
sliding windows and wood shutters can be
manually operated.

Precast concrete floor slabs with exposed
soffits provide a solid mass that can be thermally activated: in summer, the slabs are
cooled by the ingress of air at night.

Bolted sections of the load-bearing steel
structure can be dismantled and reused, as
can the precast concrete floor elements (no
composite form of construction).

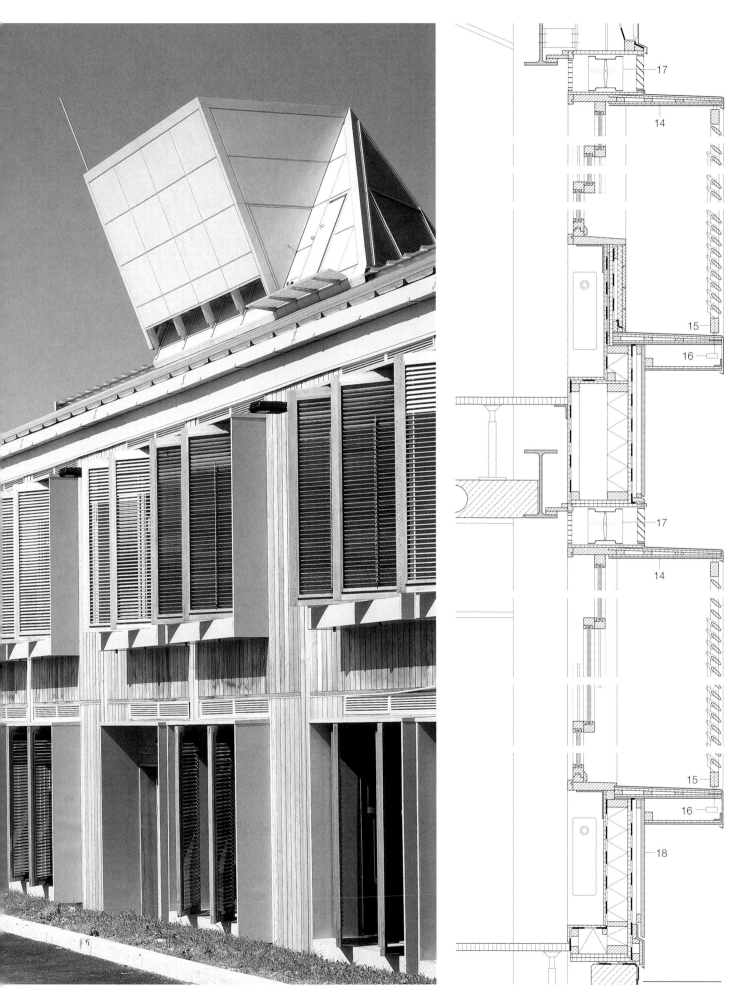

17

14

15

16

17

14

15

16

18

115

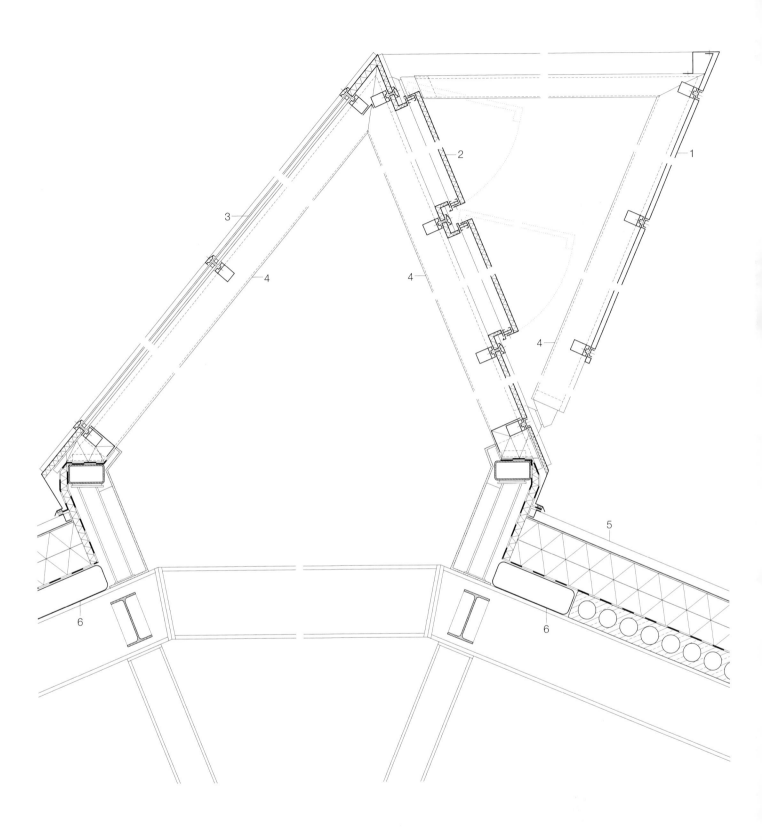

Section through
solar stack
scale 1:20

1 40 mm powder-coated
  aluminium wind baffle panel
2 40 mm insulated aluminium
  ventilation flap
3 insulating double glazing:
  6.4 mm toughened glass with

low-E coating +
22 mm cavity with
vertical sunshading louvres +
10.8 mm laminated safety glass
4 150/50/6 mm aluminium-covered
  steel RHS

5 roof construction:
  0.6 mm coated sheet steel
  260 mm mineral-wool insulation
  vapour barrier
  150 mm prec. conc. hollow slabs
6 cable duct

Administration Building in Recanati

Architects: MCA, Mario Cucinella Architects, Bologna
Mechanical services: Ove Arup & Partners, London
Daylight studies: École Polytechnique, Lausanne

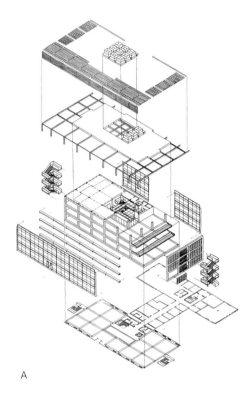

A

In the hot, dry climatic conditions of southern Europe, adequate cooling and ventilation of buildings in conjunction with optimum daylighting are essential. Erected next to an existing structure, the new headquarters of a lamp manufacturer in Recanati, Italy, were designed to allow a maximum of natural lighting and ventilation for most of the year. This rectilinear administration building with a footprint of 40 × 19.3 m is laid out around a central planted atrium and contains four floors of open-plan offices, and areas that can be partitioned off. The administration is situated on the first floor. The management occupies the top floor, where there is access to an adjoining roof terrace. Spaces for mechanical services are housed in the linking tract to the existing building.

The 100 m² atrium facilitates the ingress of daylight for the internal offices. Situated on one side of the atrium are the central staircase and lift in a metal-and-glass form of construction. The distribution of daylight and the sense of transparency in this area are enhanced by the glazed balustrades and walls to the atrium. At the top of this space, 12 lantern lights in the roof allow daylight to penetrate into the interior of the building. The form of the roof lights also supports the natural ventilation system by functioning as a central extract route for vitiated air from the various floors of the complex. At the same time, daylight entering from above is deflected in such a way as to avoid unwanted glare and shadows at the workplaces around the atrium. The south face of the building is fully glazed. A sunshading roof with fixed aluminium louvres protects the office areas within against overheating. The east and west facades are translucent. As a result of these measures, it was possible to ensure the requisite level of natural illumination for all workplaces.

A Axonometric
B Section
  scale 1:500
C System diagrams:
  ventilation • sunlighting
  • thermal mass

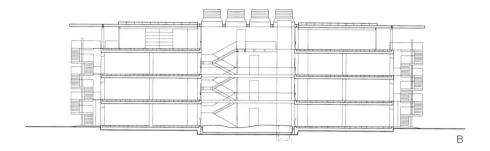

B

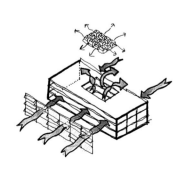

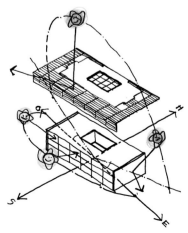

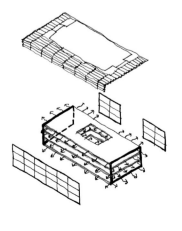

C

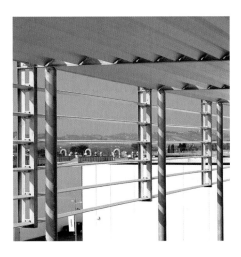

To optimize the daylighting and ventilation concepts, various measurements were made during the design and construction phases.

A Daylight studies
Taking into account various factors, such as the construction of the roof lights, the sunshading roof, the facades and the atrium, measurements showed a daylight factor of between 10.3 and 6.1 per cent with an overcast sky where there is no sunshading roof. With a sunshading roof, the daylight factor was between 10 and 5.7 per cent. With a clear sky, the corresponding figures were between 13 and 7.4 per cent and between 12.7 and 7.4 per cent respectively. The 300–500 lux illumination required for workplaces in buildings is therewith guaranteed in all areas. The highest values were calculated for the office zones around the atrium. Individually adjustable sunshade blinds were installed here to avoid glare.

B Sunshading to south facade
Daylight studies were carried out on a 1:50 model at the École Polytechnique Lausanne (EPFL) to ascertain the effectiveness of the sunshading. The measurements showed that the facade required 100 per cent shading in summer and 80 per cent shading in the transitional seasons. This served to determine the distribution and size of the aluminium louvres. The 3.70-metre-high vertical section of the sunshading roof is set 6.70 m in front of the facade and contains a series of horizontal louvres at 50 cm centres. In the horizontal plane of the roof, the louvres are fixed to the supporting structure at an angle of 45°. They are most densely grouped (at 40 cm centres) in the middle, since this zone protects the facade against the sun when it is at its zenith in summer.

C Natural ventilation and cooling
The concept was optimized in collaboration with the engineers Ove Arup & Partners.
In each of the southern facade bays, there are two opening lights in the upper and the lower areas. Fresh air flows in through the open windows at the bottom and escapes via the roof lights and the openings in the upper part of the facade. On windless days, the distribution of air layers in the atrium gives rise to a kind of stack effect, which serves to bear vitiated air out of the building at the top through the roof lights. When internal heat loads rise on extremely hot summer days, supplementary fans can be switched on to to augment the ventilation. Cooling in summer and heating in winter are aided by the solid mass of the unclad reinforced concrete floor slabs and the outer masonry walls.

Third floor plan
First and
second floor plan
Ground floor plan
scale 1:500

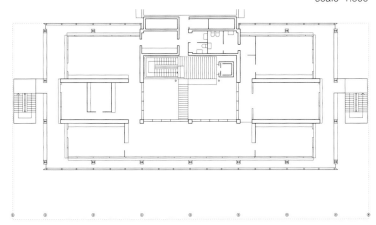

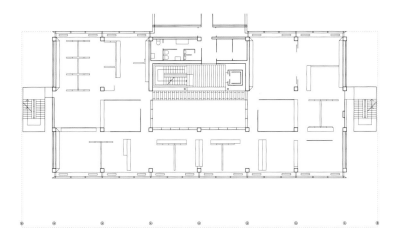

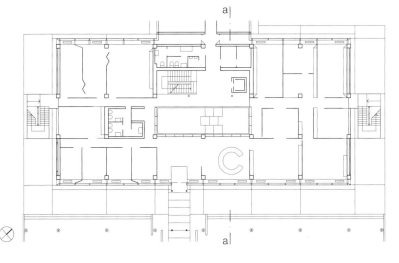

A Vertical section through edge of roof
  and roof light
B Vertical section through office space
  scale 1:20
C Horizontal section
  Facade details
  scale 1:5

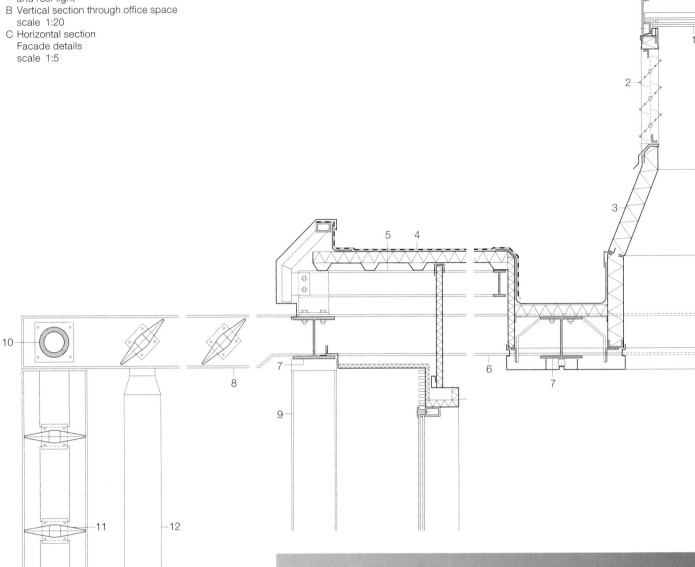

A

1 double glazing (12 + 12 + 10 mm)
2 ventilation grille with aluminium louvres
3 80 mm aluminium sandwich panel
4 roof construction:
   2 mm PVC sealing layer
   self-supporting panel with 50 mm rigid-foam
   insulation, bitumen-coated
5 steel I-beam 140 mm deep
6 steel I-beam 220 mm deep
7 steel I-beam 220 mm deep
8 steel I-beam 270 mm deep
9 steel I-column 240 mm deep
10 Ø 160/30 mm steel tube
11 aluminium sunscreen louvre
12 Ø 200/30 mm tubular steel column

122

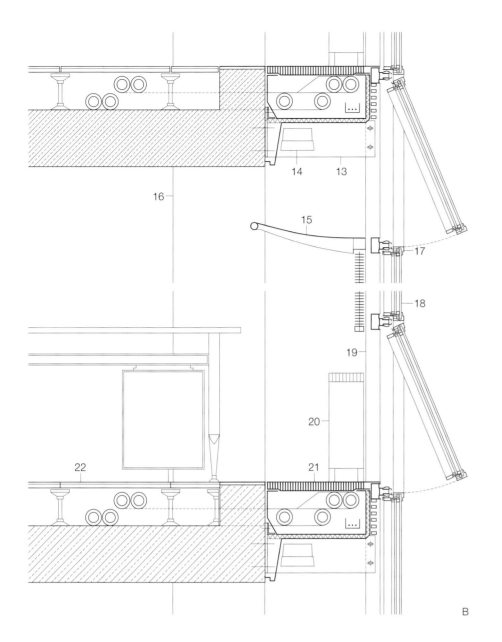

13 200/100/15 mm steel RHS
14 light fitting
15 1 mm sheet-aluminium light deflector
16 550/550 mm concrete column
17 aluminium facade rail
18 double glazing (8 + 12 + 6 mm)
19 aluminium facade post
20 radiator
21 services duct
22 hollow-floor system
23 aluminium sunscreen louvre
24 elastic seal
25 1.5 mm sheet aluminium

B

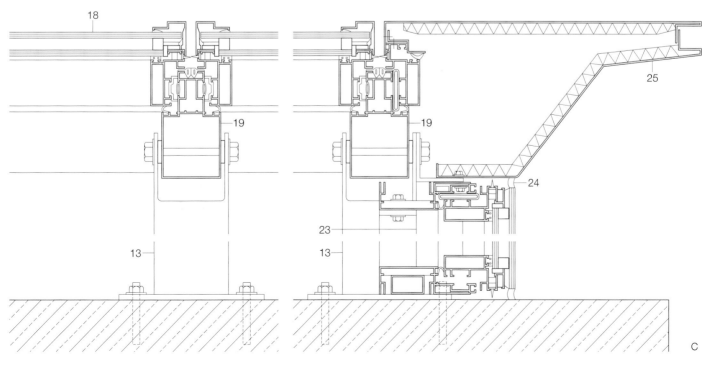

C

Administration Building in Landquart

Architects: Bearth & Deplazes, Chur
Mechanical services: Andrea Rüedi, Chur

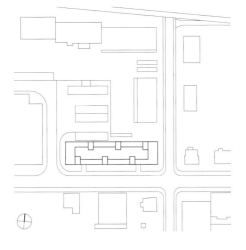

Site plan   scale 1:2000

Designed for an insurance company, this five-storey administration building is located in the station district of Landquart in the Grisons, Switzerland. The block is surrounded by a mixture of structures dating from the past three centuries. The strict cubic lines of the new development form a striking contrast to this heterogeneous urban environment, which is reflected in the steel-and-glass curtain-wall facades of the insurance building. The ventilation flaps and the moving parts of the external sunshading system are integrated flush with the outer skin. When the awnings are extended, the rectilinear form of the building is enlivened by an array of pale-green diagonal sails. In addition, coloured fabric curtains have been hung internally behind the broad areas of glazing.

The floor slabs are supported without intermediate columns by six reinforced concrete cores, which house staircases, lifts and sanitary facilities. The ground floor is laid out with a lobby and a reception area for clients. On the four upper floors, a series of colourful office landscapes has been created with open-plan spaces, combination and cellular offices. The roof storey contains conference and training rooms and a cafeteria. The individual floors are separated from each other in terms of their indoor-climate technology and are also divided along their longitudinal axes into north- and south-oriented zones. Set out along the northern face are small single-person offices and group rooms divided by transparent glazed partitions. Along the southern side, open working and service zones alternate with sitting areas.

The indoor climate is regulated by a sensor-responsive control and instrumentation system that activates the appropriate mechanical services. The system controls the automatic extension arms of the blinds as well as the motor-operated ventilation flaps in the facade. Artificial lighting within the building is activated by means of a daylight-linked mechanism.

In summer, air-extract fans can be switched on to augment the natural night-time ventilation; while two separate heating circuits on each floor – for the north and south zones – can be operated as a supplementary form of heating in winter. The control and instrumentation system is integrated in the computer network for the building, allowing members of the staff to regulate individual services via their PCs. In critical situations, an automatic control system intervenes to maintain a balance in the indoor climate. Scope is provided for the addition of further functions in the future to improve the exploitation of energy.

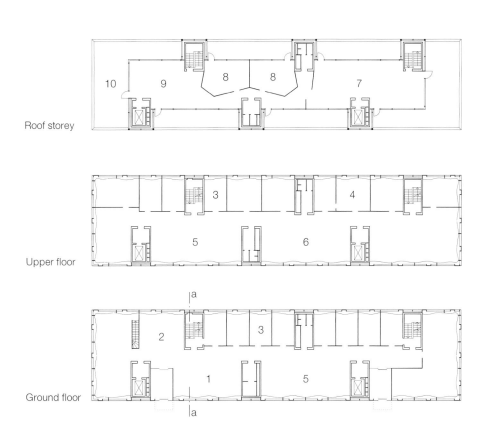

Roof storey

Upper floor

Ground floor

Floor plans
scale 1:500

1 Lobby
2 Reception
3 Single office
4 Combination office
5 Open-plan office
6 Sitting area
7 Training room
8 Conference room
9 Cafeteria
10 Roof terrace

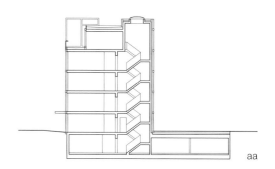

aa

	Activated	Turned off/Closed	Remarks
1. Night-time cooling (May–September):	Indoor temperature measurements at 11 p.m.		
stage 1: open windows	Ti > 22 °C and Ti ≥ Te -6K	6 a.m.	All windows on all floors open
stage 2: open windows and roof fans	Ti > 22 °C and Ti ≥ Te -2K	6 a.m.	When strong winds, only certain windows open
roof storey: ventilation with cooling	Ti > 24 °C and Ti ≥ Te -2K	6 a.m.	Cooling at full capacity / windows closed
2. External shading:	External radiation measurements on roof mast (W/m²)	High wind speeds, precipitation October–April: Ti at 6 a.m. < 22 °C	– Sunshading 24 hrs. not in operation so that solid mass of building can absorb solar heat
South-facing windows	> 200 W/m²	< 150 W/m²	
East-facing windows	> 200 W/m²	< 150 W/m²	
West-facing windows	> 200 W/m²	< 150 W/m²	
3. Heating (floor by floor):			Two reference temperatures in each case: average values for north and south zones on each floor
Northern zone	~ 21.5 °C average temperature	~ 22.5 °C	
Southern zone	~ 20.5 °C average temperature	~ 21.5 °C	
4. Controlled window ventilation:			CO_2 control measurements close to critical values: ventilation time increased
Winter: mid-November to mid-February	Air change: 0.25 (flaps opened by automatic time switch)	Saturdays, Sundays, holidays 5 p.m.–7.30 a.m.	
Summer: mid-June to end of August	Air change: 0.25 (as above)	as above	
Transitional periods:	Air change: 0.35–0.6 (flaps opened by automatic time switch)		
Roof storey (no daytime window ventilation)			Ventilation scenarios for strong wind conditions: window opening north and south zones alternately; or only every alternate flap opened in south zone
5. Ventilation in roof storey:	At Ti > 25 °C: cooling activated	Ti < 23.5 °C	Switched on when required; turned off by automatic time switch

Heating and ventilation

In winter, the building is largely heated by solar radiation, which enters through the large areas of double glazing on the south side (U = 0.8 W/m²K; g = 0.46%). Protection against glare is provided by internal fabric curtains. The solar energy is absorbed by the structure itself, which acts as a storage mass. The primary storage elements (i.e. floors, walls, furniture and fittings exposed to the direct rays of the sun) are heated first. After one to two hours, the increase in the surface temperature of the primary elements causes the internal air temperature to rise. These thermal gains are, in turn, absorbed by secondary storage elements such as the walls and ceilings that are not exposed to direct sunlight. In sunny conditions, insolation causes the internal air temperature to rise in the course of the day by 4 °C above the morning temperature of the building

components, although the control system can be programmed to provide shading or ventilation by means of air circulation. The solid structural elements along the south side form an energy reservoir and are able to react with fluctuations in temperature. The greatest changes occur on sunny days (temperature increase of about 2 °C) and on days with an overcast sky (temperature decrease of about 2 °C). With external temperatures around 0 °C, the heated storage mass can keep the building warm for one and half days without further supplies of thermal energy. To cope with longer periods of cold weather, the building should be kept at a temperature of 2–4 °C above the average target room temperature of 19 °C. A supplementary gas-fired heating system with convectors serves to maintain the solid mass of the building at a basic temperature of 20 °C.

In summer, excess heat from electrical appliances, people in the building and diffuse solar radiation is also absorbed by the solid construction members. The internal air temperature then rises a little above that of the enclosing elements. Although the structure undergoes an increase in temperature during the day, it can be cooled at night by ventilation through open window flaps. With high external night-time temperatures, ventilation fans are automatically switched on to remove internal heat. Excess cooling of the storage mass is avoided by programming the central control system to close the ventilation flaps. For most of the time in summer, one can reckon with internal temperatures below 25 °C. During heatwaves, however, these may rise to external levels. Air-extract fans in the roof storey are then automatically turned on to cool the building.

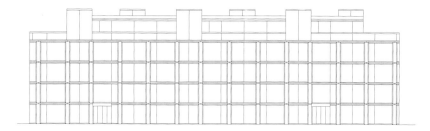

Section · Elevation
scale 1:500
Control system
parameters
Ti = internal
    temperature
Te = external
    temperature

Vertical section through facade
scale 1:20

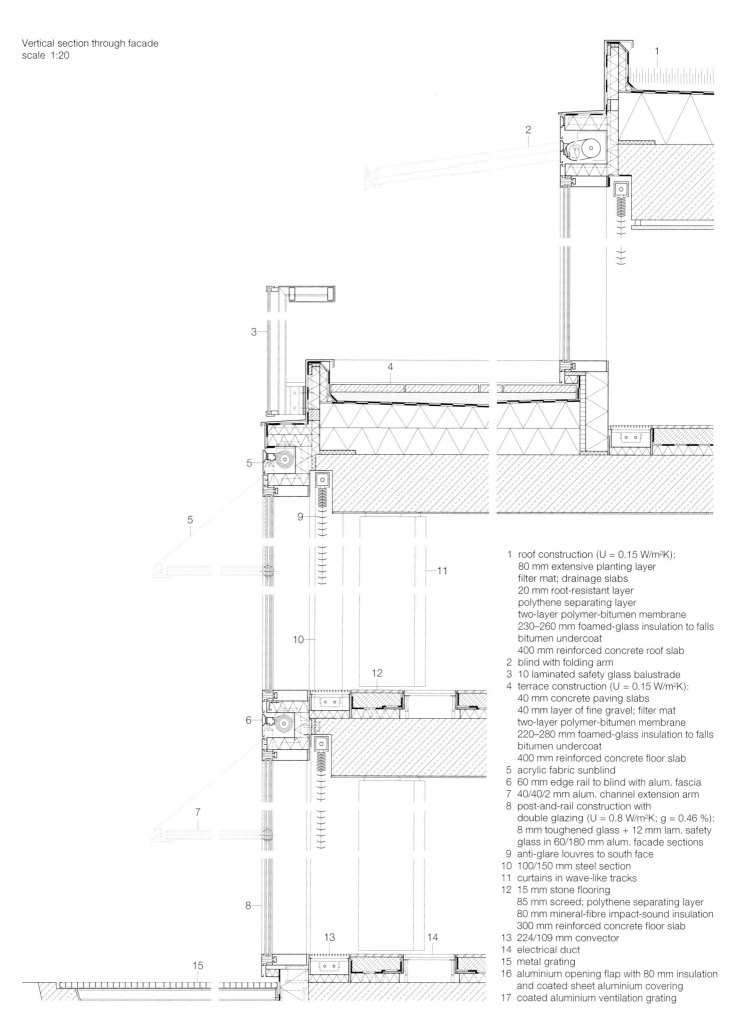

1 roof construction (U = 0.15 W/m²K):
   80 mm extensive planting layer
   filter mat; drainage slabs
   20 mm root-resistant layer
   polythene separating layer
   two-layer polymer-bitumen membrane
   230–260 mm foamed-glass insulation to falls
   bitumen undercoat
   400 mm reinforced concrete roof slab
2 blind with folding arm
3 10 laminated safety glass balustrade
4 terrace construction (U = 0.15 W/m²K):
   40 mm concrete paving slabs
   40 mm layer of fine gravel; filter mat
   two-layer polymer-bitumen membrane
   220–280 mm foamed-glass insulation to falls
   bitumen undercoat
   400 mm reinforced concrete floor slab
5 acrylic fabric sunblind
6 60 mm edge rail to blind with alum. fascia
7 40/40/2 mm alum. channel extension arm
8 post-and-rail construction with
   double glazing (U = 0.8 W/m²K; g = 0.46 %):
   8 mm toughened glass + 12 mm lam. safety
   glass in 60/180 mm alum. facade sections
9 anti-glare louvres to south face
10 100/150 mm steel section
11 curtains in wave-like tracks
12 15 mm stone flooring
   85 mm screed; polythene separating layer
   80 mm mineral-fibre impact-sound insulation
   300 mm reinforced concrete floor slab
13 224/109 mm convector
14 electrical duct
15 metal grating
16 aluminium opening flap with 80 mm insulation
   and coated sheet aluminium covering
17 coated aluminium ventilation grating

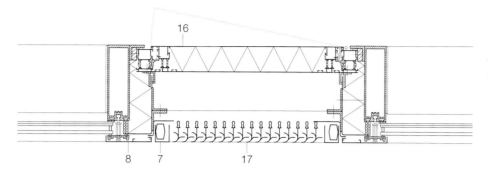

Horizontal section
though ventilation flap
scale 1:10

Administration Building in Würzburg

Architects: Webler and Geissler, Stuttgart
Mechanical services:
Ingenieurgesellschaft Püttmer IGP, Ludwigsburg

This development was designed as the headquarters of a facade manufacturing company. The form, construction and skin of the building as well as the plant and the central control technology were coordinated with each other to create a complex with a holistic solar-energy system. Fossil fuels are used to meet only peak demands. The two storeys of the building, each 4.10 metres high, were designed as open-plan spaces, with individual rooms divided off by frameless glazed partitions. The centre and visual focus of the development is a planted atrium with a pool of water and a glass roof that can be raised and slid to one side. A key element of the energy concept is the double-skin facade, which acts as a climatic buffer. The external skin is in a post-and-rail construction with fixed glazing; the internal skin consists of prefabricated elements with manually operated sliding doors and motor-operated bottom-hung lights for ventilation purposes. The fresh-air supply is drawn from the 60 cm intermediate space between the two skins. Flaps in the outer skin – in the plinth zone and in the upstand roof – serve to regulate natural vertical convection, while axial fans at the corners of the building create horizontal currents that distribute the preheated fresh air. Lightweight metal blinds reflect sunlight either away from the building, or into the interior via soffit panels lined with cotton fabric. On the south and west faces of the structure, the lower sections of the louvres have a dark coating on one side and can be adjusted separately from the upper part. Depending on the angle at which the louvres are set, the degree of thermal absorption can be increased. During the cold months of the year, they serve to preheat the air intake that flows over them. In summer, when the blinds are closed and the air flaps are open, the building is cooled by a process of convection ventilation. Additional night-time cooling is achieved via the atrium roof and the bottom-hung windows opened in a tipped position. When cooling is required, a 200-square-metre collector installation produces cold water by means of an adsorption heat pump. The water is then fed into ceiling cooling panels along the glazed facades and around the atrium. If required, the system can also provide energy for the underfloor heating. If the various elements of the system do not cover all needs, a cogenerating plant is also available to supply electricity and thermal energy. Since both the cooling soffits and the underfloor heating are water-fed systems, the two circuits can be used reciprocally. Some 250 sensors serve to measure the relevant data, on the basis of which, the control centre can respond to demands via more than 500 activating points. In addition, individual users can modulate the system via their PCs.

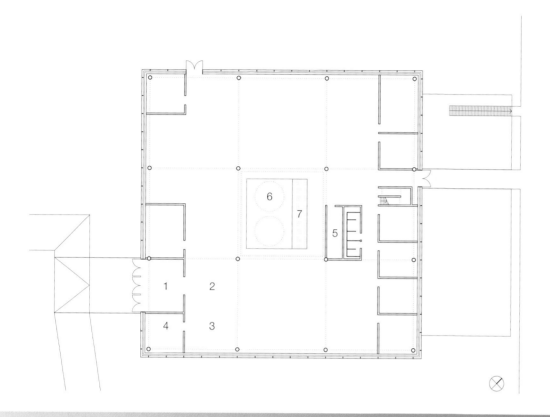

Ground floor plan
scale 1:500

1 Entrance
2 Reception
3 Waiting area
4 Conference room
5 Kitchenette
6 Planted area
7 Water pool

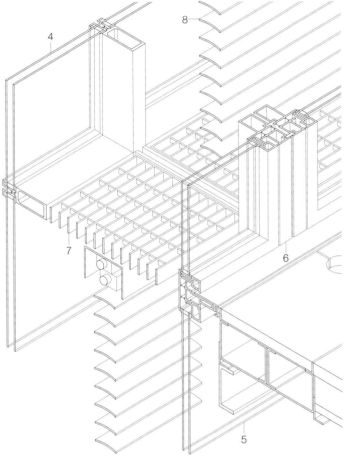

Axonometric facade detail
Sectional details of
facade   scale 1:10

1 sheet aluminium covering with
   anti-drumming coating
2 upper ventilation flap with brush
   seal at sides
3 aluminium ventilation louvres with
   fly screen
4 outer glazing skin:
   8 mm toughened glass (externally)
   22 mm cavity with inert-gas filling
   6 mm float glass with low-E coating
5 inner glazing skin:
   6 mm toughened glass (externally)

16 mm cavity with inert-gas filling
6 mm float glass with low-E
coating
6 aluminium frame, thermally
   divided
7 aluminium grating
8 perforated lightweight metal
   louvre blind:
   upper section with white coating
   on both faces;
   lower section with dark coating
   on one face;
   both sections independently
   operable
9 lower ventilation flap

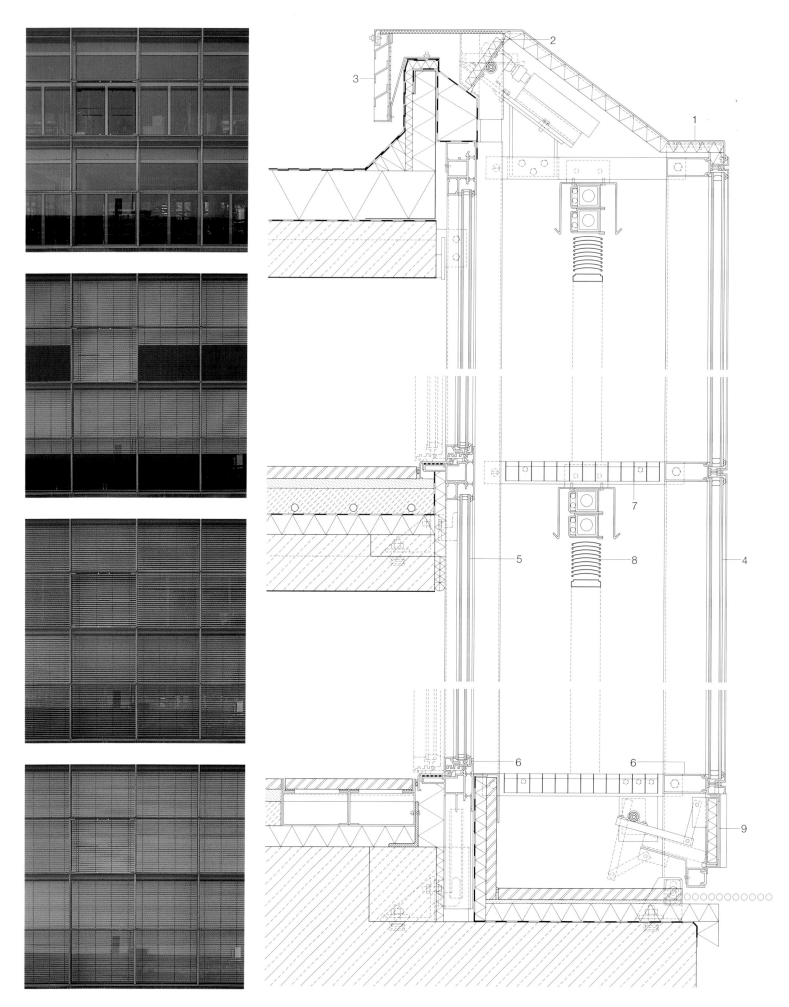

Academy in Herne

Architects: Jourda Architects, Paris
Hegger Hegger Schleiff Architects, Kassel

With the construction of the Mont-Cenis Academy for the federal state of North Rhine-Westphalia in Germany, an entire
urban district has been remodelled. The measures cover a
total area of about 60 acres and include not only the academy
itself, with a footprint of 16,000 m², but a large landscaped
park to the north and a 12-acre housing development. Within
the glazed outer skin of the structure are administration and
seminar spaces, a hotel, living quarters, a restaurant and district administration offices, together with a library and a community hall. These various functions are accommodated in
self-contained structures set within the outer enclosure. As a
result of the protection against the elements afforded by the
skin, and the passive solar energy this form of construction
yields, the hall space is in the nature of an outdoor environment with an especially mild climate. In summer and winter,
the temperatures and other climatic conditions resemble those
in Nice. The skins of the timber-clad structures within the outer
enclosure do not have to be wind- or rainproof, so that it was
possible to execute them in a simple form of construction.
Heated areas could be kept to a minimum, since access to
the internal structures is largely from within the hall.
The 2.50–3.20 square metre photovoltaic modules integrated
in the glazed roof function not only as a power-generating
system. Through the nature of their cells and the density to
which they were laid, the units also regulate the shading and
indoor climate within the outer skin and help to prevent overheating. The photovoltaic modules cover 9,300 m² of the roof
area and an additional 800 m² of the south-west facade, thus
forming the world's largest solar power plant integrated in a
building – with a total capacity of up to 1 MW and an energy
supply of approximately 750,000 kWh/a.
The initial design idea was to create a large glazed hall with a
cloud-like roof structure that would act as a "micro-climatic
skin" and generate passive solar energy. In close collaboration with specialist planners, engineers and consultants, the
architects then developed a concept for a photovoltaic installation in which the cloud-like effect would be created by varying the density of the individual modules. In the areas over the
internal building volumes, the modules are laid to a density
of 86 per cent, thereby providing the requisite sunshading. In
the transitional zones to the areas of clear glazing, a density of
58 per cent was achieved by increasing the spacings between
the modules, thus softening the contrast in brightness and creating a finely graduated lighting environment. In the central
zone, the glass roof was constructed without solar cells to
ensure adequate daylighting in the areas below. In this zone,
there are also large numbers of opening lights, which serve as

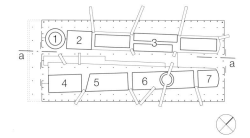

Layout plan
scale 1:3000

1 Library
2 District administration
3 Hotel
4 Community centre
5 Restaurant
6 Academy
7 Academy
   administration

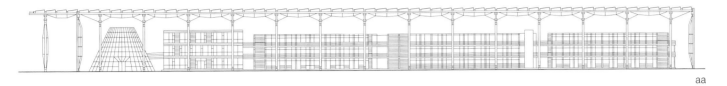

aa

Longitudinal section · Internal elevation
scale 1:1000

Solar-power installation
This development contains the world's first solar
installation in which the individual photovoltaic
elements were not simply assembled on top of
the roof, but form the actual roof surface itself.
The modules, which were specially developed for
this purpose, consist of mono- and polycrystalline
photovoltaic cells from various manufacturers.
Each unit is embedded in a 2 mm layer of high-
transparency cast resin between two layers of
toughened glass with a low-iron content: a 4 mm
outer layer facing the sun and an 8 mm inner
layer. The glass has a particularly high light-
transmission quality in the spectral range of silicon cells.
Roughly 600 decentralized modular pulse
inverters with a low saturation voltage and a
short switchover time transform the direct current
generated by the photovoltaic plant into alternating current and also condense it.

Total roof area	12,600 m²
Area of PV roof modules	9,300 m²
Area of PV facade modules	780 m²
Standard PV roof module	1.16 × 2.78 m
Standard PV facade module	1.16 × 2.40 m
No. of PV roof modules	2,905
No. of PV facade modules	280
No. of modular inverters	approx. 600
Efficiency of monocrystalline solar cells	12.8 %
Efficiency of polycrystalline solar cells	16.0 %
Inclination of roof modules	5°
Angle of facade modules	90°
Output per module	250–416 Wpeak
Total output	1 MWpeak
Reduction of CO_2 emissions	approx. 450 tonnes/a
Mean insolation	975 kWh/m²a
Energy supply	750,000 kWh/a

a means of ventilation. This not only improves the indoor climate; it also increases the effectiveness of the solar installation, which would not work efficiently if the internal space were
overheated. Along the edge of the roof are decentralized
modular inverters that convert solar energy into 220-volt alternating current. In order to achieve an overall capacity of 1 MW
and at the same time to create the desired amorphous cloud-
like effect in the roof area, solar cells from different manufacturers and of varying size and capacity were installed. At
selected points, holographic-optical elements were also incorporated in the roof. They deflect light into the conically shaped
library and reception spaces, resolving it into the colours of
the spectrum.
From the commencement of construction planning, the concept of a "micro-climatic skin" was investigated and optimized
by means of calculations and computer simulations. Simulations were also used to determine the distribution of the photovoltaic modules and to ensure the requisite daylight quality in
all zones. Light-deflecting flaps were fixed to the windows of
the structures within the outer enclosure to improve the natural
lighting in internal areas. To avoid overheating, the roof and
facade lights can be opened in summer, so that the enclosed
spaces are ventilated by cross-currents. Fresh air is supplied
to the internal structures by natural and mechanical means via
underground ducts. In winter, heating-energy requirements
are reduced by the warm air that collects beneath the glazed
roof as well as by a heat-recovery facility in the ventilation
plant. The heat given off from the internal structures is used
to preheat the fresh-air intake. In the present scheme, there
is an energy saving of roughly 23 per cent compared with
conventional buildings that have the same degree of thermal
insulation, but that are not located within a climatic skin; and
compared with a comparable air-conditioned building, there is
a roughly 18 per cent reduction in carbon dioxide emissions.
The annual thermal heating needs are less than 50 kWh.
Given optimum operating conditions, the overall energy
requirements are around 32 kWh/m²a.
The load-bearing structure and facade construction are in
timber – a regenerable raw material. Looking out at right
angles to the facades, the hall space seems to extend into the
park-like landscape beyond, whereas from an oblique angle,
one becomes aware of the principle of volumes and spaces
within a larger enveloping space.
Gas from a former mine is burned in a cogenerating plant to
produce electricity. On dull days with low atmospheric pressure, the mine gas is more plentiful and compensates for the
small solar-energy yield under these conditions.

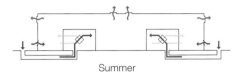

Summer

Transitional period

Winter

Sections: ventilation diagrams

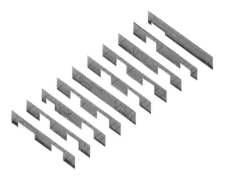

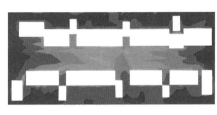

A

Temperatures and air-currents within the glazed skin

A Sequence of sections · Plan

c temperature and airstream simulations in sectional representation
d temperature and airstream simulations in plan representation

B Cross-section

a hot, windless summer day
b cold winter day; wind speed 3.5 m/s

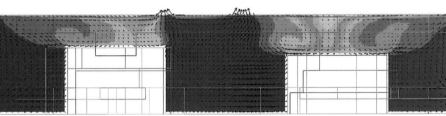

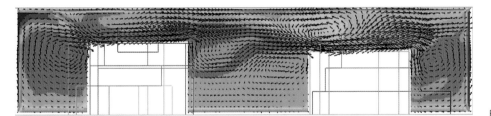

B

Ventilation diagram
The ventilation of the glazed enclosure is automatically and centrally controlled. Weather data are provided by a weather station and a sensor.

Summer
The large sliding gates in the end faces allow natural ventilation. Warm air rises to the top and escapes through the openings in the roof. In its place, fresh air is sucked in through the ventilation flaps in the lower part of the facade. Additional cooling is provided by vegetation and areas of water. The photovoltaic modules in the south-west facade and on the roof act as sunshading areas. The internal structures can be ventilated naturally and mechanically. Seven underground ducts, each one metre in diameter, are used to draw in fresh air, which is cooled and fed into the internal structures.

Winter
The building skin reduces heat losses from convection and protects against wind, precipitation and external noise. Fresh air sucked in from outside is preheated by means of insolation and the surplus heat from the internal structures, as well as by heat recoved from the vitiated air in the ventilation plant. The annual heating needs are less than 50 kWh/m²; in other words, 23 per cent less that the energy required by a conventional building of the same insulation standard. The air is preheated to around 8 °C in the underground ducts before being fed into the internal structures.

Transitional seasons
The internal structures are supplied with fresh air via the micro-climatic skin. The air enters through inlets in the lower area of the facade. Vitiated air escapes via the upper ventilation flaps.

Energy concept
The electricity generated by the photovoltaic installation is stored in lead-acid batteries with a total energy content of 1.2 MWh and a capacity of 1.5 MVA. The batteries differ from conventional lead-acid types as a result of constructional improvements and new connection technology, which result in a longer life, and greater energy effectiveness and high-current capacity. The two cogenerating units (each with a capacity of 253 kWel) produce approx. 1.9 million kWh/a of electricity and 2.7 kWh/a of heat. The use of mine gas for these units corresponds to a natural gas input of 630,000 m³/a and results in a CO_2 reduction of 10,000 t/a. The successful operation of the plant has resulted in a greater consumption of mine gas: since 2000, operations have been increased by 1 MWel and 1.2 MWth.

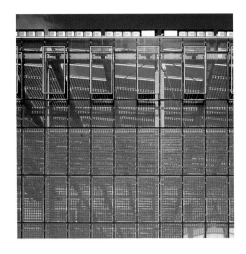

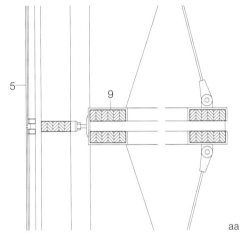

aa

Sections through outer facade
and internal structures
scale 1:20

1 laminated safety glass to roof:
  6 mm partially toughened flint glass +
  photovoltaic cells in 2 mm cast resin +
  8 mm partially toughened flint glass
2 inverter
3 galvanized steel gutter
4 fast-flow rainwater system
5 facade: 18 mm toughened glass in
  aluminium adaptor frames fixed to
  60/160 mm laminated timber facade posts
6 300/400 mm laminated timber edge beam
7 opening light
8 timber roof truss
9 vertical timber facade truss
10 380/140 mm laminated timber rail
11 steel shoe to post
12 internal roof construction:
  22 mm laminated construction board
  granular rubber mat; sealing layer
  160 mm mineral-wool thermal insulation
  vapour barrier
  200 mm reinforced concrete roof slab
13 light reflector: white-veneered wood
14 double glazing with 27 mm laminated
  safety glass inner layer
15 wall construction:
  20 mm three-ply lam. softwood boarding
  sealing layer
  100 mm mineral-wool thermal insulation
  vapour barrier
  20 mm three-ply lam. softwood boarding
16 120/40 mm wood slats on
  100 mm steel I-bearers

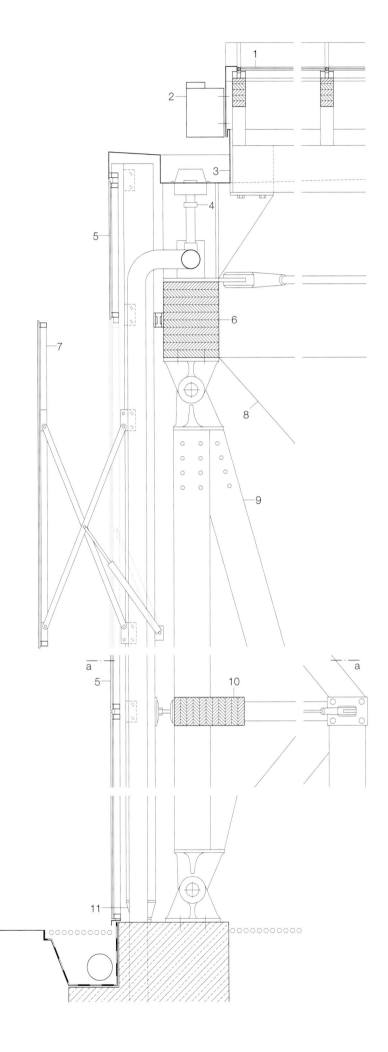

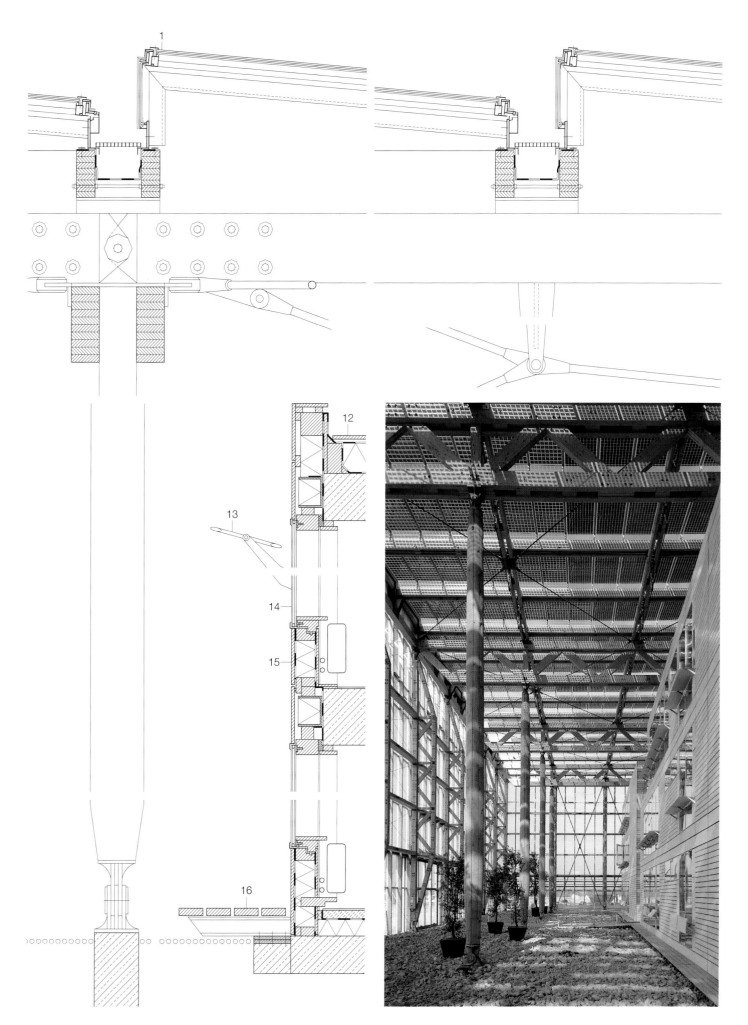

1

12

13

14

15

16

Conversion of Reichstag Building into German Bundestag in Berlin

Architects: Foster and Partners, London
Energy concept and mechanical services:
Kuehn Bauer Partner, Munich

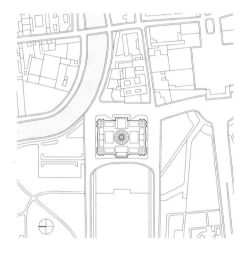

Site plan   scale 1:10,000
Section   scale 1:1500

The conversion of Paul Wallot's Reichstag building (1894) into a modern seat of parliament is the central symbol of the city of Berlin in its role as German capital. The scheme involved the redesign of the building and its restructuring internally, the insertion of a new debating chamber and the construction of a fully glazed cupola at the top. One of the main objectives was the installation of an energy supply system that would conserve resources. The planning of this new parliamentary building aimed to achieve clear energy savings in combination with a reduction of the use of fossil fuels. Elements of the mechanical services system developed for the Reichstag a hundred years ago were also incorporated. In view of the large mass of the building, the structure itself acts as an energy store. An even indoor climate is achieved throughout the year by heating and cooling with a minimum supply of energy. The thermal activation of the structural elements allows the heating requirements in winter to be covered at low-temperature levels. In summer, the system is reversed, and heat is removed from the building by a constant process of cooling the structure.
As a symbol of the renewal of a building that remains largely unchanged outwardly, the new cupola, which is visible over a great distance, is not merely a reconstruction of the historical dome. Internally it is accessible via a visitors' ramp in the form of a double helix with a public viewing platform at the top. Through the glazed inner roof, one has a view into the debating chamber below. At the same time, the dome is an important element of the daylighting, heating and ventilation systems. The 24 curved steel ribs of the cupola, which have a triangular cross-section of varying depth, are supported on the roof of the building by a circular box girder. The ribs are also welded at the top to a circular tie beam and are braced by 17 horizontal ring beams, to which they are connected by cast-steel nodes welded on to the ribs. The scale-like glazing to the entire surface of the cupola consists of laminated safety glass in aluminium frames. A 300 m² photovoltaic installation with a peak capacity of 40 kW supplies energy to the ventilation plant and the sunshading system in the dome. Two motor-operated power plants generate the electrical energy for the complex of parliamentary buildings in a heat-and-power cogenerating plant fuelled by vegetable oil. Surplus heat from the firing process is fed into a seasonal store, which can be tapped when needed. This combination of different, mutually complementary measures reduces CO_2 emissions from about 7,000 tonnes to 1,000 tonnes per annum.

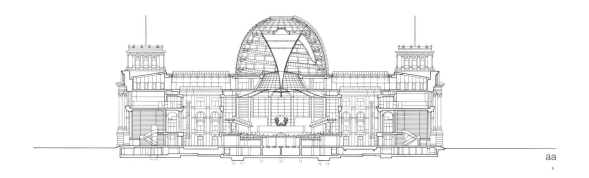

aa

Solar energy and energy reservoirs
The energy supply for the Reichstag building forms part of a network operated in conjunction with other parliamentary buildings in the Spree-bogen area. The supply concept is based on a system of decentralized motor-operated plants that function parallel to the public grid. These electrical generators work on a cogenerating principle, producing heat and power. The generators are fuelled with vegetable oil methylester (also known as bio-diesel). Through the use of this regenerable source of energy, it was possible to reduce CO_2 emissions by more than 50 per cent in comparison with fossil fuels. With an electrical capacity of roughly 3.2 MVA, the cogenerating plants cover approximately 80 per cent of the electrical needs of the Reichstag; while the sur-plus heat produced in this process covers roughly 90 per cent of the heating needs of the building.

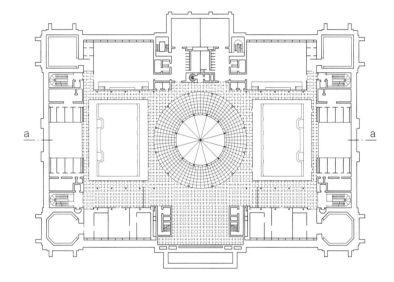

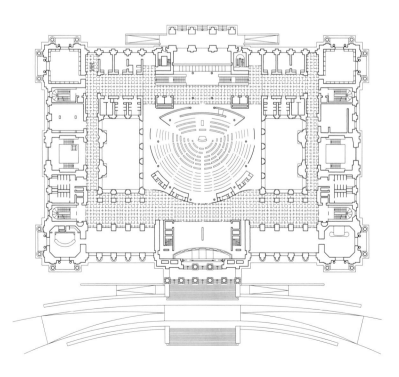

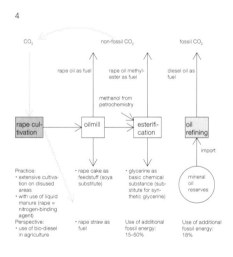

Fourth floor plan · Ground floor plan
scale 1:1500

Use of vegetable oil as renewable raw material to generate the energy supply
Energy stored in aquifer reservoirs
A Temperature curve for cooling reservoir
B Temperature curve for heating reservoir

If neither heating nor cooling, but only electricity is required, surplus heat from the generating process is fed in the form of hot water into a 300-metre-deep aquifer reservoir. Salt water at a natural temperature of 20 °C is pumped to the surface via one of two bore holes about 800 metres apart. The water is heated to approximately 70 °C with the excess thermal energy from the cogenerating plant and pumped down the other bore hole. The maximum capacity of this system is 100,000 litres per hour. A strata of boulder clay above the zone of warm groundwater acts as an insulation layer and prevents heat rising to the surface. A lateral dissipation of the thermal energy is not possible either, since there are no groundwater currents. In winter, the energy in the aquifer reservoir can be used for the low-temperature heating system (approx. 65 °C), in which case, the direction of flow is reversed. The water then yields its heat to the building via heat-exchange units, after which it is pumped back below ground at a temperature of approx. 20 °C.

In order to store water at a mean temperature of approx. 50 °C, salt-water-bearing layers 300 m beneath the earth's surface are used. A layer of Rupelean clay ensures a natural separation of the heated lower layer and the cool, water-bearing layers above. Exploiting the temperature of the warm water drawn from the reservoir, it is possible to operate air-heating grids, underfloor heating systems, etc. If the temperature is not high enough, a CFC-free heat pump can be switched on.

As a means of cooling the building and the air in summer, groundwater can be drawn via a number of bore holes from a second aquifer reservoir at a depth of 30–60 m. The maximum rate of flow in this case is approx. 300,000 l/h. The cold water, with a temperature of 5–10 °C, absorbs heat from the building and excess heat from the cooling plant. The temperature of the water is increased via a heat-exchange unit to a maximum of 28–30 °C. Cooling for the combined district energy system is thus generated with a minimum of additional primary energy: 55 per cent direct cooling from the aquifer cooling reservoir, 40 per cent from surplus heat (dessicative and evaporative cooling and absorption) and 5 per cent from electrically operated compressors. The energy balance near the surface remains unaffected. Since a constant supply of heat to the groundwater would be environmentally unacceptable, the heated water is cooled again in winter by means of absorption heat pumps. The use of the aquifer reservoir allows the cogenerating plant to be operated at an optimum capacity.

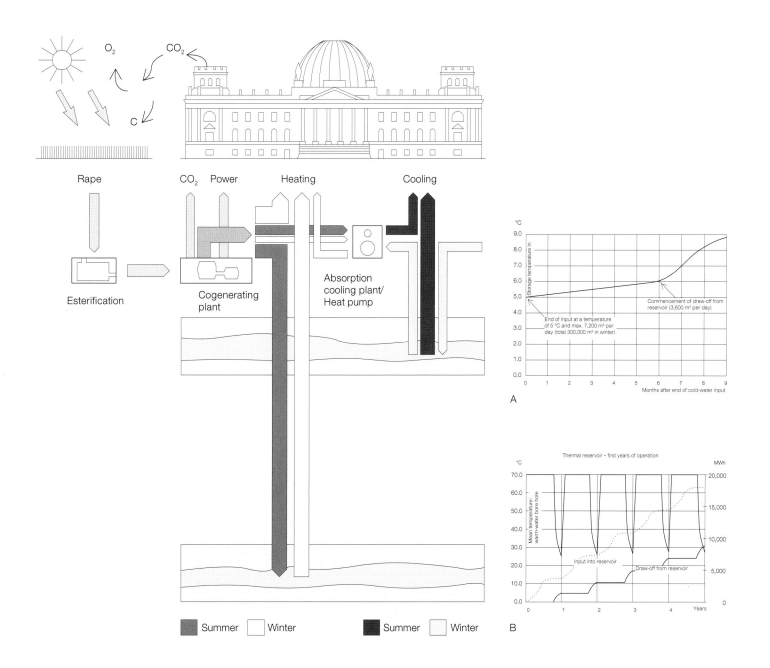

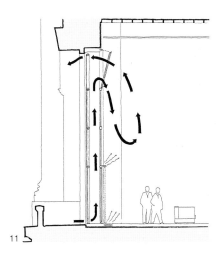

11

Natural ventilation

The use of double-skin facades with motor-operated and/or manually openable windows facilitates the natural ventilation of the internal spaces. The two skins of glazing in elliptical aluminium sections consist of an inner, thermally divided glazing layer, a cavity containing movable sunshading elements, and a fixed outer pane of glass with a peripheral ventilation joint. Depending on the external temperature and wind conditions, between half and five times the air volume of the rooms can be changed every hour. Sensors also allow the windows to be opened by a central control system. As a result, natural ventilation is possible for a large part of the year. Since the outer skin of glazing protects the inner skin, the latter can be left open as a means of night-time cooling.

Vertical section through double-skin facade
scale 1:10

1 steel bearers, adjustable in three dimensions
2 stainless-steel anti-pigeon wires
3 rock-wool thermal insulation
4 sheet-aluminium lining to reveal
5 air seal and vapour barrier
6 silicone seal
7 extruded aluminium section with integrated guide for cable and heating runs
8 concealed electrical chain operation
9 thermally divided extruded aluminium section, with wet-look silver finish
10 low-E double glazing:
   8 mm toughened glass + 10 mm laminated safety glass (U = 1.1 W/m²K)
11 extruded aluminium frame for fixed glazing
12 electrically operated sunshading and anti-glare blind; louvres 50 mm wide
13 plastic guide track
14 aluminium head strip
15 facade heating element with stainless-steel fixings for water-bearing copper pipes
16 fixed glazing: 12 mm toughened glass, fixed in extruded aluminium sections with silicone adhesive
17 sliding door
18 extruded aluminium fixed ventilation louvres
19 track for sliding door
20 stainless-steel tray with stainless-steel grating

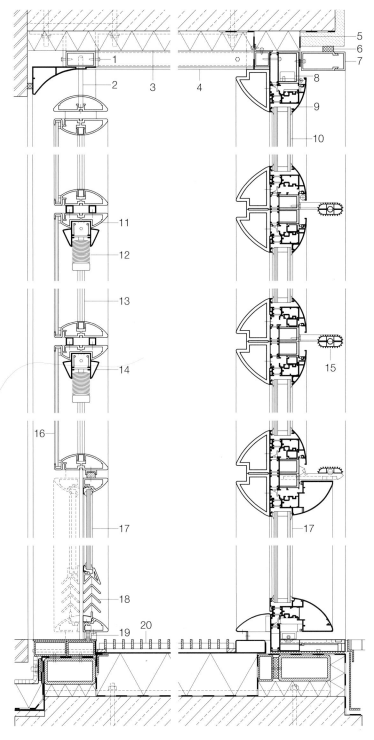

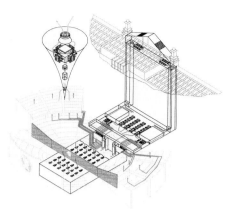

Ventilation of debating chamber
Large-scale ventilation shafts created in the building 100 years ago are today used for the fresh-air supply to the debating chamber. Air is drawn in over the western portico and flows through large shafts and collector spaces. Low airstream speeds and the small degree of resistance in the ducts mean that pressure losses within the system are reduced to a minimum. The fresh air is heated or cooled by large heat-exchange units. Slowly rotating fans propel the conditioned air over a large area into a plenum beneath the debating chamber, from where it is fed through perforated mesh in the floor and through the loose-weave carpet into the parliamentary space. The air is slowly distributed throughout this space, rising to the top as it increases in temperature. The warm, vitiated air is extracted via openings in the funnel-shaped daylighting cone at the centre of the cupola. Within this structure is a large ventilation plant. Heat is recovered from the vitiated air by means of heat-exchange units. The waste air is finally emitted at the top of the cone – at the level of the viewing platform – and escapes through the 9-metre-diameter central opening in the cupola. The floor-level air-input system, intuitively developed in 1883 for this building, formed the basis of the present ventilation concept. Elaborate numerical simulations of the airstream patterns within the debating chamber in relation to the level of occupation were carried out to tune the ventilation system to an optimum level.

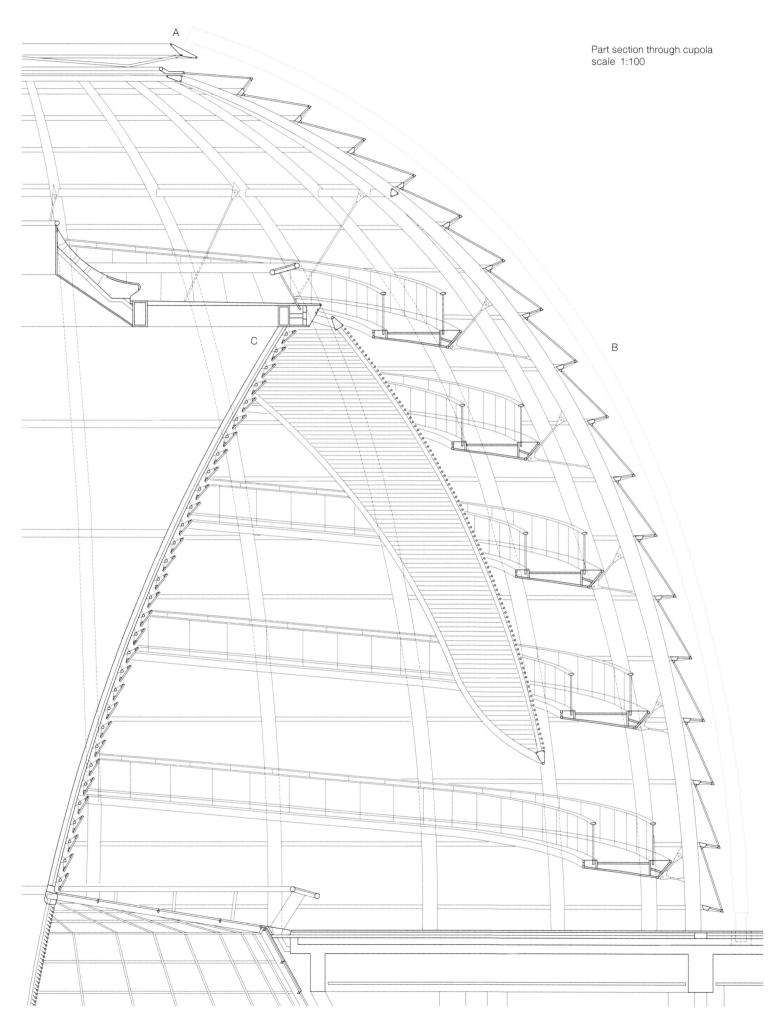

A

Part section through cupola
scale 1:100

C

B

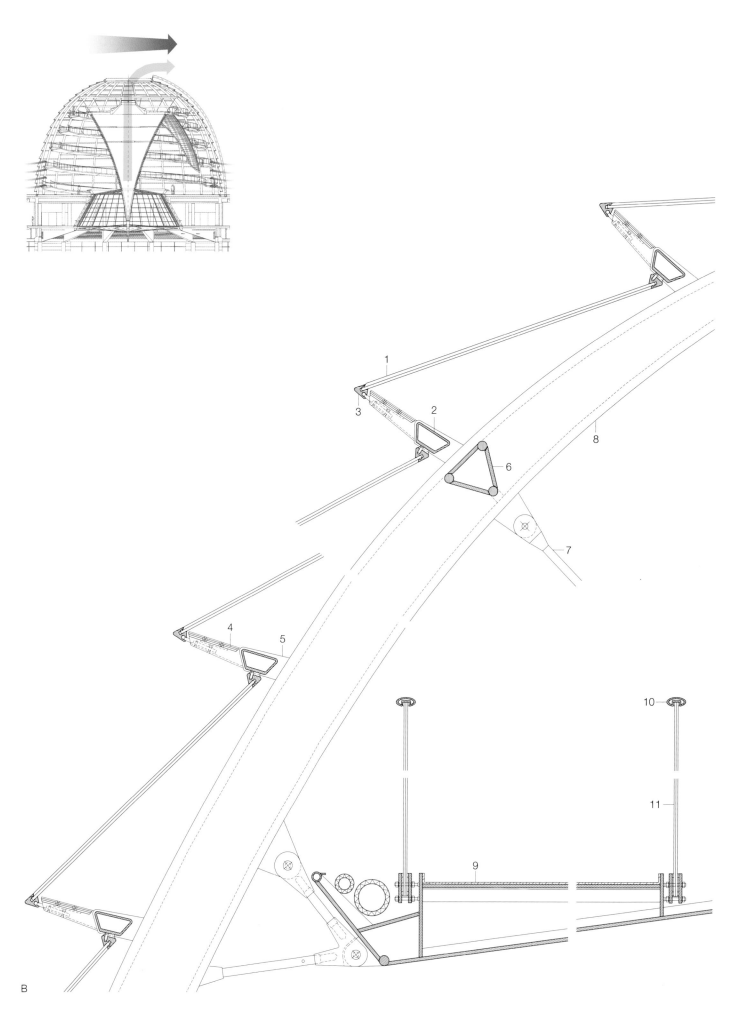

B

156

A

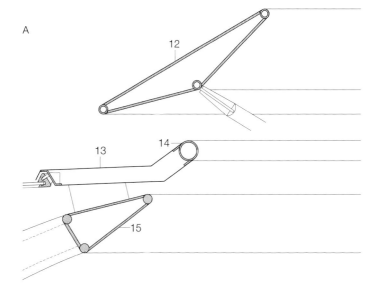

Air supply and extract in debating chamber;
air-conditioning plant
Sectional details through cupola
scale 1:20

 1 laminated safety glass:
   2× 12 mm toughened glass
 2 210/100 mm steel trapezoidal hollow section
 3 aluminium glazing section
 4 laminated safety glass:
   2× 8 mm toughened glass
 5 cast-steel node
 6 ring beam: Ø 50 mm round steel members
   20 mm sheet steel
 7 Ø 60 mm steel hanger for viewing platform
 8 dome rib: Ø 50 mm round steel members
   23 mm sheet steel
 9 10 mm synthetic mortar on 15 mm steel plate
   with 4 mm metal damper plate, adhesive
   fixed beneath
10 stainless-steel handrail
11 laminated safety glass balustrade:
   2× 8 mm toughened glass
12 6 mm sheet-steel wind deflector
13 3 mm sheet steel
14 Ø 114.3/4 mm steel tube
15 ring beam: Ø 50 mm round steel members
   10 mm sheet steel

Vertical section through cone
scale 1:20

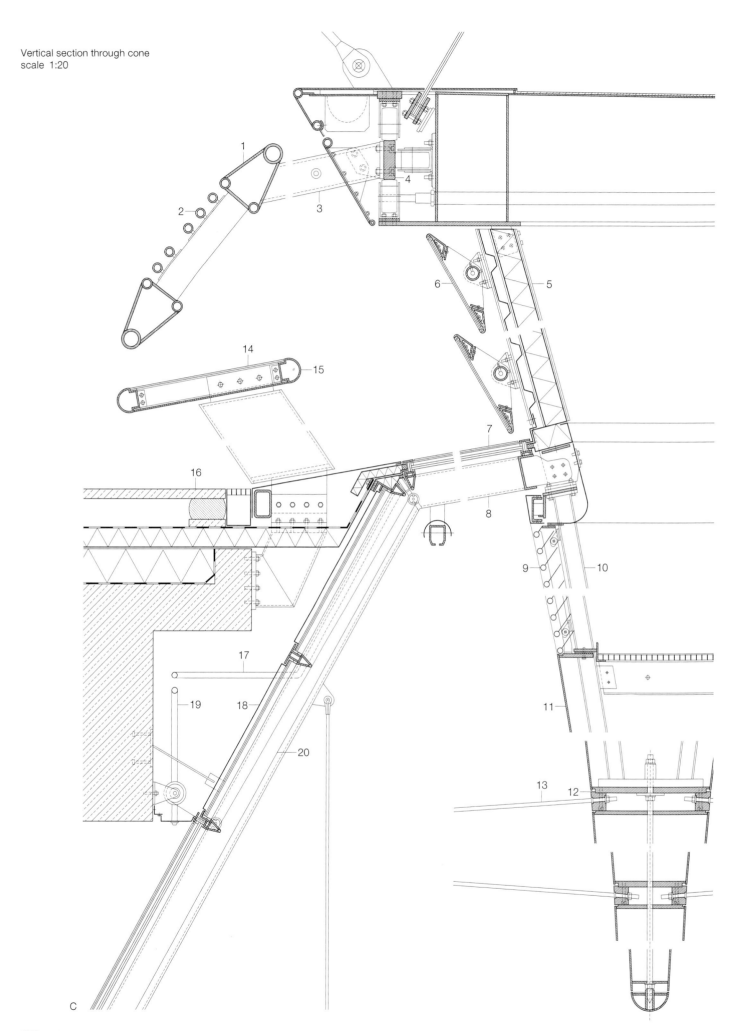

1

2

3

4

5

6

7

8

9

10

11

12

13

14

15

16

17

18

19

20

C

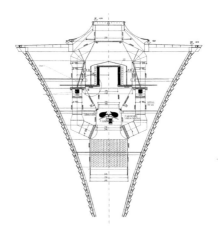

Daylighting

In contrast to the historical dome by Paul Wallot, the new glazed cupola is used for daylighting the interior and forms an integral part of the energy concept. A concave conical steel construction with a maximum diameter of 15 m and lined with 360 mirror units was inserted within the cupola and reflects daylight into the debating chamber below. A 12-metre-high shading element that rotates about the cone protects against glare and reduces the amount of energy required for cooling. The exact position of this element is computer controlled on the basis of data provided of 24 measurement points. The deflection of daylight into the chamber helps to reduce the energy consumption for electric lighting. A daylight-related dimming system reduces the power needs even further. At night, in contrast, the cupola is a radiant beacon on the skyline, reflecting out the internal illumination via the mirrors.

1 adjustable sunshading element:
    edge beam consisting of Ø 51/6.3 mm and
    Ø 101.6/10 mm steel tubes, with
    12 mm sheet steel
2 Ø 50/3 mm aluminium tubes
3 180/180/15 mm steel SHS
4 200/60 mm steel ring beam
5 wall construction:
    202 mm welded steel bearers
    120/550/1.25 mm insulated sheet-steel panels
    trapezoidal-section ribbed metal
    sheeting 35/201 mm
6 mirror element in aluminium frame
7 55 mm glazing: 2x laminated safety glass
8 65/180/8 mm welded steel triangular section
9 3 mm sheet stainless-steel ventilation louvres
10 steel I-section 100 mm deep
11 5 mm sheet stainless steel
12 Ø 625.9/100 mm stainless-steel ring
13 Ø 20 mm stainless-steel rod
14 8 mm toughened safety glass covering
15 Ø 114 mm aluminium section
16 80 mm concrete slabs on mortar pads
17 sprinkler supply
18 3 mm sheet-steel panel
19 heating supply pipe to metal sections
20 cable runner for acoustic insulation sail

Environmental factors

The Sun

The sun is the centre of our solar system and contains nearly 98 per cent of its mass.

Mass (kg)	1.989×10^{30}
Mass (earth = 1)	332830
Equatorial radius (km)	695000
Equatorial radius (earth = 1)	108.97
Mean surface temperature (photosphere)	6000 °C
Mean core temperature	15000000 °C

The radiation of the sun reaches the earth's atmosphere with an intensity of roughly 1340 W/m². It is reduced to approximately 100 W/m² by the atmospheric influence of a cloudless sky, and drops to 50 W/m² on overcast winter days. In southern regions with predominantly clear skies, such as the Sahara, insolation is 2200 kWh/m² per year, in Germany approximately 900–1200 kWh/m² depending on location.
This is nevertheless a considerable energy potential: 1000 kWh is the numeric equivalent of the calorific value of 100 l heating oil. Global radiation is the measurable solar radiation on the earth's surface. It is composed of diffuse sky radiation and direct solar radiation.

The Earth

Mass (kg)	5.976×10^{24}
Equatorial radius (km)	6378.14
Rotation duration (days)	0.99727
Rotation duration (hours)	23.9345
Period of revolution (days)	365.256
Mean revolution speed (km/s)	29.79
Equatorial surface gravitation (m/s²)	9.78
Average surface temperature	15 °C
Atmospheric pressure (bar)	1.013

The earth's diameter is 12756.3 km. The earth consists of different layers with varying chemical and seismic characteristics (depth in km):

0–40	crust
40–400	solid outer mantle
400–650	transition zone
650–2700	plastic inner mantle
2700–2890	D-layer
2890–5150	liquid outer core
5150–6378	solid inner core

Thermal flow/wind

Thermal flow (thermal convection) occurs when surfaces of differing composition warm to different degrees. While light surfaces reflect most of the sun's radiation, dark surfaces absorb it. The latter warm up more quickly in the morning, warm air pockets detach from the ground as it warms up and warm air rises. Cooler surrounding air flows in from below to fill these pockets, resulting in a low-pressure area. In a high-pressure area, air coming from above flows into the low-pressure area from the side. The air is warmed and simultaneously increases in density and decreases in humidity. During this process the air contracts. New air masses stream into the area and prevent the formation of clouds.

A mean surface temperature is measurable on the earth during all these processes. It does not fully correspond to the real temperature near the surface of the earth, because incident electromagnetic waves cause the atmospheric particles to oscillate. This process is referred to as greenhouse effect and threatens to compromise the temperature balance of the earth.

Heat, water, air

71 per cent of the earth's surface is covered in water. The thermal storage capacity of the oceans is essential for the stabilization of the earth's temperature. Liquid water is the cause of erosion and weather formations above continents.
The earth's atmosphere contains 7 per cent nitrogen and 21 per cent oxygen with traces of argon, carbon dioxide and water. The minute portion of 0.03 per cent trace gases in the atmosphere plays a key role in maintaining the surface temperature since the trace gases absorb the long-wave heat radiation from the earth. This natural greenhouse effect raises the mean global temperature to 15 °C. Without this effect, the temperature of the earth would by roughly 33 °C colder.

The release of gases that impact the climate and accumulate in the atmosphere triggers a man-made greenhouse effect in addition to the natural greenhouse effect. The former causes a dramatic rise in global temperatures. These effects result in a wide range of climate changes.

Absorber
The most important component of the solar collector ($\rightarrow$ p.166), which collects incident solar radiation, transforms it into heat and transfers it to a carrier medium. The absorber is usually composed of metal plates with good thermal conductivity, dark coating and integrated heat-transfer tubes.

Absorptance α
Ratio of absorbed radiant energy H_α to the total incident radiant energy H_o ($H_\alpha = H_o \cdot \alpha$).

Absorption chiller
Device for generating cold energy in a thermo-dynamic process by means of absorption. Absorption is the dissolving of gases by liquids. It is limited and decreases with rising temperatures. A refrigerant, which reaches the boiling point at a very low temperature, is warmed in the device. The refrigerant evaporates and extracts heat from the surrounding field. The vapour condenses and releases the previously absorbed heat in the liquefier. This system is a viable application when cooling cycles result in the availability of excess heat at sufficiently high temperatures, because cooling energy is principally generated with thermal energy.

Adiabatic cooling/evaporative cooling
The cooling that occurs when a liquid evaporates as a result of extraction of the "evaporation heat" required for evaporation is referred to as evaporative or adiabatic cooling. The evaporation process is accelerated when the resulting vapour is rapidly flushed out by a dry stream of air, allowing a constant influx of fresh, unsaturated air.

Adsorption
Surface retention of water molecules from the air on a porous solid substance.

Adsorption chiller
Conditioning device in which humidity is extracted from the air by means of $\rightarrow$ adsorption. Humid air flows through large heat wheels (drying rotors) with many small channels, which increases their surface ratio. The surface of the channels is covered in an adsorptive coating. For dehumidification, humid air is drawn in and transported through the rotor. The strongly hygroscopic (water-absorbing) adsorptive coating extracts humidity from the air and binds it to the rotor. As the water vapour condenses, latent (humid) heat is transformed into sensible heat and transferred to the air. The dry air is therefore warmed as it exits from the device. A second blower heats the air to over 100 °C. This second stream of hot air is also transported through the rotor in a cycle that is separated from the humid air. The water retained in the pipe (channel) is expelled and absorbed by the warm air. This air from the regenerating cycle is expelled to the outside. The two air streams – process air and regeneration air – are separated by special sealing barriers, with the constant revolution of the rotor perpetuating the alternation of the adsorptive and regenerative cycles and thus allowing for continuous operation.

Aerogel
Highly porous, homogenous silicate glass structure, the conductivity of which lies below that of the value for static air. Solar radiation is not reflected from the inner pore surface; aerogels are therefore suitable as transparent thermal insulation between two glass panes.

Air change [h^{-1}]
Indicates the frequency with which the air volume in a room is exchanged per hour. An air change of 1 h^{-1} means that the entire volume of air is exchanged each hour.

Air collector
Solar collector with air as carrier medium. For applications where the warmed air is used directly in the subsequent or connected process (warm air heating, industrial dryers). ($\rightarrow$ p. 166)

Air distribution/-duct
Air ducts constructed from aluminium sheet, galvanized sheet steel, masonry and concrete, etc., are used to transport air from the outside to the conditioning and ventilation devices, into the rooms and then again to the outside. Air distribution in the rooms should be even and draught-free. The ducts must conform to fire-safety and sound-protection standards.

Air mass (AM)
Equivalent relative air mass used to describe the length travelled by light passing through the atmosphere. AM0 corresponds to the solar spectrum in space, AM1 is the average spectrum at the equator. AM1.5 is the reference spectrum for all standard test conditions for solar installations and corresponds to the mean spectrum at 45 ° latitude.

Air-only system
In air-only systems, the transport and distribution of all required thermal energies is effected exclusively via air volume flow, which are conditioned (warmed/cooled) in a centralized or decentralized system arrangement.

Air velocity
Comfort parameter in a room. Air velocity over 10 cm/s is perceived, and velocities over 20cm/s are experienced as uncomfortable.

Amorphous cells/silicon ($\rightarrow$ p. 164)

Annual heating requirement Q_h [kWh/a]
Heating requirement of a building over the course of a year.

Annual primary energy requirement Q_p [kWh/m^{2}a]
Energy required to cover the total energy requirement in consideration of the energy required for processes outside of the building for harnessing, transforming and distributing the relevant fuel.

Aquifer
$\rightarrow$ Seasonal energy storage

Auxiliary energy
Energy required to operate system components such as circulating pumps, controls, etc.

Available daylighting
Percentage of annual lighting provided by daylight.

A/V-ratio [m^{-1}]
Unit of measure expressing the compactness of a building form through the ratio of the heat-transmitting surrounding area (A) to the heated building volume (V).

Azimuth angle ϕ
Deviation of angle of collector or photovoltaic surface from geographical south orientation. $\phi = 0°$ means that the surface orientation is true south (west $\phi = +90°$; east $\phi = -90°$).

Biogas
Combustible gas generated from the bacterial decomposition of animal and vegetable wastes with a calorific value of approximately 5 kWh/m^3. ($\rightarrow$ biomass)

Biomass
Reproductive fuels of organic or animal origin regenerate within a given period by comparison to fossil fuels. Biomass is generated by biochemical transformation of sunlight (photosynthesis) and is, therefore, stored solar energy. The use of biomass as an energy source means that the CO^2 cycle remains largely unchanged. This differentiates biomass from other renewable resources such as solar energy, wind- and water power.

Blower-door-test
Standardized test procedure employed to determine the air tightness of buildings. A fan set into the external wall (e.g. door opening) is used to blow air into the building. The positive pressure resulting in the interior forces air to escape to the outside through leaks in the building components. The volume of escaping air is measured.

Boreholes
Depending on the type of ground, boreholes are rammed, injected or drilled, to a depth ranging from 8 to 30 m, even deeper in rock (deeper boreholes can also be operated without anti-freezing agents). Different borehole lengths are used to create heat or cold sumps, e.g., for air-conditioning or free cooling in summer. If the ground has a good storage capacity, excess solar- and $\rightarrow$ CHP waste heat can be stored for later use. Consistent performance is achieved by combining boreholes and heat pumps.

Building component heating/-cooling
System employed to activate the thermal mass of building components for the purpose of heating and cooling. Building component heating/cooling is usually effected via floors, ceilings or walls into which water-filled coiled pipes are integrated. The temperatures of the carrier medium are similar to the room temperature. Up to approximately 28 °C are required for heating and up to approximately 18 °C for cooling.

Bus/bus system
The bus system represents a link for data exchange between several communicating building system devices, sensors and control terminals and the building automation system. Sensors record current state data, actors transmit all registered changes to the recipients in the form of specially coded switching signals. LON (Local Operating Network) or EIB (European Installation Bus) systems are commonly used to control building functions.

Bypass diode
Protects the cells of a PV modules against thermal damage when individual cells are partially shaded while other cells are fully exposed to radiation.

CIS semi-conductor
Copper-indium-diselenide semi-conductor for photocells in thin-film technology.

Collector ($\rightarrow$ S. 166)

Combined heat and power plant (CHP)
A generator produces electrical power and heat in a coupled heat-and-power process by means of the combustion of fossil fuels, biogas, rape-methyl ester or wood. High efficiency is ensured

through the utilization of the waste heat and low transfer losses in decentralized systems.

Condensing gas boiler
Optimized gas boiler, which utilizes the fuel efficiently and also harnesses the latent condensing heat through cooling of the fuel gas.

Conditioning systems
Conditioning systems regulate air temperature and humidity throughout the year, maintaining desired values. They unify all four air-handling functions in one system and feature: humidifier, cooler (simultaneous dehumidifier) and heater. Return air and outside air are mixed in a mixing chamber and filtered.

Conductivity λ (Lambda) [W/mK]
Value of heat [W], which is conducted in 1 h through 1 m² of a 1-m-thick material layer, at a constant temperature difference of 1 K between the surfaces. Low conductivity means that the material has excellent insulating characteristics.

Crystalline cells/silicon cells (→ p. 164)

Daylight autonomy
Annual percentage of work hours illuminated by means of daylighting.

Daylight deflection
Technology employed to direct diffuse daylight deep into a room with the help of mirrors or light-directing systems.
(→ Light direction)

Daylight factor
Ratio of illuminance at a point in the interior to the external illuminance under an overcast sky. The daylight factor diminishes the greater the distance between the point and the window.

DEC installation
(Desiccant and Evaporative Cooling)
Installation for the cooling and dehumidification of outside air for building ventilation. It extracts humidity from the fresh supply air by warming the exhaust air. The warmer the exhaust air, the more humidity is extracted from the outside air in the exchanger unit. Air is cooled with the help of evaporative humidifiers. High-performance collectors can be used to generate the required process heat.
(→ Sorption technology)

Dew point temperature θ (Theta) [°C]
Temperature at which the vapour content of air is saturated. When the temperature falls below the dew point, the excess vapour is expelled as condensation.

Diffusion equivalent strength of air layer s_d [m]
Indicates the diffusion behaviour of a material layer of the strength (thickness) s across the required distance of static air layer in order to achieve the vapour diffusion resistance μ of the a building component. $s_d = μ \cdot s$ [m]

Displacement ventilation (→ Ventilation by convection)

District-heating/district-heating grid
(→ Solar district-heating)

Drinking water heating demand
Heat required to warm the desired volume of drinking water.

Earth collectors
An exchange cycle filled with brine collects earth heat in a system of pipes installed at a depth of roughly 2 m below ground. In a modified version, the foundation slab itself is designed as an energy absorber for cooling purposes.

Efficiency η (Eta)
Ratio of effective energy to supplied energy.

Energy Conservation Regulation (EnEV)
On the Federal Republic of Germany the EnEV replaces the Insulation Regulation from 1995 (WSchV 95), which prescribes the maximum annual heating requirement, and the Heating Installation Regulation (HeizAnlV). For the first time, the building in its entirety is taken into considering, rather than each individual building component. The EnEV regulates the primary energy requirement for building heating, ventilation and domestic water heating; this requirement incorporates all insulating and system technological measures. The EnEv was drafted to achieve a considerable reduction of CO_2 in accordance with the Kioto Protocol.

Energy factor
Defines the energy consumed in the building. Power and heat consumption are "added" to arrive at this factor.

Energy piles
The foundation piles are designed with integrated pipes as heat exchanger units. They are in direct contact with the soil or the groundwater.

Energy roof (→ Solar roof)

Envelope area
The sum of all areas that enclose a building from the exterior, soil and unheated rooms.

Environmental factors
(→ p. 160)

ETFE film
Ethylene tetrafluoroethylene film with low own weight (350 g/m² for 200 μm) and high light- and UV-permeability. It is employed as a multi-layered, mechanically or pneumatically pre-stressed structure.

Evacuated tube collectors (→ p. 166)

Flat plate collectors (→ p. 166)

Fluorescent lamp
In the discharge lamp, the supplied energy is transformed into UV-radiation by means of mercury vapour discharge; the UV-radiation causes the materials coating the inner side of the glass tube to emit light in the desired colour. The high → luminous efficacy diminishes the energy requirement in comparison with an incandescent lamp by 75 per cent.

Forced air heating
Forced air heating generally operates with circulating air systems. The air is usually directly heated with an oil or gas boiler. A system of ducts distributes the heat across all rooms that are equipped with a supply and exhaust air outlet. By comparison to warm water heating, forced air heating warms up quickly, is less expensive and cannot freeze. On the other hand, the movement of air through the ducts generates noise and the circulation of large volumes of air increases dust levels. It is difficult to regulate temperatures individually per room.

Fossil fuels
Raw materials extracted from the earth's crust such as coal, natural oil, natural gas and blended products such as oil sand or oil shale. The former can be directly transformed into heating energy by combustion. The latter require additional energy to separate the mineral materials. All fossil fuels release a high CO_2-content during combustion.

Fuel cell
System for the generation of power and heat where chemically stored energy is directly transformed into electrical power and heat at a very high rate of efficiency. This is achieved, for example, within the context of a controlled reaction of hydrogen (H_2) and oxygen (O_2) to deliver the end product water (H_2O). The required hydrogen is produced beforehand in an electrolytic process by means of photovoltaic current. High-temperature fuel cells transform natural gas into electrical power with a high degree of efficiency and generate waste gases in the process, which can be utilized for heating purposes.

Geothermal energy
Energy stored in the form of heat below the surface of the earth. The principal source of geothermal energy is the heat released upon the disintegration of radioactive isotopes in the earth's interior.

Geothermal heat exchanger
Outside air is conducted through underground pipelines to condition the supply air for a building.

Global radiation
Energy composed of direct solar and diffuse sky radiation on the surface of the earth.

Gravitational ventilation
Free ventilation as a result of the suction caused when windows, doors or eaves/ridge elements are opened.

Gross density [kg/m³]
Mass of a material in relation to volume. The greater the gross density, the greater the capacity of a material for thermal storage and for conductivity.

Groundwater utilization
Groundwater is extracted for the purpose of producing energy. This is a laborious process, because groundwater regulations must be considered and suction and sump wells require constant maintenance. Utilizing groundwater becomes a viable economic option in areas with a natural → aquifer in which underground → seasonal heat and cold storage units are created by installing suction and sump wells at the relevant location.

g-value
→ Total solar energy transmission

Heat Q [J] or [Ws]
Form of energy. 1 Joule [J] = 1 Watt second [Ws]. $3.6 \cdot 10^6$ Ws = 1 Kilowatt hour [kWh]

Heating degree-days
Value for heating energy demand within a heating period, defined as the sum of daily differences between the mean room temperature of 20 °C and the mean outside air temperature during the days of the heating period. The mean daily temperature on a degree-day is below 15 °C. Values have been defined for many locations based on meteorological records.

Heating energy requirement
Energy required to heat a building taking into account the heating demand and the losses incurred in heat transfer, distribution and production.

Heating, ventilation and air-conditioning systems (HVAC-Anlagen)
The systems are classified according to the number of air-treatment functions they fulfil, that is, none, one, two, three or four functions (cooling, heating, humidifying and dehumidifying). Air circulation is carefully controlled with the help of fans (controlled air condition, flow direction and velocity, etc.) to adapt to user needs.

Heat output requirement Q_n [kWh/a]
Amount of heat, which must be supplied by the heating system to maintain the nominal temperature in heated rooms. The heat output requirement is determined by drawing up a balance sheet of heat losses and heat gains. Indicator of the heating efficiency of a building.

Heat protection glass
Insulating glazing with a very low → U-value and at least one coated surface facing the interstitial space between panes to reduce heat dissipation. The cavity is frequently gas-filled (e.g., argon, krypton or xenon).

Heat requirement Q [kWh]
The heat requirement is the product of heat losses and heat gains. Precise data on the amount, temperature level and temporal distribution of the required heat are established as prerequisites to designing a solar installation.

Heat transmission
Transmission of heat energy through a building component in the direction of the course of temperature.

Holograms
Transmission holograms are integrated into glazing to direct light at a defined incidence angle. The transmission produces spectral colour separation as in a prism. White light holograms are used to remix the rainbow colours into white light.

Hot-spot effect
Overheating of an individual cell in a solar module. Occurs in case of partial shading.

Hybrid cells
To optimize efficiency, hybrid cells consist of a monocrystalline → wafer surrounded by two layers of amorphous silicon.

Hybrid solar systems
Photovoltaic- and thermal solar systems are employed in the form of "solar power-heat coupling" to increase the efficiency in the utilization of solar energy since photovoltaic systems can only transform 15 per cent of radiation into electrical energy. The rest is transformed into heat.

Illuminance E in lux [lx]
Ratio of incident luminous flux to the size of the illuminated area. There are set illuminance quotients according to room use.

Incidence angle
Angle at which a ray of light falls onto a surface.

Infrared transmission
Ability of a material to permit the transmission of heat radiation at wavelengths of 780 nm–2800 nm.

Internal heat gains Q_i [kWh/a]
Heat gains from heat radiating from equipment, lighting and building occupants.

Joint transmission coefficient a
Unit of measure for air exchange via window sashes and frames during a given time and for a specific air pressure difference (→ Blower-door-test). Uncontrolled air exchange is a key factor in the heat losses of a building.

Kilowatt hour [kWh]
Unit of measurement for energy: output of 1000 Watt [W] over one hour [h]. 1kWh =3600 kJ

Kilowatt peak [kWp]
Normal output of solar modules under standardized test conditions.

Latent heat storage
Latent heat storage utilizes melting heat and is tied to a fixed temperature – the melting temperature. When heat is stored, the material begins to melt and does not increase in temperature until it is fully melted. Since there is no notable rise in temperature despite the addition to heat, the heat stored during this phase transition is also called "hidden" or latent heat. Latent heat storage systems possess tremendous storage capacity.

Light-directing glass
Light-directing glass is used to bring daylight into interiors. In cast glass, the surfaces are deformed to such a degree that the radiation that is incident on the first glass surface is directed onto the next surface, then on to the bright ceiling of the room and from there into the room itself. In insulating glass, curved plastic elements are installed in the interstitial space between panes to direct light into the room from above.

Light-directing louvered blind
Daylight is directed into the depth of the room via the concave upper surfaces of reflecting louvers.

Light direction
Light direction is used to direct daylight or artificial light into the further recesses of a room and to utilize it at some distance from the light source. Daylight direction is dependent on numerous structural and local parameters.

LON-control (→ Bus system)

Low-energy house
In Germany, a building meets the low-energy standard if it consumes 30 per cent less energy than set forth in the Energy Conservation Regulation.

Luminance
Unit of measurement for the brightness emitted by a light source or illuminated surface.

Luminance distribution
Indicates the brightness values in a room. According to DIN 5035 the maximum difference in brightness between the brightest and darkest surface near the working plane should not exceed 3:1; between the working plane and the surroundings at some distance from it, the maximum difference in luminance should lie below 10:1.

Luminous efficacy η [lm/W]
Ratio of the luminous flux emitted and the required output.

Luminous flux φ in lumen [lm]
Luminous flux, given in lumen, quantifies the luminous output of a light source in all directions.

Luminous intensity I in candela [cd]
The unit of measurement of the luminous intensity I, called candela [cd], describes the luminous flux emitted by a light source in a given direction and solid angle.

Massive storage
Massive components of a building, or components with good storage capacity, for example, exposed concrete ceilings and walls.

Microcrystalline/micromorphous cells
(→ p. 164)

Minimum illuminance
The minimum illuminance is defined in DIN 5035 for a wide variety of room uses, (e.g., 500 lx at an office workstation).
(→ Illuminance)

Monocrystalline cells/silicon (→ p. 164)

MPP (Maximum Power Point)
Power point on the variable current-voltage curve at which the PV-cell generates maximum output (silicon cell roughly 0.45 V).

Nominal energy demand
Energy, which the heating system must emit under standardized conditions to cover the heating requirements and the drinking water heating requirement.

Nominal illuminance
Expression used to describe the desired illuminance for a specific room use independent of the age of the light sources.

Off-grid operation/off-grid system (insular systems)
Self-sufficient photovoltaic system for the generation of electrical energy without connection to a supply grid, usually operated with batteries as energy storage.

On-grid system
Photovoltaic system linked to public power grid, used to compensate for supply deficiency in case of diminished solar radiation and to feed excess energy into the grid.

Partial conditioning system
Systems that do not feature all the functions of a standard conditioning system, among others air heater and air humidifier. They are used to control relative humidity in winter, but do not provide cooling in summer. Air heaters and air coolers can cool the supply air in summer, they cannot control relative humidity in winter.

Passive house
The passive house is a progression of the German low-energy house standard. It consumes 75–85 per cent less heating energy than stipulated in the Energy Conservation Regulation. The annual heating requirement is less than 15 kWh/m²a.

Phase displacement [h]
Temporal displacement of the internal temperature curve in relation to the external temperature curve. Gradual thermal transmission (optimum 12 h) shifts the external temperature peaks to the evening in the interior.

Photovoltaics

Photovoltaics

Solar cell material (laboratory)	Cell efficiency (production)	Cell efficiency (mass production)	Module efficiency
monocrystalline silicon	24.7 %	18.0%	14.0%
polycrystalline silicon	19.8 %	15.0 %	13.0 %
amorphous silicon	13.0 %	10.5 %	7.5 %
CIS	18.8 %	14.0 %	10.0 %
CdT	16.4 %	10.0 %	9.0 %
micromorphous silicon	12.0 %	10.7 %	9.1 %
hybrid cell	20.1 %	17.3 %	15.2 %
colour cell	12.0 %	7.0 %	5.0 %

Source: Fraunhofer ISE, 26th IEEE PVSC, NREL, spec sheets from various manufacturers

Photovoltaics is the direct transformation of light into electrical energy by means of the photo-electric effect in semiconductors. Solar cells are usually constructed with silicon. We differentiate three different cell types: monocrystalline, poly-crystalline and amorphous, according to surface structure, colouring and efficiency.

The semiconductor material is doped to create a solar cell. Chemical elements are introduced to create a positive charge surplus (p-junction semiconductor layer) or a negative charge surplus (n-junction semiconductor layer). When two distinct and differently doped regions adjoin, the resulting boundary is known as an n-p junction. At this transition, two thin layers of positively and negatively charged region form and create an electrically charged field. The electrical current, approximately 0.5 V for silicon, can be tapped off via contacts printed onto the surface. The current intensity increases proportionate to the radiation intensity, while the voltage is hardly affected by the incidence of light. Higher cell temperatures cause a drop in electrical output (current x voltage) and diminish efficiency. Solar cells are most efficient when radiation and cell temperature are stable. To achieve a desired voltage or output, the individual cells are connected in series (higher current) or in parallel (higher voltage). Photovoltaic modules achieve a nominal output of 10 W_p–100 W_p. The generated power can be fed into a self-sufficient system with battery storage or into a network integrated with the public power grid.

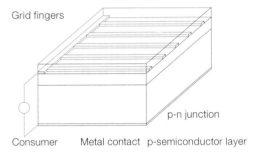

Antireflex coating

n-semiconductor layer

Grid fingers

p-n junction

Consumer   Metal contact p-semiconductor layer

A Diagram of a crystalline solar cell

PV-module with monocrystalline cells
In the production of monocrystalline cells, a silicon rod (diameter 10–20 cm) with a completely regular crystalline structure is formed from melted silicon. The monocrystalline rod is cut into thin disks (wafers). Structural etching ensures improved light absorption. In the next step, several silicon atoms in each wafer are replaced by foreign atoms through gaseous diffusion to enable the photoelectric effect. Contacts are then printed onto the front and bottom sides. An antireflex coating is added to minimize light losses by reflection; the coating changes the appearance of the cells from the original silver-grey to a darker hue ranging from dark-blue to black.

PV-module with polycrystalline cells
Polycrystalline cells are manufactured by pouring melted silicon into a mould. As the silicon cools, many small crystals are formed, whereby the position of each individual crystal to the other is random. Within each crystal, however, the atoms are arranged in a regular formation. The cooled block is cut into rectangular wafers. The separation of the individual crystals in the cells compromises the photovoltaic effect and is responsible for the diminished efficiency of this type of cell. The production method, on the other hand, is both energy- and cost-efficient.

PV-module with thin-film cells with copper-indium-diselenide (CIS)
For the manufacture of amorphous thin-film cells, gaseous silicon is bonded to a carrier medium (e.g. glass) resulting in a thin layer (strength <1 μm) of non-directional silicon. A solar module is then produced in one piece; a laser divides the coated surface in narrow strips and, as a result, individual areas are connected in series. The production costs for this manufacturing process are less than those for crystalline cells since only 1 to 2 per cent of the amount of silicon is required. The low efficiency of these modules translates into a larger area requirement.

Monocrystalline silicon

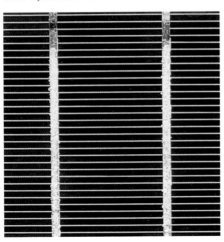

Polycrystalline silicon

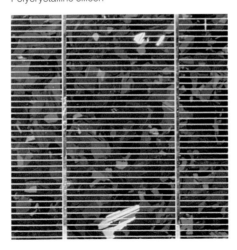

Thin-film cell

The terms used to describe the direct transformation of light into electrical energy. (→ p. 164)

Photovoltaic generator
Totality of connected photovoltaic modules in a solar power plant.

Photovoltaic module
Unit of connected → solar cells.
(→ p. 164)

Photovoltaic system (self-sufficient, hybrid, ongrid)
(→ p. 164)

Plate heat exchanger
Plate heat exchangers usually consist of thin plastic or aluminium plates, which are arranged in closely-spaced layers. Media (e.g. air) flow past each other in the interstitial space between plates without mixing. The difference in temperatures causes heat to be transferred from one medium to the other.

Plus-energy houses
Buildings that generate more energy in a year than they consume.

Polycrystalline cells/silicon (→ p. 164)

Power point
Point at which a PV-module or –generator produces power defined by the electric potential and the strength or intensity of current. The power point at which the highest performance is achieved is called the (→ MPP).

Receptors
In the human eye, light stimuli are transformed into neuronal impulses by two receptor systems. The evenly distributed and light-sensitive rod receptors enable wide-angle vision at low illuminance and the cone receptors provide focus and colour vision.

Reflected glare
Glare can be caused directly by a light source or as reflected glare from the reflection of a light source.

Relative humidity
Ratio of absolute water vapour W contained in the air to the water vapour saturation volume WS. The capacity of air to absorb water vapour increases with rising temperatures. Relative humidity diminishes when the moisture content is constant and the air temperature increases.

Resistance to thermal transmittance R_t [m^2K/W]
The sum of the resistance to thermal transmission R and the resistance factors R_{si} and R_{se} to surface heat transfer serves as an intermediate value in determining the thermal transmission coefficient U.

Roof-integrated installation
Collectors or solar models are structurally integrated into the roof skin.

Seasonal energy storage
Long-term storage in large tanks ($\geq$ 10,000 m^3 water) to compensate for the seasonal differences in solar radiation.
(→ Groundwater utilization)

Self-regulating facades
Facades, which automatically change their permeability by means of → switchable glass according to daylight and solar radiation.

Semiconductor
Basic material for the manufacture of solar cells whose electrical conductivity is intermediate between that of a conductor and an isolator. It is strongly temperature-dependent: in contrast to metals, the resistance of the semiconductor decreases with increasing temperature or incident light, and its conductivity increases.

Silicon
Silicon is the second most common element in the earth's crust and is used as a semiconductor material in the production of solar cells.

Solar cells
Semiconductor building component, in which solar radiation is transformed into electrical voltage through relevant structure of layers.

Solar collector (→ p. 166)

Solar district heat
Semi-central, solar thermal supply for closed housing developments with warm water and space heating. The heating energy gained in collector installations is centrally stored to compensate for diurnal and seasonal differences in solar radiation. The heating demand is generally also covered with the support of other, auxiliary energy carriers. However, complete coverage of the demand with solar energy is also possible, albeit only with the provision of very large storage volumes (up to 20 000 m^3).

Solar factor fa
Percentage of energy requirement to be covered by solar energy: a solar installation for domestic water heating, for example, can achieve an annual solar coverage rate of roughly 55 per cent. In summer, the coverage may be as high as 90 per cent, falling to below 30 per cent in winter.

Solar generator
Photovoltaic installation comprising solar modules that are switched in series or parallel.

Solar heat gains Q_S [kWh/a]
Heat gains from diffuse sky and direct solar radiation on the building components of a building.

Solar roof
Large, segmented collector installation, which simultaneously serves as roof covering.

Solar thermal cooling processes
(→ Adsorption chillers, → Sorption technology)

Sorption-assisted cooling (SAC)
(→ Sorption technology)

Sorption technology
Alternative to conventional, power-driven chillers with a process to generate cooling energy on the basis of desiccation with subsequent evaporative cooling. Water replaces CFC- or FC-containing refrigerants in other chillers. The advantage of → DEC installations with sorption technology in comparison with conventional chiller systems is the diminished connect load because the need for a chiller is obviated; other advantages are the resulting reduction in power consumption and the low annual water consumption; moreover, there is no need to recool the chillers.

Specific heat or calorific capacity c
[kWh/kgK] or [kJ/kgK]
Heat, which generates a temperature increase by 1 K per mass or volume unit of a material.

Specific transmission heat loss coefficient HT
[W/m^2K]
Heat flux through external building components per 1 degree Kelvin temperature difference.

Stacked cells
Photovoltaic cells with two or three layers stacked one above the other (tandem- or triplecells). To improve the efficiency, each layer is designed for a different spectral range (short-, medium- and long-wave radiation).

Standard test conditions
Test conditions employed to determine the nominal output of solar modules. Insolation: 1000 W/m^2; cell temperature: 25 °C; spectrum AM1.5

Switchable glass
To control solar gains, types of glass with controllable (switchable) transmission characteristics have been developed. The prototypes now available have not yet gone into mass production. The types of glass modify their radiation transmission coefficient either in response to a change in temperature or an applied voltage. We differentiate thermotropic and thermochromic, electrochromic and gasochromic systems as well as those operating with liquid crystals.

Surface heat flux, heat flux density q [W/m^2]
Indicates heat volume [J], which flows through 1m^2 of a material cross-section in 1 second.

Surface temperature θ (theta) [°C]
The θ symbol is used for surface temperatures to differentiate them from air temperatures.

System components
Components of the PV network aside from the generator, such as installation structure, switches, controls, meters and storage.

System requirement coefficient e_p
Describes the energy efficiency of a total installation system as an expression of the ratio of the total primary energy absorbed by the system technology to the released thermal energy. The small the requirement coefficient, the greater the efficiency of the system.

Tandem-/triple cells (→ Stacked cells)

Thermal bridges
Area of the building skin with increased heat loss. There is a risk of falling below the dew point temperature and resulting moisture damage.

Thermal flux Φ (Phi)[W]
Heat volume per unit of time.

Thermal or heat absorption factor a
[$Ws^{0.5}$/m^2K]
Factor of thermal absorption capacity of a material. The higher the factor, the faster a building component will absorb heat.

Thermal transmittance, U-value [W/m^2K]
The constant expresses the transmission heat lost in Watt per m^2 of heat transmitting area at a temperature difference of 1 K.

Thermal transmission coefficient $\Lambda\lambda$ [W/m^2K]
Thermal flux, which flows through the material layer of a strength s at a constant temperature difference of 1 K between the surfaces.

Thermal solar energy
The transformation of the radiation energy of the sun into usable heat.

Solar Collectors

Collector type	Conversion factor	Thermal loss Factor [W/m²]	Temperature range [°C]
Absorber (no cover)	0.82 – 0.97	10 – 30	up to 40
Flat plate collector	0.66 – 0.83	2.9 – 5.3	20 – 80
Evacuated flat plate collector	0.81 – 0.83	2.6 – 4.3	20 – 120
Evacuated tube collector	0.62 – 0.84	0.7 – 2.0	50 – 120
Storage collector	approx. 0.55	approx. 2.4	20 – 70
Air collector	0.75 – 0,90	8 – 30	20 – 50

1

Air collectors
Air collectors harness solar radiation for the direct heating of air. The absorber is placed in an insulated housing under glass. Air flows through or circulates around the absorber inside the housing. Air collectors can be operated as fresh air or circulated air systems. In fresh air systems, the outside air is warmed and utilized without further processing. In circulated air systems, air, as the carrier medium, is circulated in a closed cycle. The heat collected in this cycle is then available for use via heat exchangers. The circulated system provides protection against dirt accumulation and is easier to maintain. The fresh air system, on the other hand, obviates the need for heat exchangers and the heat losses associated with them. Air collectors are suitable for applications that utilize the warmed air in a direct manner (forced air heating, industrial dryers).

Flat plate collectors
Flat plate collectors consist of dark absorber surfaces with integrated tubes, usually in serpentine arrangement. The heat collected by the absorber passes through the tube wall to the heat carrier medium. A transparent cover of solar toughened glass with a high transmission ratio in the short-wave spectral range prevents heat emission from the absorber (greenhouse effect) and heat losses by convection. The cover is closely attached to the housing; it protects the absorber against the elements and diminishes the heat losses of the collector by conduction. In evacuated flat plate collectors, the air is evacuated from the interior of the collector housing to further minimize heat losses. Flat plate collectors are a cost-efficient technology for space and drinking water heating.

Evacuated plate collectors
The absorbers are installed inside an evacuated, compression-proof glass tube, which is mounted to rotate for optimized utilization of the solar radiation. The heat carrier medium flows directly through the absorber. The collector comprises several tubes, connected in series and linked to a collecting tube. When temperatures are low, the heat carrier evaporates inside the tube. The vapour rises, transfers the heat to the medium in the collecting tube via a heat exchanger, condenses and flows back again. For this process to occur, the collector must be installed on a minimal incline. It operates very efficiently with high absorber temperatures and moderate to low radiation and is a suitable option for the generation of process heat. The high efficiency in winter and in the transitional seasons results in an increase of 30 to 50 per cent of the average energy gains.

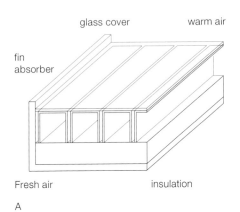

A

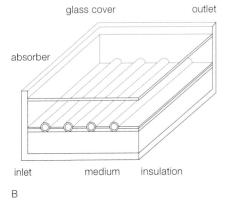

B

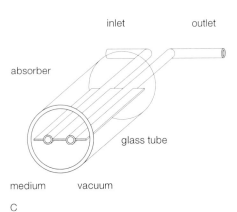

C

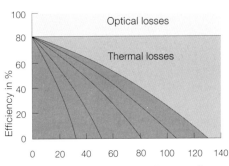

2

3

1 Conversion- and thermal loss factors for different types of collectors (Source: solarserver.de)

2 Efficiency curve of a solar collector depending on solar radiation

3 Efficiency curves and operative ranges of different collector types when exposed to solar radiation of 1000 W/m²

Thermal storage
A material stores thermal energy in accordance with its mass.

Thermal storage factor S [Wh/m³K]
Volume-specific thermal storage capacity of a building component.

Thermal transmission resistance R [m²K/W]
Inverse value of thermal transmission coefficient; indicates the insulating effect of a material layer in the form of resistance. A high resistance value represents a good insulating effect.

Thermo-active ceiling ($\rightarrow$ Building component cooling)

Thin-film technology
Production of thin photovoltaic cells by depositing gaseous silicon on glass, metal or plastics. This technology is used in the production of cells with amorphous silicon (a-Si), cadmium-telluride (CdTe), copper-indium-diselenide (CIS) and gallium-arsenide (GaAs).
($\rightarrow$ p. 164)

Total energy requirement
Energy required to cover the annual heating demand Q_P and the domestic water heating demand Q_W of the building under observation.

Total solar energy transmission g
Energy quotient of incident solar radiation, which is transmitted through the glazing into the interior. This value should be maximized in order to achieve solar gains in the overall energy balance of a building.

Transmission
Ability of a material to allow light to pass through.

Transparent Cells
"Transparent" polycrystalline cells and their fascinating optical effects are a new technology in photocell design. A special process is used to cut the front and underside of the $\rightarrow$ wafer in parallel grooves. The (micro-)holes that result at the intersecting points somewhat diminish the area output, but create the impression of a transparent cell.

Transparent Insulating Material (TIM)
External building insulating material, which allows light to penetrate into the interior without being transparent. In addition to insulation, the material's ability to direct daylight glare-free into large room depths is another advantage. In combination with storage masses, wall structures with TIM can also be used for heat storage.

Usable area
Area in buildings not used for living purposes. The usable area is divided into principal and ancillary usable areas.

Utilizing geothermal energy
($\rightarrow$ Energy piles, earth collectors, geothermal heat exchanger, bore holes, groundwater utilization)

Ventilation by convection
Cool air flows into the area to be ventilated and forms a "sea of air" at floor level. Thermal convection causes the air to rise along warm bodies, draws fresh, unmixed air into the space and provides complete air flow through the room. Soundless and draught-free, it absorbs heat and is extracted at the ceiling.

Ventilation heat loss Q_L [kWh/a]
Heat loss resulting from the air exchange with cold outside air through ventilation and leaks in the joints ($\rightarrow$ Joint transmission coefficient).

Ventilation system with supply and exhaust air system
The identical transportation capacity (identical sizing of supply and exhaust air fans) prevents pressure changes from occurring in the room. In order to avoid unwelcome odour in adjacent rooms, the exhaust air flow, e.g. in kitchens, is sized to be greater than the supply air flow (slight negative pressure).

Ventilation systems with supply air fans
Supply air injected into the room with the help of a fan. A positive pressure is created, which results in excess air escaping, usually in an uncontrolled fashion, through windows, doors, etc.

Wafer
Thin silicon disks with diameters of up to 300 nm, which are used as carrier material in the manufacture of computer chips and photocells.

Warm water collector ($\rightarrow$ p. 166)

Wood-chip heating
Wood waste and scraps machine-cut into small chips (size roughly 3 cm) is used as fuel for modern, automated wood-chip combustion. The calorific value of the chipped material is roughly 2–5 kWh/kg, its combustion is CO_2-neutral. ($\rightarrow$ Biomass)

Wood pellet heating
Pellets stoves (up to 11 kW) and central pellet heating systems (up to 35 kW) utilize wood waste as an energy source for CO_2-neutral combustion. Wood shavings and sawdust are pressed into small pellets without binding agent (length 20–50 mm, Ø 6–8 mm, calorific value roughly 5 kWh/kg (= 0.5 l heating oil). Pellets are fed into the combustion boiler either manually or automatically (worm conveyor or suction system) depending on the system. The pellets are automatically combusted in the combustion chamber. A digital control system optimizes combustion air, fuel volume and operating temperature to achieve low waste gas values and an efficiency of up to 95 per cent. Pellet heating is generally used as an auxiliary system for thermal solar installations when solar radiation is insufficient.

Bibliography

A Green Vitruvius. Principles and Practice of Sustainable Architectural Design. University College Dublin, the Architect's Council of Europe, Softtech and the Finnish Association of Architects, London 1999

Achilles; Braun; Seger; Stark; Volz: lasklar, produkte und technologien zum einsatz von glas in der architektur. Munich 2003

Ackermann, Thomas: Energieeinsparverordnung. Wiesbaden 2003

Althaus, Dirk: Fibel zum ökologischen Bauen. Berlin 2000

Behling, Sophia und Stefan: Sol Power. Die Evolution der solaren Architektur. Munich 1996

Birnbacher, Dieter (ed.): Ökophilosophie. Ditzingen 1997

Brand, Cornelius: Die neuen Energiesparhäuser. Aktuelle Entwicklungen – Zeitgemäße Architektur. Munich 1997

Brandi, Ulrike; Geissmar-Brandi, Christoph: Lichtbuch. Die Praxis der Lichtplanung. Basel 2001

Brown, G.Z.; DeKay, Mark: Sun, Wind and Light. Architectural Design Strategies. New York 2001

Bundesarchitektenkammer (ed.): Energiegerechtes Bauen und Modernisieren. Basel 1996

Buonocore, Pablo; Critchley, Michael A.: Tageslicht in der Architektur. Sulgen 2001

Compagno, Andrea: Intelligente Glasfassaden. Material, Anwendung, Gestaltung, 5th Edition. Basel, 2002

Crowe, Norman; Economakis, Richard; Lykoudis, Michael (ed.): Building Cities, Towards a Civil Society and Sustainable Environment. London 1999

Daniels, Klaus: Advanced Building Systems. A Technical Guide for Architects and Engineers Basel 2003

Daniels, Klaus: Technologie des ökologischen Bauens. Grundlagen und Maßnahmen, Beispiele und Ideen. Basel 1995

Danner, Dietmar; Dassler, Friedrich H.; Hajek, Kristina: Die klima-aktive Fassade. Leinfelden-Echterdingen 1999

Deecke, Günther Olesen: Die Betonkernaktivierung. Norderstedt 2003

Detail. Zeitschrift für Architektur + Baudetail, Solares Bauen, 1993/6,1997/3,1999/3,2002/6

Deutsches Architekturmuseum; Volz, Michael: Die ökologische Herausforderung in der Architektur. Nachhaltigkeit, Bilanzierung, Normung, Recycling.Tübingen 1999

Deutsches Kupferinstitut (ed.): Architektur & Solarthermie. Darmstadt 2002

Dietz, Bernhard: Zur Nutzung solarer Strahlung für die permanente Kälteerzeugung. Stuttgart 2002

EMPA-Akademie (ed.); Bleich, Jürgen et al.: Die Gebäudehülle. Konstruktive, bauphysikalische und umweltrelevante Aspekte. Stuttgart 2000

Farmer, John; Richardson, Kenneth (ed.): Green Shift, Changing Attitudes in Architecture to the Natural World. Oxford 1999

Fischer, Udo: Tageslichttechnik. Cologne 1982

Fox, Ulrich: Sonnenkollektoren. Thermische Solaranlagen. Stuttgart 1998

Ganslandt, Rüdiger; Hoffmann, Harald: Handbuch der Lichtplanung. Braunschweig 1992

Gauzin-Müller, Dominique: Nachhaltigkeit in Architektur und Städtebau. Basel 2002

Gfeller-Corthésy, Roland: Bartenbach Lichtlabor: Bauen mit Tageslicht, Bauen mit Kunstlicht. Braunschweig 1998

Graf, Anton: Neue Passivhäuser, 25 Beispiele für den Energiestandard der Zukunft. Munich 2003

Graham, Peter: Building Ecology. Oxford 2003

Grimm, Friedrich: Energieeffizientes Bauen mit Glas. Munich 2003

Grobe, Carsten: Passivhäuser, Grundlagen, Bauphysik, Konstruktionsdetails, Wirtschaftlichkeit. Munich 2002

Gunßer, Christoph: Energiesparsiedlungen. Konzepte, Techniken, Realisierte Beispiele. Munich 2000

Guzowski, Mary: Daylighting for Sustainable Design. New York 1999

Hagan, Susannah: Taking Shape. A New Contract between Architecture and Nature. New York 2001

Hagemann, Ingo B.: Gebäudeintegrierte Photovoltaik. Architektonische Integration der Photovoltaik in die Gebäudehülle. Cologne 2002

Herzog, Thomas (ed.): Solarenergie in Architektur und Stadtplanung. Munich 1996

Huber; Müller; Oberländer: Das Niedrigenergiehaus. Stuttgart, Berlin, Cologne 1996

Hullmann, Heinz: Photovoltaik in Gebäuden. Stuttgart 2000

Humm, Othmar (ed.): NiedrigEnergie- und Passiv Häuser. Staufen 1998

Humm, Othmar; Toggweiler, Peter: Photovoltaik und Architektur. Basel 1993

Kaiser, Yvonne; Hastings, S.R.: Niedrigenergie-Solarhäuser. Systeme, Projekte, Technologien. Basel 1998

Kaltenbach, Frank (ed.): Detail Praxis, Transluzente Materialien. Glas, Kunststoff, Metall. Munich 2003

Kramer, Heinrich; von Lorn, Walter: Licht – Bauen mit Licht. Cologne 2002

Krapmeier H.; Drössler E.: CEPHEUS. Wohnkomfort ohne Heizung. Vienna 2002

Landesinstitut für Bauwesen des Landes Nordrhein-Westfalen (ed.), Zeine, Carl: Stromsparpotentiale in Landesbauten. Aachen 1997

Lewis, Owen; Goulding, Jon: European Directory of Sustainable and Energy Efficient Building. London 1999

Lloyd Jones, David; Hudson, Jennifer: Architektur und Ökologie, zeitgenössiche bioklimatische Bauten. Stuttgart 1998

Lüling, Claudia (ed.): Architektur unter Strom. Berlin 2000

Meyer, Roland: Das EnergieEinsparHaus. Taunusstein 2001

Mürmann, Herbert: Wohnungslüftung. Kontrollierte Lüftung mit Wärmerückgewinnung: Systeme, Planung, Ausführung. Heidelberg 1999

Ökologisches Bauen-Phase II. "Stand und zukünftige Entwicklungen." (Dissertation),, Bauhaus Universität, Weimar, 1/1999

Oesterle; Lieb; Lutz; Heusler: Doppelschalige Fassaden. Munich 1999

Österreichisches Institut für Baubiologie und -ökologie, Donau Universität Krems, Zentrum für-Bauen und Umwelt (ed.); Mötzl, H.; Zelger,T.: Ökologie der Dämmstoffe. Grundlagen der Wärmedämmung, Lebenszyklusanalyse von Wärmedämmstoffen. Optimale Dämmstandards. Vienna 2000

Oswald, Philipp: Wohltemperierte Architektur. Neue Techniken des energiesparenden Bauens. Heidelberg 1994

Porteous, Colin: The New Eco-Architecture. Alternatives from the Modern Movement. London 2002

Reiners, Holger: Energie effektiv nutzen. Die besten Einfamilienhäuser. Munich 2002

Reyer, Eckhard, et. al.: Kompendium der Dämmstoffe. Stuttgart 2002

Roaf, Sue; Fuentes, Manuel; Thomas, Stephanie: Ecohouse: A Design Guide. Oxford 2002

Schittich, Christian (ed.), Building Skins. Concepts, Layers, Materials. Munich, Basel 2001

Schittich, Christian; Staib, Gerald; Balkow, Dieter; Schuler, Matthias; Sobek, Werner: Glasbau Atlas. Munich, Basel 1998

Schneider, Astrid (ed.): Solararchitektur für Europa. Basel 1996

Schüle, R., et. al.: Thermische Solaranlagen. (Market survey. A guide to buying solar and domestic water systems.) Staufen 1997

Websites

Seltmann, Thomas: Fotovoltaik: Strom ohne Ende. Berlin 2000

SIA Schweizerischer Ingenieur- und Architekten Verein: Kriterien für nachhaltige Bauten. Zurich 2000

Slessor, Catherine: Eco-Tech. Umweltverträgliche Architektur und Hochtechnologie. Ostfildern 1997

Sliwinski, Sigismund; Stach, Edgar: Sustainability in Architecture. University of Tennessee 2002

Smith, Peter F.: Architecture in a Climate of Change. A Guide to Sustainable Design. New York 2001

Suttor, Wolfgang; Müller, Armin: Das Mini-Blockheizkraftwerk. Eine Heizung die kostenlos Strom erzeugt. Heidelberg 2000

Thierfelder, Anja (ed.): Transsolar – Climate Engineering

Thomas, Randall (ed.); Fordham, Max: Photovoltaics and Architecture. London, New York 2001

Treberspurg, Martin: Neues Bauen mit der Sonne. Ansätze zu einer klimagerechten Architektur, 2nd edition. Vienna 1998

UIA Berlin 2002 e.V. (ed.): Resource Architecture (4 publications: congress proceedings, poster session, exhibition catalogue, student competition). Basel 2002

Umweltforum Bau e.V. (ed.): Niedrigenergiehäuser. Karlsruhe 1997

Weik, Helmut: Expert-Praxislexikon, Sonnenenergie und solare Techniken. Renningen 2000

Weik, Helmut: Sonnenenergie für eine umweltschonende Baupraxis. Renningen 1995

Wigginton, Michael; Harris, Jude: Intelligent Skins. Oxford 2002

Zimmermann, Mark: Handbuch der passiven Kühlung. Rationelle Energienutzung in Gebäuden. Stuttgart 2003

Bauhaus – University of Weimar
www.uni-weimar.de/architektur/oekologisches_bauen

Federal Ministry of Building and Development
www.urban21.de

Federal Ministry of the Environment
www.bmu.de

Databases, projects, grants, subsidies, manufacturer information, products
www.solarinfo.de

German Society for Solar Energy
Up-to-date information on renewable energy resources and the rational use of energy
www.dgs-solar.org

Energieinstitut Voralberg
www.energieinstitut.at

Eurosolar
European Association for Renewable Energy Sources
www.eurosolar.org

Glossary with extensive explanations on solar energy technologies
www.regio3.ch/solarregion/inhalt.htm

International research forum for regenerative energy sources
www.iwr.de/solar

Cost-efficient passive houses as European standard
www.cepheus.de

Network for solar and ecological building
www.agsn.de

Öko-Insitut e.V., Institute of Applied Ecology
www.oeko.de

Passivhaus Institut
www.passiv.de

Praxis-Informationen und Hilfen zur Anwendung der Energieeinsparverordnung (EnEV)
www.enev-online.de

Solarcity
www.solarcity.org

Solarenergie Informations-und Demonstrationszentrum
www.solid.de

Sunrise 2002: "Die europäischen Märkte für Solarthermie und Photovoltaik," (Market survey)
www.deutsche-energie-agentur.de

Comprehensive information on all topics relating to solar energy
www.solarserver.de

VDB Berufsverband Deutscher Baubiologen e.V.
www.baubiologie.net

Website for students of architecture
www.candarch.de/links_architektur/oekologie.htm

Zeitschrift für EnergieEffizientes Bauen
www.e-bauen.de

Passive row house in Dornbirn, Austria

Architects:
Johannes Kaufmann Architektur
JKA, Dornbirn
www.jkarch.at

Johannes Kaufmann
Born 1967 in Bezau;
since 1993 independent architecture studio;
1996–2000 office partnership with
Oskar Leo Kaufmann.

Client:
Errichtergemeinschaft Falkenweg
Energy concept:
Planungsteam E-PLUS
Kaltheier &Partner OEG, Egg
Tel.: +43 5512 26068
Fax: +43 5512 26068-17
Physics: Lothar Künz, Hard
Tel.: +43 5574 778510
Fax: +43 5574 61689
Structural engineer:
Merz Kaufmann Bauingenieure
(timber structure), Dornbirn
Tel.: +43 5572 36031-0
Fax: +43 5572 36031-40
Mader & Flatz Ziviltechniker GmbH
(concrete structure), Bregenz
Tel.: +43 5574 44129-0
Fax: +43 5574 44129-33
Completion: 2002

Timber construction:
Kaufmann Zimmerei, Reuthe
Tel.: +43 5514 2209
Fax: +43 5514 3275
Master builder:
Strohmeier Bau GmbH, Lauterach
Tel.: +43 5574 64260-0
Fax: +43 5574 77299
Roofer + Sprengler:
Heinzle Sprenglerei,
Kohlbach-Götzis
Tel.: +43 5523 62343
Fax: +43 5523 62343-18
Windows:
Böhler Fenser GmbH, Wolfurt
Tel.: +43 5512 74550
Fax: +43 5512 77390
Heating engineer:
Steurer Installationen
Energietechnik GmbH,
Schwarzenberg
Tel.: +43 5512 2958
Fax: +43 5512 2958-8
Electrician:
Elektro Vögel,Mellau
Tel.: +43 5518 2232
Fax: +43 5518 22324

Housing ensemble in Kolding, Denmark

Architects:
3XNielsen, Århus
Team members:
Christian Platz, Palle Holsting,
Jørgen Søndermark, Lars Poulsen,
Malene Knudsen, Carsten Olsen
www.3xn.dk

Lars Frank Nielsen
Born 1951 in Esbjerg;
since 1986 independent office with
Kim Herforth Nielsen.

Kim Herforth Nielsen
Born 1954 in Sønderberg;
since 1986 independent office with
Lars Frank Nielsen.

Client:
AAB Kolding
Building systems/structural and
energy engineering:
COWI, Vejle
General contractor:
Højgaard & Schulz Vest,
Kolding
Tel.: +45 7551 7088
Fax: +45 7551 7075
Completion: 1998

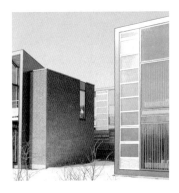

Passive terraced houses in Ulm, Germany

Architects:
Brucker Architects, Stuttgart
Team members:
Peter Lell, Jürgen Groß
Tel.: 49 711 611663

Johannes Brucker;
since 1986 independent office;
lecturer at Stuttgart University.

Client:
Bauherrengemeinschaft
Sonnenfeld GbR, Ulm
Building systems/electrical
engineer/building physics:
ebök, Tübingen
Structural engineer:
Harry Lieb, Ulm
Landscape design:
Johannes Brucker,
Stuttgart
Completion: 2001

Shell work:
Härle Hoch- und Tiefbau
Betonfertigteile GmbH,
Maselheim

Tel: 07351 1587-0
Fax: 07351 9501331
Häufele & Sohn GmbH &Co. KG,
Ulm
Tel.: +49 731 40194-0
Fax: +49 731 40194-40
Carpentry/wood construction:
Lehner GmbH,
Bonndorf-Wellingen
Tel.: +49 7703 919347
Fax: +49 7703 919367
Windows:
Pazen GmbH,
Zelting-Rachtig
Tel.: +49 6571 90450
Fax: +49 65713602
Heating and ventilation:
Prestle, Biberach
Tel.: +49 7351 5000-13
Fax: +49 7351 5000-55
Insulating sandwich board:
Wilhelm Frank, Ulm
Tel.: +49 731 37636
Fax: +49 731 36782
Roof insulation/sealing:
Deutsche Asphalt GmbH, Ulm
Tel.: +49 731 93611-0
Fax: +49 731 93611-99
Sarnafil GmbH,
Feldkirchen
Tel.: +49 89 90480859
Fax: +49 89 99145100
Masonry: limestone
Kontor Südwest GmbH,
Karlsruhe
Tel.: +49 721 981640
Fax: +49 721 814083

Detached houses in Innsbruck, Austria

Architects:
Baumschlager & Eberle, Lochau
Project management:
Gerhard Zweier, Wolfurt
office@be-g.com

Carlo Baumschlager
Born 1956; since 1985
office partnership with Dietmar
Eberle; teaching since 1985.

Dietmar Eberle
Born 1952; since 1985
office partnership with Carlo
Baumschlager; teaching since
1983;
since 1999 professor at the
ETH Zurich.

Client:
Neue Heimat Tirol, Gemeinnützige
Wohnungsbau- und
Siedlungsgesellschaft mbH,
Innsbruck
Building systems:
GMI Gasser & Messner, Dornbirn
Klimatherm, Rum
HVS/Solar technology:
Ortner GmbH, Innsbruck
Tel.: +43 512 224910
Fax: +43 512 2825302
Ventilation:
Hermes electronics (Genvex),
Essen
Tel.: +49 201 89911-0
Fax: +49 201 89911-20
Structural engineer:
Marc Wallnöfer, Innsbruck
IFS Ziviltechnik GmbH, Innsbruck
Gerhard Neuner, Rum
Electrical engineer:
Obwieser GmbH, Absam
Landscaping:
Kienast +Vogt, Zurich
Completion: 2000

Folding shutters, facade:
Meyer GmbH und Co. KG,
Nüziders
Tel.: +43 5552 63548-0
Fax: +43 5552 63548-22
Glazing contractor:
Foidl Bau- und Kunstglas,
St. Margarethen
Tel.: +43 5244 626668
Fax: +43 5244 626669
Joiner windows/interior doors:
Kienpointner GmbH,
Waidring
Tel.: +43 5353 53485
Fax: +43 5353 5950
Gas heater:
Vaillant GmbH, Innsbruck
Tel.: +43 512 580464
Fax: +43 512 580464-15
Solar collectors:
Teufel & Schwarz
Heizungsgroßhandel GmbH, Going
Tel.: +43 5358 3939
Fax: +43 5358 3900
Doma Solartechnik, Satteins
Tel.: +43 5524 5353
Fax: +43 5524 5353-10
Heat exchanger/solar storage:
Forstner Speichertechnik,
Dornbirn
Tel.: +43 5572 26274
Fax: +43 5572 26274
Air handling/fresh air pre-warming:
Weger Luft- und Klimatechnik,
Lienz
Tel.: +43 4852 7126-0
Fax: +43 4852 7126-020
Ventilation equipment:
Pichler GmbH, Klagenfurt
Tel.: +43 463 32769
Fax: +43 463 37548
Rainwater barrels:
Freudenthaler GmbH & Co. KG,
Inzing
Tel.: +43 52 38 5 30 45
Fax: +43 52 38 5 30 464
Dry construction:
Linder GmbH, Baden
Tel.: +43 5223 46700
Fax: +43 5223 46700-70

Screed:
Kronbichler GmbH, Ebbs
Tel.: +43 5372 43575
Fax: +43 5372 42932
Parquetry/natural stone:
Freisinger GmbH &Co. KG, Ebbs
Tel.: +43 5372 42209
Fax: +43 5372 42209-2
Terrazzo:
Maccione GmbH, Rum
Tel.: +43 512 263163
Fax: +43 512 263163-4
Master builder:
Porr AG, Rum
Tel.: +43 512 2405
Fax: +43 512 2405-59
Water-proof concrete:
Zementol GmbH, Dornbirn
Tel.: +43 5572 2435-0
Fax: +43 5572 2435-05

Law office in Röthis, Austria

Architects:
Reinhard Drexel, Hohenems
Team members:
Sabine Schneider, Eveline Drexel
Reinhard Drexel

Born 1967;
1994–1996 associate in the office
of Baumschlager-Eberle;
independent office since 1997;
since 2000 teaching at the
HTL-Rankweil.

Client: Hatto Frick, Sylvia Frick
Controlled building ventilation with
heat recovery:
Drexel Solarlufttechnik und
Lüftungsbau GmbH, Bregenz
Tel.: +43 5574 71856-0
Fax: +43 5574 71856-7
Structural engineer:
bhm-Ingenieure, Rankweil
Tel.: +43 5522 46101
Completion: 2001

Carpentry:
Summer-Holzbau, Röthis
Tel.: +43 5522 45217
Fax: +43 5522 47803
Shading components:
Manfred Köb, Bregenz
Tel.: +43 5574 70583
Fax: +43 5574 70584
Wood-frame windows:
Schertler, Lauterach

Tel.: +43 5574 6888-0
Fax: +43 5574 70108
Mastic asphalt with smoothed
surface: BITU–Terrazzo, Hard
Tel.: +43 5574 65870
Fax: +43 5574 65874

Gymnasium in Wängi, Switzerland

Architects:
Fent Solare Architektur, Wil
www.fent-solar.com

Guiseppe Fent
Born 1952 in Hemberg;
since 1995 specialized in solar
architecture;
invention of Lucido-facade.

Client:
Volksschulgemeinde und
Politische Gemeinde Wängi
Projekt- und Bauleitung:
Almer + Almer AG,
Wängi
Energy calculations,
facade construction:
Lucido Solar AG, Wil
Building systems:
Martin Eisenbart,
Münchwilen
Structural engineer:
Steiner Jucker Blumer,
Frauenfeld
Electrical engineer:
Bächler, Frauenfeld
Landscape design:
Fent Solar Architektur
Completion: 2002

Timber construction:
Arge Blumer-Lehmann, Isenring,
Ammann, Blumer Lehmann AG,
Erlenhof windows:
Fensterfabrik, Albisrieden

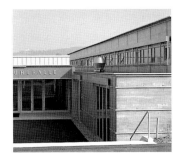

School building in Klaus, Austria

Architects:
Dietrich I Untertrifaller Architects
Project management:
Peter Nußbaumer
Team members:
Tobias Dieng, Thomas Spiegel
www.dietrich.untertrifaller.com

Helmut Dietrich
Born 1957 in Mellau;
since 1986 independent architect;
working partnership with Much
Untertrifaller; 1994 foundation of
Dietrich I Untertrifaller Architects.

Much Untertrifaller
Born 1959 in Bregenz; 1982–85
associate in the firm of Much
Untertrifaller Senior; since 1986
independent office with Helmut
Dietrich and Much Untertrifaller
Senior;
since 1994 Dietrich I Untertrifaller
Architects.

Client:
Gemeinde Klaus
Immobilienverwaltungs
GmbH & Co. KEG
Construction supervision:
E.Gmeiner BaugmbH, Schwarzach
Construction coordination:
BAM GmbH, Götzis
HSV-engineering:
IGT Consulting & Engineering
GmbH, Hohenems
Physics: Bernhard Weithas, Hard
Structural concrete engineering:
Mader Flatz Zivilingenieure,
Bregenz
Structural timber engineering:
Merz Kaufmann Partner, Dornbirn
Cost management:
JM Projektabwicklung GmbH,
Feldkirch
Electrical engineer:
Hecht Licht- und Elektroplanungs
OEG, Rankweil
Acoustics:
Karl Brüstle, Dornbirn
Geotechnics:
Plankel-Pelzl & Partner, Lauterach
Landscape architects:
Rotzler, Krebs Partner, Winterthur
Completion: 2003

Artificial lighting/photovoltaics:
Heinzlemänner Elektroinstallationen
GmbH, Götzis
Fixed glazing:
Glas Marte GmbH, Bregenz
Passive house windows:
Heinrich Manahl GmbH, Bludenz
Bings
Heating, sanitation:
Markus Stolz GmbH & Co. KG,
Bludenz
Ventilation:
Lippuner Energie und Metall-
bautechnik GmbH, Weiler
Shading system:
Fesal- Sonnen- u.Wetterschutz
Sonderegger GesmbH, Koblach
Master builder:
Dobler Bau GmbH
Thomas Heiß, Helmut Gartler, Klaus
Peschl, Polier, Röthis

Congress and exhibition building in Osnabrück, Germany

Architects:
Herzog + Partner
Architekten BDA GbR
Team members:
Stefan Sinning, Kirsten Braun,
Patrick Bröll, Peter Gotsch,
Matthias Lettau,
Sybille Fries
www.herzog-partner-architekten.de

Thomas Herzog
Born 1941 in Munich;
independent office since 1973;
since 1974 professor, from 1993 at
the TU Munich.

Hans Jörg Schrade
Born 1951 in Stuttgart;
since 1994 in partnership with
Thomas Herzog.

Client:
Deutsche Bundesstiftung Umwelt,
Osnabrück
Projection management and
construction supervision:
Reinders & Partner GbR
Architekten BDA, Osnabrück
Ground analysis:
Jagau & Partner, Syke
Topography: surveyors
Werner Flüssmeyer,
Osnabrück
Sound protection-noise emission:
Kötter Consulting Engineers GmbH
Structural engineer:
Barthel & Maus,
Munich
Test engineeer:
Speich, Hinkes und Partner,
Hanover
Energy and systems technology:
ZAE Bayern e.V., Garching
Building and room acoustics,
Physics:
Müller BBM, Planegg
Landscape design:
Latz & Partner,
Kranzberg
Media technology:
MedienSL GmbH, Kürten,
Membrane roof experiments:
Universität GH Essen,
Bauwesen, Essen
Environmental stress analysis of
excavation material:
Chemisches Laboratorium
Weißling GmbH, Hanover

Completion: 2002

Shell work and tiling work:
Kleine-Kuhlmann GmbH,
Ankum
Exterior:
Heinrich Steinhake GmbH,
Osnabrück
Timber load-bearing structure/
sealing/ Fibrated concrete:
Holzbau Brüggemann
GmbH & Co. KG,
Neuenkirchen
Membrane roof:
B & O Hightex GmbH,
Rimsting/Chiemsee
Facade/windows and
overhead glazing:
LANCO,
Göttingen
Daylighting/
installation of daylighting modules:
H. & J. Harms,
Zwickau
Sonnenschutztechnik GbR,
Shading, linear drive and
eletr. controls:
RSI-Schröder & Imhof GbR,
Großwallstadt
Structural steel work:
Heinrich Rohlfing GmbH,
Stemwede
Screed work:
Fußboden Krause GmbH,
Versmold
Elevators:
OSMA-Aufzüge A. Schenk
GmbH & Co. KG,
Osnabrück
Sanitation/heating:
Eckhard Senger GmbH & Co. KG,
Osnabrück
Air-handling systems:
Kuhr GmbH, Meppen
Electrical engineer:
OSMO-Anlagenbau,
Georgsmarienhütte

Office building in Solihull, England

Architects:
Arup Associates, London
Daniel Jang Wong
www.arupassociates.com

Ove Arup,
1895–1988,
since 1938 with Arne Arup
Arup & Arup Ltd;
since 1946 Ove Arup & Partners.

Client:
BVP Developments Ltd.,
The Arup Group, Solihull
Building system engineering:
Arup Associates, London
Peter Worburton, Patrick Regan,
Malcolm Wallace
Structural engineering:
Arup Associates, London
Terry Raggett, Damian Eley
Lanscape design:
Bernard Ede in collaboration with
Roger Griffiths
Associates, Rugby
Construction supervision:
Rob Saunders,
The Arup Group
General contractor:
Interserve Project Sevices,
Birmingham
Tel.: +44 121 3444888
Fax: +44 121 3444677
Completion: 2001

Steel construction:
Green & Sons Ltd., Spalding, Lincs
Tel.: +44 1406 370585
Fax: +44 1406 370766
Down & Francis Ltd., Birmingham
Tel.: +44 121 4333300
Fax: +44 121 4599222
Fire-protection coating for steel
structure:
Fire Management Ltd., Shrewsbury
Shropshire
Tel.: +44 1939 291210
Roof structure:
Laubeuf UK Ltd.,
Sheffield
Tel.: +44 1484 667745
Fax: +44 114 2482894
Roofing contractor:
Richard Lees Steel Decking Ltd.,
Ashbourne, Derbyshire
Tel.: +44 1335 300999
Sharkey and Company,
Birmingham
Tel.: +44 121 3803700
Fax: +44 121 3803710
Wood floors:
Tarmac Topfloor Ltd.,
Ashbourne, Derbyshire
Tel.: +44 1335 360601
Fax: +44 1335 360014
Weather boarding:
Swift Horsman,
Ware Hertfordshire
Tel.: +44 1920 466795
Fax: +44 1920 461026
Joiners:
Joinery Shoppe Ltd.,
Aldridge, Walsall
Tel.: +44 1922 455 997
HVS:
Haden Young Ltd.,
Birmingham
Tel.: +44 121 7061116
Fax: +44 121 7065229
Elevator:
Express Evans Lifts,
Lichfield, Staffordshire
Rotating door:
Boon Edam,
Ashford, Kent
Exterior:
Kevin Pickering,
Wotton Fields, Northampton

Administration building in Recanati, Italy

Architect:
MCA Mario Cucinella Architects,
Bologna;
www.mcarchitects.it

Mario Cucinella,
since 1992 independent office;
since 1999 office partnership with
Elizabeth Francis in Bologna;
lecturer at the University of Ferrara.

Client:
iGuzzini Illuminazione, Recanati
Tel.: +39 071 75881
Fax: +39 071 75881
Building systems engineering:
Domenella Engineers, Civitanova
Marche,
Natural ventilation concept:
Stephen Jolly, Alistair Guthrie
Ove Arup & Partners, London
Energy concept:
EDAS, Energy Design Advice
Sheme
Brian Ford, London
Daylighting concept:
MCA in collaboration with
Polytechnikum Lausanne
Steel construction and facades:
Promo, Corridonia
Tel.: +39 0733 433542
Fax: +39 0733 433433
Control system:
Johnson Controls SpA,
Sesto San Giovanni Milan
Concrete, structural engineering:
Stefano Sabbatini, Recanati
Completion: 1997

Shell work:
GM, Civitanova Marche
Execution building systems:
General Impianti, Recanati
Atrium garden: Mauro Paccamiccio
Vivaista, Recanati

Administration building in Landquart, Switzerland

Architects:
Bearth & Deplazes Architekten AG,
Chur
Team members:
Bettina Werner, Marlene Wallimann,
Roger Durrer, Urs Geiger,
Andreas
Egger
www.deplazes.arch.ethz

Valentin Bearth
born 1957 in Tiefencastel;
1984–1988 associate in the studio
of Peter Zumthor, Haldenstein;
since 1988 joint office with
Andrea Deplazes; since 2000
visiting lecturer at the Accademia di
architettura, Mendrisio; since 2001
Bearth + Deplazes AG, Chur.

Andrea Deplazes
born 1960 in Chur; since 1988 joint
office with Valentin Bearth; since
1997 professor of Architecture +
Construction, ETH Zurich;
since 2001 co-owner of
Bearth +Deplazes AG, Chur.

Client:
ÖKK Graubünden Stiftung,
Landquart
Construction supervision:
Toscano AG, Thusis
Energy- and ventilation concept:
Andrea Rüdi, Chur
Waldhauser Haustechnik AG,
Münchenstein
Building systems/HVS-engineering:
ARGE, Landquart
Hans Gadient, Trimmis
Structural engineer: Conzett
Bronzini Gartmann AG, Chur
Physics: Edy Toscano AG, Chur
Electical engineer:
Elkom Partner AG, Chur
Interiors: Abitare Hürlimann, Chur
Completion: 2002

Manufacturing building in Braunschweig, Germany

Architects:
Banz + Riecks Architekten BDA,
Bochum
www.banz-riecks.de

Elke Banz
1990 –1992 associate in the office
of Eckhardt Gerber, Dortmund;
1992 –1993 associate in the office
of Jörg Friedrich, Hamburg;
since 1994 freelance work in
Bochum.

Dietmar Riecks
since 1994 freelance work in
Bochum; 1995–2000 lecturer at
University of Dortmund.

Client:
Solvis Energiesysteme
GmbH &Co. KG,
Braunschweig
Energy- and daylighting concept:
Fraunhofer Institut für Solare
Energiesysteme ISE, Freiburg
Physics:
Robert Borsch-Laaks,
Büro für Bauphysik, Aachen
Building systems:
Solares Bauen GmbH,
Freiburg
Blower-Door testing:
Ingenieurgesellschaft
Bauen + Energie + Umwelt,
Springe/Eldagsen
Structural engineer:
Burkhard Walter, Ingenieurbüro
für Bauwesen, Aachen
Factory coordination and produc-
tion logistics:
Vollmer und Scheffczyk GmbH,
Hannover
Test engineers:
Ingenieurbüro kgs, Hildesheim
Soil analysis:
Suckow & Zarske GbR,
Braunschweig
Fire protection:
Neumann Kex & Partner,
Schmallenberg
Completion: 2002

Administration building in Würzburg, Germany

Architects:
Webler + Geissler,
Architekten BDA,
Stuttgart;
www.webler-geisler.de

Garnet Geissler
Born 1958 in Würzburg;
1985–1989 associate at Norman
Foster, London; since 1990 joint
office with Martin Webler;
1992–1993 lecturer at Stuttgart
University.

Martin Webler
Born 1957 in Hanover;
1984–1987 associate at
Norman Foster, London;
since 1990 joint office with
Garnet Geissler;
1988–1989 lecturer at Stuttgart
University.

Client:
Herrmann Püttmer, Kirchberg an
der Murr
Building systems and BAS:
Ingenieurgesellschaft Püttmer IGP,
Ludwigsburg
Tel: +49 7141 9915125
Fax: +49 7141 99151296
Structural engineer:
Ingenieurbüro für Bauwesen Wolff,
Stuttgart
Tel: +49 711 712263
Fax: +49 711 7189410
Electrical engineer:
Ingenieurbüro Klausch & Partner,
Erfurt
Construction contractor:
Götz GmbH, Fellbach
Shading:
WAREM, Marktheidenfeld/Main
System wall, system ceiling:
Webler + Geissler, Architects BDA,
Stuttgart
Ingenieurgesellschaft Püttmer,
Ludwigsburg
Götz GmbH, Würzburg
Energy/cooling systems/CHP:
Gesellschaft für Bodenanalytik,
Mannheim
Gesellschaft für Energietechnik,
Bremen
Solar collectors: Ingenieurges-
ellschaft Püttmer,
Ludwigsburg
Götz GmbH, Würzburg
Steel construction: steel structure
hall, hall facade:
Götz GmbH, Würzburg
Glazing: SANCO,Nördlingen
Completion: 1995

Academy in Herne, Germany

Architects:
Jourda Architectes, Paris
Hegger Hegger Schleiff, Kassel;
Team members:
Andreas Wiege, Gerhard Greiner
www.hhs-architekten.de

Françoise-Hélène Jourda
Born 1955; 1979–1983 lecturer;
professor at TU Vienna.

Manfred Hegger,
since 1980 partnership
HHS Planer + Architekten;
since 1973 lecturer at various
universities; since 2001 professor
at the TU Darmstadt.

Client:
Land Nordrhein-Westfalen
Energy concept:
HL Technik, Stuttgart
Photovoltaics:
Pilkington Solar International,
Cologne
Tel.: +49 221 92597062
Fax: +49 221 2581117
Flabeg Solar Int. GmbH, Colonge
Tel.: +49 221 925970-0
Fax: +49 221 2581117
Structural engineering:
Schleich Bergermann und Partner,
Stuttgart
inverter:
E.U.S.Gesellschaft für innovative
Energieumwandlung und
-speicherung mbH,
Gelsenkirchen
Tel.: +49 209 162210
Fax: +49 209 1672201
Glass skin:
Schneider, Stimpfach
Tel.: +43 5574 804140
Fax: +43 5574 804100
Construction and foundation work:
Echterhoff-Holland
Hoch- und Tiefbau GmbH,
Bochum
Tel.: +49 234 92211-0
Fax: +49 234 287345
Züblin AG, Duisburg
Tel.: +49 203 2820-0
Fax: +49 203 27283
Gutehoffnungshütte
Baugesellschaft mbH,
Oberhausen
Tel.: +49 208 6788-0
Fax: +49 208 6788-299
Ground recovery/recycling:
BSR GmbH, Bochum
Tel.: +49 234 68789-0
Fax: +49 234 9129633
Timber construction:
Kaufmann Holz AG, Reuthe
Tel.: +43 5574 804-0
Fax: +43 5574 804-201
Building climate:
GfA-Gesellschaft für
Aerophysik mbH, Munich
Tel.: +49 89 7233081
Fax: +49 89 7233082
Completion: 1994

Bundstag in Berlin, Germany

Architects:
Foster and Partners,
London
www.fosterandpartners.com
Norman Foster
Born 1935 in Manchester;
1961 foundation of Team 4 with
Richard Rogers; since 1967 Foster
Associates.

Building services:
Kuehn Bauer Partner, Beratende
Ingenieure GmbH, Hallbergmoos
www.kbp.de

Client:
Bundesbaugesellschaft Berlin im
Auftrag der Bundesrepublik
Deutschland
Energy concept/technology
engineering:
Kaiser Bautechnik, Duisburg
Fischer Haustechnik, Wehrheim
Amstein und Walthert, Zurich
Planungsgruppe Karnasch-
Hackstein
Structural engineering:
Ove Arup Partnership, London
Schleich Bergermann und Partner,
Stuttgart
Leonhard und Andrä, Stuttgart
Acoustics/sound protections:
Müller BBM GmbH, Planegg
Georg Plenge, Egling-Thanning
Lighting engineer:
Claude Engle
Facade engineer:
Emmer und Pfenniger,
Münchenstein
Physics:
Bobran Ingenieure,
Stuttgart
Heritage conservation consultants:
Acantus, Bristol
Fire protection:
Wolfram Klingsch,
Wuppertal
Built in: 1894
Conversion: 1999

ARGE Reichtag dome
Waagner-Biro AG,
Vienna/Munich
Tel.: +43 1 28844544
Fax: +43 1 288447842
Götz GmbH, Dillingen
Tel.: +49 9071 70 00
Fax: +49 9071 6343

Authors

Christian Schittich (editor)

Born 1956
Studied architecture at the Technical University, Munich, followed by seven years of practical experience in the field; publicist; since 1991 member of the editorial team at DETAIL, since 1992 co-editor; since 1998 editor in chief; author and editor of numerous books and journal articles.

Manfred Hegger

Born 1946
Studied architecture at the University of Stuttgart, the Hochschule für Gestaltung in Ulm, the Technical University of Berlin and the London School of Economics and Political Science;
1969–1970 Partnership Arbeitsgruppe Nutzungsforschung,
1979–1982 OECD consultant, Paris;
since 1980 partnership HHS Planer + Architekten GbR, Kassel;
1973–1990 Lecturer at the Institute for School Architecture at Stuttgart University,
1977–1979 Visiting professor for architecture at Kassel University;
since 1979 at the Institute for Design and Architecture at Hanover University (lecturer, assoc. professor); since 2001 professor at the Faculty of Design and Energy-efficient Building at the Technical University of Darmstadt, Faculty of Architecture.

Roland Krippner

Born 1960
Trained machinist;
Studies in architecture at the Polytechnic Kassel;
1993–1995 independent practice;
since 1995 staff member/assistant in the faculty of building systems,
Prof. Thomas Herzog, Technical University, Munich;
Publications since 1994.

Michael Kuehn

Born 1941
Since 1960 studies in electronics at the Technical University Hanover; since 1970
director of energy technology, Kraftanlagen Heidelberg AG;
1980 foundation of engineering firm Kuehn Bauer Partner,
concepts, studies, research and development, integrated planning,
implementation of urban plans and high-rise projects.

Dirk Mattner

Born 1965
Studies in machine engineering at the Technical University in Braunschweig and
at the Technical University in Stuttgart, focus energy systems; since 1994 partner
at Kuehn Bauer Partner, Munich, project manager TGA,
studies, research, concept development, planning and implementation.

Helmut F.O.Müller

Born 1943
Studies in architecture at the University of Hanover, Stuttgart University and the
London University College, certificate in 1972;
1972–1982 Planning and research in construction at various engineering firms
and Stuttgart University, PhD. in 1979;
1982–1993 Professor of architecture at the Polytechnic of Cologne;
1991–1997 Founder and director of the Institute for Lighting and Building Engineering at the Polytechnic Cologne (ILB);
since 1993 professor at the Faculty for climate-conscious architecture at the
University of Dortmund;
since 1997 managing partner of the GLB, Gesellschaft für Licht und Bautechnik
mbH, Dortmund;
publications since 1979.

Heide Schuster

Born 1969
Studies in architecture at the Polytechnic Darmstadt, certificate 1997;
1997–1998 Postgraduate scholarship,
Master of Arts at the Architectural Association, London 1998;
freelance architect since 1997; since 2000 associate at the Faculty for climate-
conscious architecture at the University of Dortmund;
publications since 1999.

Illustration credits

The authors and editor wish to extend their sincere thanks to all those who helped to realize this book by making illustrations available. All drawings contained in this volume have been specially prepared in-house. Photos without credits are form the architects' own archives or the archives of "DETAIL, Review of Architecture". Despite intense efforts, it was not possible to identify the copyright owners of certain photos and illustrations. Their rights remain unaffected, however, and we request them to contact us.

- All Air Charter, Berlin: p. 150
- BASF Schweiz, Zürich: 2.11
- Bonfig, Peter, München: 2.16, p. 12
- Bryant, Richard/Arcaid, Kingston-upon-Thames: pp. 153, 159
- Cook, Peter/View, London: pp.112–113, 115, 117
- de Calan, Jean, Paris: pp. 118–123
- Feiner, Ralph, Malans: pp. 125–127, 129
- Fischer, Hans-Dieter, Herne: p. 142
- Fraunhofer Institut Solare Energie-systeme, Freiburg: 2.10
- Gesellschaft für Licht und Bautechnik mbH, Dortmund: 5.16, 5.25
- Gilbert, Dennis, London: 1.2
- Halbe, Roland/artur, Köln: 5.14, pp. 130–131, 132 top, 134–135
- Hegger, Manfred, Darmstadt: 2.2
- Heinrich, Michael, München: 4.25
- Helbling, Bruno, Zürich: 3.8
- Hempel, Jörg, Aachen: 1.3
- Holzherr, Florian, München: pp. 94–97
- Hand&Errico, Tricase: pp. 98–101
- Hueber, Eduard, New York: pp. 88–89
- Huthmacher, Werner, Berlin: 5.12
- Kaltenbach, Frank, München: pp. 38, 91, 92, 144
- Kämpfen, Beat, Zürich: 2.4
- Keller, Andreas/artur, Köln: 5.13
- Klomfar & Partner, Wien: pp. 103, 105, 107
- Kober, Bertram/Punctum, Leipzig: pp. 108–111
- Krase, Waltraud, Frankfurt: 4.11
- Lehrstuhl für klimagerechte Architektur, Universität Dortmund: 5.17, 5.21, p. 145
- Martínez, Ignacio, Lustenau: pp. 72–73, 76–77,
- Mjell, Ivar, Irhus: pp. 79, 81

- Müller, Helmut F.O., Dortmund: 5.26
- Müller-Naumann, Stefan, München: pp. 56, 132
- Nikolic, Monika/artur, Köln: p. 143
- Ott, Thomas, Mühltal: 5.23
- Richters, Christian, Münster: pp. 136–138, 139 right and left, 140–141, 146–147
- Rosenberg, Simone, Berlin: 4.3
- Roth, Lukas, Köln: p. 26
- Schittich, Christian, München: 1.1, 2.4, 2.5, 2.6, 3.6, 4.23, 5.5, pp. 8, 104, 149, 152, 157
- Schodder, Martin, Stuttgart: 5.9
- Schuster, Heide, Dortmund: 5.2, 5.8
- Soratroi, Ernst, Innsbruck: p. 90
- Spiluttini, Margherita, Wien: 2.12, 3.12
- Südwestdeutsches Archiv für Architektur und Ingenieurbau Karlsruhe, Photo: Horstheinz Neuendorf, Baden-Baden: 4.19, 4.21
- Tollerian, Dietmar, Linz: 3.7
- Walti, Ruedi, Basel: 5.24
- Weber, Jens, München: 4.2
- Young, Nigel, London: pp. 154, 164 left and middle
- Zentrum für Sonnenenergie- und Wasserstoff-Forschung Baden-Württemberg: p. 164 right
- Zwickert, Gerhard, Berlin: 3.9

from books and journals:

- Bode, Peter, M. et al., Entscheidung zur Form, Wien-München, 1973: 4.14, 4.15, 4.17
- Daniels, Klaus; Technologie des ökologischen Bauens. Grundlagen und Maßnahmen, Beispiele und Ideen, Basel, 1995: 2.8, 2.9
- Danner, Dietmar; Dassler, Friedrich H.; Hajek, Kristina, Die klima-aktive Fassade, Leinfelden-Echterdingen, 1999: 5.10
- DBZ Deutsche Bauzeitschrift, 8/2001: 3.10
- DIN 5034: 5.11
- Koppelkamm, Stefan, Künstliche Paradiese, Berlin, 1988: 2.3
- Lange, Horst, Handbuch für Beleuchtung, Landsberg am Lech, 1992: 5.4
- Produktinformation Firma Siemens: 5.7
- Schirmer, Wulf (Ed.), Egon Eiermann 1904–1970 Bauten und Projekte, Stuttgart, 2002: 4.18, 4.22

Articles and introductory b/w photos:

p. 8; The Sun, Source of Solar Energy
p. 12; Parish Centre in Schwindkirchen; arc Architekten, Munich
p. 26; Museum of Archaeology, Herne; von Busse Klapp Brüning, Essen
p. 38; Swiss Re Headquarters, London; Foster and Partners, London
p. 56; Munich Airport, Terminal 2; Koch + Partner, Munich

Dust-jacket photo:

Steel Dome of the Reichstag, Berlin
Architects: Foster and Partners
Photo: Christian Schittich